1st International Workshop on Language Technology Platforms (IWLTP 2020)

Marseille, France
11 – 16 May 2020

Editors:

Georg Rehm
Kalina Bontcheva
Khalid Choukri

Jan Hajic
Stelios Piperidis
Andrejs Vasiljevs

ISBN: 978-1-7138-1264-7

LREC 2020 Workshop
Language Resources and Evaluation Conference
11–16 May 2020

**IWLTP 2020 – 1st International Workshop on
Language Technology Platforms**

PROCEEDINGS

Edited by:
Georg Rehm, Kalina Bontcheva, Khalid Choukri,
Jan Hajič, Stelios Piperidis, Andrejs Vasiļjevs

Proceedings of the LREC 2020 Workshop
IWLTP 2020 – 1st International Workshop on
Language Technology Platforms

Edited by: Georg Rehm, Kalina Bontcheva, Khalid Choukri, Jan Hajič, Stelios Piperidis, Andrejs Vasiļjevs

Acknowledgement: this work has received funding from the EU's Horizon 2020 research and innovation programme through the contract ELG (grant agreement no. 825627).

https://www.european-language-grid.eu/iwltp-2020/

**EUROPEAN
LANGUAGE
GRID**

For more information:
European Language Resources Association (ELRA)
9 rue des Cordelières
75013, Paris
France
http://www.elra.info
Email: lrec@elda.org

Preface

With the increasing number of platforms, grids and infrastructures in the wider area of Language Technologies (LT), NLP, NLU, speech, interaction and language-centric AI, there is also a growing need for sharing experiences, approaches and best practices to learn and benefit from the work of others and also, practically, to start a collaboration towards platform interoperability.

The 1st International Workshop for Language Technology Platforms (IWLTP 2020) addresses all smaller and larger language grids, language-related infrastructures, platform initiatives as well as collaborative research projects that touch upon LT platforms, especially platform interoperability and related topics, both in Europe and world-wide. Its objective is to exchange and discuss observations, experiences, solutions, best practices as well as current and future challenges. The workshop also addresses the issue of fragmentation in the Language Technology landscape. Instead of "platform islands" that simply exist side by side, possibly even competing with each other, initiatives should discuss how their platforms can be made interoperable and how they can interact with one another to create synergies towards a productive LT platform ecosystem.

The EU project European Language Grid (ELG; 2019-2021) is creating a platform that will provide thousands of data sets and hundreds of LT services. ELG aims to promote technologies tailored to all European languages and cultures, adapted to their social and economic needs. At the same time, there are several established platforms or infrastructure-related initiatives as well as emerging new ones, both on the European but also on the national level as well as on other continents. Some of the initiatives are more language-related and have a strong industry focus, others are mainly research-oriented. Moreover, there are digital public service initiatives, and platforms, in which language is only one aspect of many. With all these established and emerging initiatives, there is a risk of even stronger fragmentation in the Language Technology field, which is already highly fragmented, at least in Europe. Our approach is to bring these initiatives together to discuss ways not only of preventing further fragmentation but, crucially, of reversing it. This will only be possible if interoperability and mutual data exchange is ensured and if metadata formats and technical requirements are compatible, among others.

A total of 30 papers were submitted to IWLTP 2020, 17 of which were accepted (acceptance rate: 56.7%). The organisers would like to thank all contributors for their valuable submissions and all members of the Programme Committee for reviewing the submitted papers. Due to the ongoing SARSCoV-2 pandemic, the workshop cannot be held as originally foreseen. Together with the organisers of LREC 2020 we will explore if we can organise the workshop at a later point in time or if we can organise it as a virtual event.

G. Rehm, K. Bontcheva, K. Choukri, J. Hajič, S. Piperidis, A. Vasiljevs   May 2020

Organising Committee and Programme Committee

Organising Committee

Georg Rehm (DFKI GmbH, Germany) – main editor and chair
Kalina Bontcheva (University of Sheffield, UK)
Khalid Choukri (ELDA, France)
Jan Hajič (Charles University, Czech Republic)
Stelios Piperidis (ILSP, R. C. "Athena", Greece)
Andrejs Vasiļjevs (Tilde, Latvia)

Programme Committee

Albina Auksoriūtė (Institute of the Lithuanian Language, Lithuania)
António Branco (University of Lisbon, Portugal)
Gerhard Budin (University of Vienna, Austria)
Walter Daelemans (University of Antwerp, Belgium)
Christian Dirschl (Wolters Kluwer, Germany)
Maria Gavriilidou (ILSP, R. C. "Athena", Greece)
Stefan Geißler (Kairntech, France)
José Manuel Gómez Pérez (Expert System Iberia, Spain)
Manuel Herranz (Pangeanic, Spain)
Ilan Kernerman (K Dictionaries, Israel)
Svetla Koeva (Bulgarian Academy of Sciences, Bulgaria)
Simon Krek (Jožef Stefan Institute, Slovenia)
Cvetana Krstev (University of Belgrade, Serbia)
Krister Lindén (University of Helsinki, Finland)
Dora Loizidou (University of Cyprus, Cyprus)
Jean-Pierre Lorré (Linagora, France)
Bernardo Magnini (Fondazione Bruno Kessler, Italy)
Jan Odijk (Utrecht University, Netherlands)
Maciej Ogrodniczuk (Polish Academy of Sciences, Poland)
Christoph Prinz (Sail Labs, Austria; LT Innovate, Belgium)
Sören Räuchle (3pc, Germany)
Artem Revenko (Semantic Web Company, Austria)
Eiríkur Rögnvaldsson (University of Iceland, Iceland)
Bolette Sandford Pedersen (University of Copenhagen, Denmark)
Inguna Skadiņa (University of Latvia, Latvia)
Marko Tadić (University of Zagreb, Croatia)
Dan Tufiș (Romanian Academy of Sciences, Romania)
Tamás Váradi (Hungarian Academy of Sciences, Hungary)
Phillippe Wacker (LT Innovate, Belgium)
Andy Way (Dublin City University, Ireland)
François Yvon (CNRS – LIMSI, France)
Matteo Zanioli (Alpenite, Italy)

Table of Contents

Proceedings of the 1st International Workshop on Language Technology Platforms (IWLTP 2020), pages 1–7
Language Resources and Evaluation Conference (LREC 2020), Marseille, 11–16 May 2020
© European Language Resources Association (ELRA), licensed under CC-BY-NC

Infrastructure for the Science and Technology of Language
PORTULAN CLARIN

António Branco,[1] **Amália Mendes,**[2] **Paulo Quaresma,**[3]
Luís Gomes,[1] **João Silva,**[1] **Andrea Teixeira**[1]

[1]*University of Lisbon*
NLX—Natural Language and Speech Group, Department of Informatics
Faculdade de Ciências
Campo Grande, 1749-016 Lisboa, Portugal
[2]*University of Lisbon*
Center of Linguistics, School of Arts and Humanities
[3]*University of Évora*
Escola de Tecnologia

Abstract

This paper presents the PORTULAN CLARIN Research Infrastructure for the Science and Technology of Language, which is part of the European research infrastructure CLARIN ERIC as its Portuguese national node, and belongs to the Portuguese National Roadmap of Research Infrastructures of Strategic Relevance. It encompasses a repository, where resources and metadata are deposited for long-term archiving and access, and a workbench, where Language Technology tools and applications are made available through different modes of interaction, among many other services. It is an asset of the utmost importance for the technological development of natural languages and for their preparation for the digital age, contributing to ensure the citizenship of their speakers in the information society.

Keywords: research infrastructure, language science, language technology

1. Introduction

This paper presents the PORTULAN CLARIN Research Infrastructure for the Science and Technology of Language,[1] which is part of the European research infrastructure CLARIN ERIC[2] as its Portuguese national node, and belongs to the Portuguese National Roadmap of Research Infrastructures of Strategic Relevance.[3] It ensures the preservation and fostering of the scientific heritage regarding natural languages, supporting the preservation, promotion, distribution, sharing and reuse of language resources, including text collections, lexicons, processing tools, etc.

PORTULAN CLARIN includes a repository of language resources and tools, as well as a workbench with language processing services. The expanding list of resources and services results largely from a wide network of implementation partners, formed by 3 proponent partners and over 20 research centers working in Computer Science, Linguistics, Psychology, etc., from Portugal and Brazil.

The mission of PORTULAN CLARIN is to provide services to all kinds of users that in one way or another have to handle or process language, which naturally includes researchers from Artificial Intelligence, Humanities, Cognitive Science, etc.

PORTULAN CLARIN fosters Open Science practices by supporting its users in making their results and resources accessible to all sectors of an inquiring society.

It represents an asset of the utmost importance for the technological development of natural languages and to their preparation for the digital age, contributing to ensure the citizenship of their speakers in the information society.

In this paper we present the goals, target users, and mission of the infrastructure in Section 2. The repository and the workbench are described in Sections 3 and 4, respectively. Section 5 introduces the organization of the Help Desk and Consultancy support to the users of the infrastructure, and Section 6 the sharing and licensing options offered by the platform. Finally, we present in Section 7 the certifications received by PORTULAN CLARIN and in Section 8 its system of governance and network of implementation partners, before offering the concluding remarks in Section 9.

2. Mission

2.1. All about human natural languages

The mission of PORTULAN CLARIN is to support researchers, innovators, citizen scientists, students, language professionals and users in general whose activities resort to research results from the Science and Technology of Language. This is pursued by means of the distribution of scientific resources, the supplying of technological support, the provision of consultancy, and the fostering of scientific dissemination.

2.2. All scientific and cultural domains served

This infrastructure supports activities in all scientific and cultural domains with special relevance to those that are more directly concerned with language—whether as their immediate subject, or as an instrumental mean to address their topics. This includes, among others, the areas of Artificial Intelligence, Computation and Cognitive Sciences, Humanities, Arts and Social Sciences, Healthcare, Lan-

---

[1]`https://portulanclarin.net/`

[2]`https://www.clarin.eu/`

[3]`https://www.fct.pt/apoios/equipamento/`
`roteiro/index.phtml.en`

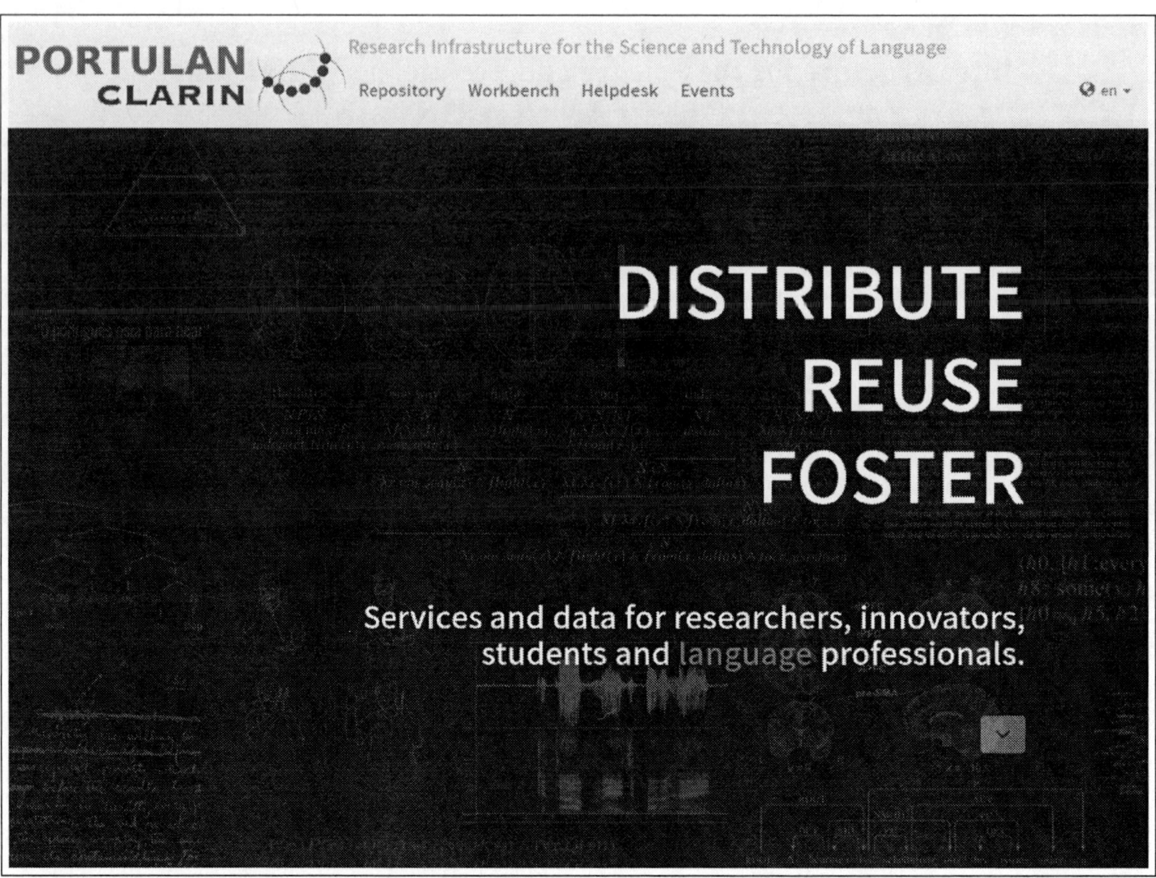

Figure 1: Front page of the PORTULAN CLARIN research infrastructure

guage Teaching and Promotion, Cultural Creativity, Cultural Heritage, etc.

2.3. All results from research on language shared

The infrastructure serves all those whose activity requires the handling and exploration of language resources, including language data and services:

- in all sorts of modalities—spoken, written, sign, multimodal, etc.

- in all types of representations—audio, text, video, records of brain activity, etc.

- and in all types of functions—instrument for communication, symbolic object, cognitive ability to be stimulated through formal education in native language, knowledge vehicle, ability to be exercised in the acquisition of a second language, reflection of mental activity, natural form of interaction with artificial agents and devices, etc.

It is used when it is necessary, for example:

- to use a language processing tool—e.g. conjugators, terminology extractors, concordancers, part-of-speech taggers, parsers, named entity recognizers, deep linguistic processing grammars, etc.

- to access data sets—e.g. linguistically interpreted corpora, terminology data bases, EEG records of neurolinguistic experiments, transcriptions, collections of literary texts, etc.

- to obtain a data sample—e.g. video recording of deaf children sign language, words for concepts in the Organization subontology, etc.

- to use specific research support applications—e.g. lemma frequency extractors, treebank annotators, etc.

- to use an appropriately equipped online workbench of tools—to support field work on the documentation of endangered languages, to do research on translation, etc.

The front page of the infrastructure is displayed in Figure 1.

2.4. All users welcome

PORTULAN CLARIN favors and promotes Open Science, Open Access, Open Data and Open Source policies. Accordingly, all users are welcome to use and benefit from the scientific resources it distributes, with no user registration needed.

To ensure the quality of the scientific resources it distributes, depositors of resources are requested to register before depositing and distributing their resources through the infrastructure. This is a very lean procedure, asking only for a user name, email and affiliation.

3. Repository

A major pillar in PORTULAN CLARIN mission is the distribution and preservation of language resources, including language data and language processing tools.

3.1. Deposit

Resource archival is ensured by maintaining a repository to which these scientific resources, together with their corresponding metadata information, may be deposited by registered users for long-term archiving and access, and from which any visitor can obtain copies of resources that are relevant for them.

Basic curation of the resources submitted to the repository is performed by checking the completeness and well-formedness of the metadata. The resource submission process relies on online forms, and on a workflow that ensures that the depositor is prompted when required information is lacking and that the required steps are performed for a submission to be completed and accepted.

After the metadata is submitted to the repository, the basic curation process is continued by the repository staff by means of manual assessment of the metadata and by means of checking its correspondence to the resource to be deposited.

Resource depositors are prompted, as it is in their best interest, to provide in the relevant metadata field a canonical citation for the resource being deposited.

Every resource in the repository is assigned a persistent identifier (PID) for long-term referencing.

Resources are being uploaded at a good pace by users, with the repository containing a large number (hundreds) of resources and growing.

3.2. Retrieval

The scientific resources stored and distributed through the repository can be searched by keyword match on the resource name and on its description, with faceted search bringing further filtering on metadata fields, such as the language, modality type, media type, etc.

Periodically, the metadata records are automatically harvested to the Virtual Language Observatory (VLO),[4] which acts as a central search hub for the whole, pan-European CLARIN ecosystem of repositories.

Note that the keyword search runs over the name and description metadata fields, not over the data content of the resource. Search over the data content of some resources is possible through the Federated Content Search (FCS) functionality of CLARIN.[5] This functionality allows running a query from a central location over multiple data sets, distributed over different national CLARIN nodes.

Figure 2(a) shows the search page of the PORTULAN CLARIN repository, with the list of resources ordered alphabetically. The text box on the top is used for keyword search, while the options of the right allow performing faceted search, which filters the results by multiple criteria (e.g. the language, the modality, etc). Figure 2(b) shows an example of a landing page for a resource.

3.3. Technological underpinnings

The repository is built with the Django[6] Web framework. The underlying database schema and workflow logic have been developed as an enhancement of the previously available METASHARE[7] repository software.

The repository website is created with the Bootstrap[8] CSS front-end framework, which provides a consistent and responsive interface that gracefully handles access from desktop and mobile platforms.

The keyword search functionality relies on Apache Solr[9] for efficient indexing.

The automatic metadata harvesting to the VLO central search hub is done using the OAI-PMH[10] protocol for repository interoperability.

4. Workbench

Another important part of PORTULAN CLARIN mission is to provide access to Language Technology tools and applications. This is accomplished through a workbench that makes available a wide range of processing tools and applications, whose display is grouped by categories, e.g. POS tagging, named entity recognition, sentiment analysis, etc. There are now about a couple of dozen services available, and their number is growing. A screenshot of the main workbench page is shown in Figure 3(a).

4.1. Modes of usage

The tools and applications are made available through different modes of interaction, namely through the browser, through file processing and through web services.

Using the tools and applications through the browser allows the user to directly enter the input, press a button and immediately get the result. Figure 3(b) shows an example of this mode of interaction.

While direct interaction through the browser is useful for short amounts of input, or as a demonstration of the capabilities and output format of a tool, large amounts of input need different modes of interaction. For relevant tools, the workbench also makes available a file processing mode of interaction which allows uploading files to be processed. The task of processing the uploaded files will be added to a queue and handled asynchronously. After the files are processed, the user will be notified by email and will be able to download the result from a unique URL generated when the task was submitted.

A third mode of interaction permits accessing the tools and applications as web services. This is particularly useful for end-users wanting to integrate some of the tools into their own processing workflow without having to be concerned with installing the tools locally on their own machines, or

---

[4]`https://vlo.clarin.eu/`

[5]`https://contentsearch.clarin.eu/`

[6]`https://www.djangoproject.com/`

[7]`http://www.meta-share.org/`

[8]`https://getbootstrap.com/`

[9]`https://lucene.apache.org/solr/`

[10]`https://www.openarchives.org/pmh/`

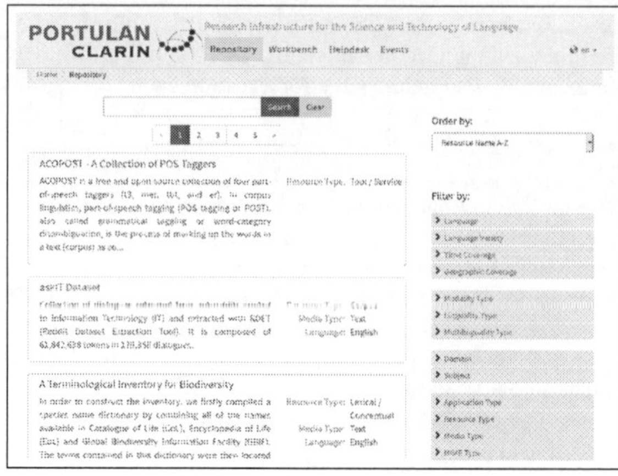

(a) Search page of the repository

(b) Landing page of a resource

Figure 2: Screenshots of the repository

to depositors that wish to make the functionality of a tool accessible to end-users without releasing the tool itself.

Tools that are made available as a web service expose a programmatic interface that can be seamlessly invoked remotely. Their usage can be combined with the help of the CLARIN Language Resources Switchboard facility,[11] which provides a central location from where to find and connect webservices that are part of the wider CLARIN ecosystem.

4.2. Technological underpinnings

The tools and applications in the workbench may vary a lot in terms of the software used to implement them (C, Java, Perl, Python, etc.) and in terms of the supporting software libraries they require. To better cope with this heterogeneous environment, all tools and applications are organized into separate Docker containers. This greatly facilitates their configuration, minimizes system-wide dependencies and, by employing multiple instances of a container, allows performing load-balancing in a straightforward way.

Communication between tools is accomplished by the standard XML-RPC protocol. The same protocol is used for the web services.

The workbench website is also created with the Bootstrap framework, providing a consistent and responsive interface throughout the whole of PORTULAN CLARIN.

5. Help Desk and Consultancy

An important component of PORTULAN CLARIN mission is to provide support to the community of users of language technology. This is done through a help desk service for the infrastructure itself, and through a Language Technology consultancy service for the community at large.

5.1. Help desk

PORTULAN CLARIN staff runs a help desk that provides a user support service for the infrastructure, for the data sets in its repository and for the processing tools and services it makes available. This is useful for all users, but particularly suited for early career students and also for research from scientific domains with less ICT technical skills.

Besides providing help on how to use the scientific resources in the infrastructure and with troubleshooting issues, user support also involves the enhanced curation of submitted resources. This permits, for instance, to provide help in converting the deposited resources to formats other than their original formats, including standard formats, which should be particularly useful for users that lack the technical expertise to do the format conversion.

5.2. Consultancy

Another goal of CLARIN is to share knowledge, thus ensuring that the expertise that exists distributed over the various member countries of CLARIN is readily accessible, both within the infrastructure and to the research community as a whole. This is accomplished through the establishing of Knowledge Centres (K-centers), which are entities centrally certified by the CLARIN as being able to provide expert advice on some field.

PORTULAN CLARIN is recognized as a K-Centre specialized for the Science and Technology of the Portuguese Language, addressing all topics concerning this language: from Phonetics to Discourse and Dialogue; considering all language functions, from communicative performance to cultural expression; approached by all disciplines, from Theoretical Linguistics to Language Technology; covering all language variants, from national standard varieties across the world to dialects of professional groups; and taking into account all media of representation, from audio to brain imagiology recordings.

6. Depositing and Licensing

6.1. Deposit license

To deposit a resource, the user needs to fill in a respective metadata record and submit an instance of the deposit agreement template. This agreement grants a non-exclusive license for distribution of that resource to the PORTULAN

---

[11] https://switchboard.clarin.eu/

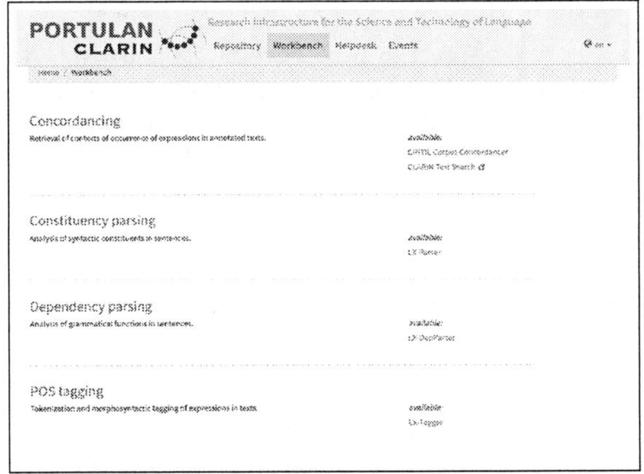

(a) Workbench page showing the list of tools

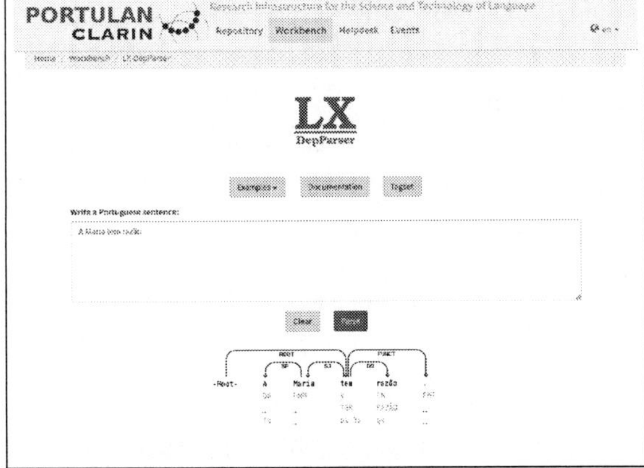

(b) A tool (dependency parser) used in-browser

Figure 3: Screenshots of the workbench

CLARIN research infrastructure, and therefore does not prevent the user from exercising their rights to distribute or publish the resource elsewhere.

This license is for distribution only, and therefore does not transfer the property or moral rights to the infrastructure.

6.2. Usage licenses

While PORTULAN CLARIN adheres to Open Science, Open Access, Open Data and Open Source policies, it does not impose them on its users.

In order to ensure the distribution of and access to the widest possible collection of scientific resources, the scientific resources in the repository are licensed by the respective depositors with the license set of their choice. This includes licensing resources for restricted usages, e.g. research, non commercial only, etc., and thus requiring that the end user proceeds to identify himself under the terms that may be required by the depositor.

When the depositor needs help in finding a suitable license for a resource, PORTULAN CLARIN provides support via its help desk and with online advice services like the CLARIN License Category Calculator.[12]

The license of a resource is stored as part of its metadata and is presented to any user attempting to have access to it. To eventually get access to a resource, a user has to explicitly accept the respective license. In order to obtain a copy of a resource with special restrictions or sensitive data, the user may be directed to the respective depositor in order to arrange for the compliance with the specific terms of that licensing.

The PORTULAN CLARIN repository provides long-term storage and distribution of data. The responsibility of following disciplinary and ethical norms for data storage and distribution lies with the repository. The responsibility of following disciplinary and ethical norms for the creation and gathering of data lies with the depositor of the data. As noted above, to deposit a resource in PORTULAN

CLARIN, the depositor has to fill in and submit a depository agreement. In this agreement, it is explicitly stated that disciplinary and ethical norms were complied with when the resource was created. The depositor also has to specify whether the resource contains confidential data that could potentially be disclosed and the presence of such data will restrict the set of possible licenses that can be associated to the resource and end users that can have access to it.

7. Certification

PORTULAN CLARIN complies with the highest standards for research infrastructures. This is certified at different levels, by different entities.

7.1. International

PORTULAN CLARIN holds the international CoreTrustSeal[13] certification.[14] This certificates the compliance with a systematic range of organizational and technical requirements, such as its long-term sustainability plan, compliance to disciplinary and ethical norms, guarantees of data integrity and authenticity, software and hardware stability, data security, among many others.

7.2. European

As one of its national nodes, PORTULAN CLARIN is part of the CLARIN ERIC, which holds the European ESFRI-European Strategy Forum on Research Infrastructures[15] certification[16] as a landmark research infrastructure.[17]

Additionally, PORTULAN CLARIN holds the European

---

[12]https://www.clarin.eu/content/clarin-license-category-calculator

[13]https://www.coretrustseal.org/

[14]https://www.coretrustseal.org/wp-content/uploads/2019/12/PORTULAN-CLARIN.pdf

[15]https://www.esfri.eu/

[16]http://roadmap2018.esfri.eu/projects-and-landmarks/browse-the-catalogue/clarin-eric

[17]http://roadmap2018.esfri.eu/

CLARIN ERIC certification as a Knowledge Centre[18] and the European CLARIN ERIC certification as a national centre.[19]

7.3. National

FCT—Foundation for Science and Technology,[20] from the Portuguese Ministry of Science, Technology and Higher Education, is the national funding agency for scientific research. PORTULAN CLARIN holds the national certification from FCT as a research infrastructure of the National Roadmap of Research Infrastructures of Strategic Relevance.[21]

8. Governance and network

8.1. Network of implementation partners

The implementation of the infrastructure was undertaken under a project whose three core proponents partners are the Faculty of Sciences of the University of Lisbon, the School of Arts and Humanities of the University of Lisbon and the University of Évora.

Additionally, the implementation project is supported by a wide network of implementation partners. This network is open to further partners and currently encompasses over twenty research centers and organizations from the large range of scientific domains served by the infrastructure. There are partners from Brazil and Portugal, from all regions of Portugal, including the Azores islands. The Camões Institute, the Portuguese national organization responsible for the Portuguese language policy, is also part of the network and helps to pursue that part of the mission of the infrastructure concerned with the promotion of the Portuguese language.

The implementation partners are actively involved in depositing scientific resources and in the enhancing of the infrastructure. The list of implementation partners is open to further contributions and, as the infrastructure will evolve, it will include more organizations from all domains, including from the Humanities, Artificial Intelligence, Neuroscience, etc.

A list of the current network centers is provided in the Annex A.

8.2. Governance and staff

The infrastructure staff members have a large experience in the development of linguistic resources, data curation, natural language data processing, technical maintenance and software development. Most of them are also experts in the field of Language Technology who publish on, and attend, top-ranked scientific conferences in their domains of expertise.

The governance of the infrastructure includes a Board of Directors and a Management Team:

- Board of Directors
  - Director General: António Branco
  - Executive Director: Amália Mendes
  - Executive Director: Paulo Quaresma
- Management Team
  - Technical Manager: Luís Gomes
  - Scientific Resources and Users Support Manager: João Ricardo Silva
  - Communication and Administrative Manager: Andrea Teixeira

9. Conclusion

This paper presented the PORTULAN CLARIN Research Infrastructure for the Science and Technology of Language, which is the Portuguese national node of the pan-European research infrastructure CLARIN ERIC, with 20 member countries, and is part of the Portuguese national Roadmap of Research Infrastructures of Strategic Relevance.

Its mission is to support the widest range of users who need to resort to research results from the Science and Technology of Language. This is pursued through three main pillars in the infrastructure: (i) a *repository* for long-term archiving and access of language resources, be them language data or tools; (ii) a Language Technology *workbench* that makes available a wide range of language processing tools and applications, through various modes of interaction; and (iii) *help desk and consultancy* services that provide support to its users.

The infrastructure adheres to the principles of Open Science and its services are open to all users with no need of user registration or other dispensable access barriers.

Acknowledgements

The results reported here were partially supported by POR-TULAN CLARIN—Research Infrastructure for the Science and Technology of Language, funded by Lisboa2020, Alentejo2020 and FCT—Fundação para a Ciência e Tecnologia under the grant PINFRA/22117/2016.

Annex A   Network of implementation partners

- Cristina Martins and Margarita Correia, Centro de Estudos de Linguística Geral e Aplicada (CELGA-ILTEC), Faculdade de Letras Universidade de Coimbra, Portugal

- Pilar Barbosa and Cristina Flores, Centro de Estudos Humanísticos (CEHUM), Universidade do Minho, Portugal

- Augusto Silva, Centro de Estudos Filosóficos e Humanísticos, Faculdade de Filosofia, Universidade Católica de Braga, Portugal

- José Augusto Leitão, Centro de Investigação do Núcleo para os Estudos e Intervenção Cognitivo-Comportamental (CINEICC), Faculdade de Psicologia, Universidade de Coimbra, Portugal

---

[18] https://www.clarin.eu/content/knowledge-centres

[19] https://www.clarin.eu/content/clarin-centres

[20] https://www.fct.pt/index.phtml.en

[21] https://www.fct.pt/apoios/equipamento/roteiro/index.phtml.en

- Amália Mendes, Centro de Linguística da Universidade de Lisboa (CLUL), Faculdade de Letras, Universidade de Lisboa, Portugal

- Fátima Oliveira, João Veloso and Rui Silva, Centro de Linguística da Universidade do Porto (CLUP), Faculdade de Letras, Universidade do Porto, Portugal

- Maria do Céu Caetano and Francisca Xavier, Centro de Linguística da Universidade Nova de Lisboa (CLUNL), Faculdade de Ciências Sociais e Humanas, Universidade Nova de Lisboa, Portugal

- Luís Gomes, Centro ALGORITMI, Universidade dos Açores, Portugal

- São Luís Castro, Centro de Psicologia da Universidade do Porto (CPUP), Faculdade de Psicologia e Ciências da Educação, Universidade do Porto, Portugal

- António Branco, Faculdade de Ciências (FCUL), Universidade de Lisboa, Portugal

- Paulo Quaresma, Laboratório de Ciência da Computação e Informática (NOVA LINCS), Instituto de Engenharia de Sistemas e Computadores (INESC), Escola de Ciências e Tecnologia, Universidade de Évora, Portugal

- Nuno Mamede, Instituto de Engenharia de Sistemas e Computadores (INESC), Instituto Superior Técnico, Universidade de Lisboa, Portugal

- Ricardo Campos, INESC TEC, Laboratório de Inteligência Artificial e Apoio à Decisão (INESC TEC/LIAAD), Centro de Investigação em Cidades Inteligentes (Ci2 – IPT), Instituto Politécnico de Tomar, Portugal

- Fernando Perdigão, Instituto de Telecomunicações Coimbra (IT Coimbra), Faculdade de Ciências e Tecnologia, Universidade de Coimbra, Portugal

- Gabriel Lopes and Nuno Marques, Laboratório de Ciência da Computação e Informática (NOVA LINCS), Faculdade de Ciências e Tecnologia, Universidade Nova de Lisboa, Portugal

- Eugénio Oliveira and Henrique Lopes Cardoso, Laboratório de Inteligência Artificial e Ciência de Computadores (LIACC), Faculdade de Engenharia, Universidade do Porto, Portugal

- Vera Strube de Lima and Renata Vieira, Faculdade de Informática (FACIN), Pontifícia Universidade Católica do Rio Grande do Sul, Brasil

- Aline Villavicencio and Vera Strube de Lima, Instituto de Informática, Universidade Federal do Rio Grande do Sul, Brasil

- Thiago Pardo, Núcleo Interinstitucional para a Linguística Computacional (NILC), Instituto de Ciências Matemáticas e Computação, Universidade de São Paulo, Brasil

- Rui Vaz, Camões — Instituto da Cooperação e da Língua, Portugal

Proceedings of the 1st International Workshop on Language Technology Platforms (IWLTP 2020), pages 8–15
Language Resources and Evaluation Conference (LREC 2020), Marseille, 11–16 May 2020
© European Language Resources Association (ELRA), licensed under CC-BY-NC

On the Linguistic Linked Open Data Infrastructure

Christian Chiarcos[1], Bettina Klimek[2], Christian Fäth[1], Thierry Declerck[3], John P. McCrae[4]
[1] Goethe-Universität Frankfurt am Main, Germany
[2] Universität Leipzig, Germany
[3] DFKI GmbH, Multilinguality and Language Technology Lab, Saarbrücken, Germany
[4] Data Science Institute/Insight Centre for Data Analytics, NUI Galway, Ireland
[1]{chiarcos,faeth}@informatik.uni-frankfurt.de, [2]klimek@informatik.uni-leipzig.de
[3]declerck@dfki.de.de, [4]john@mccr.ae

Abstract

In this paper we describe the current state of development of the Linguistic Linked Open Data (LLOD) infrastructure, an LOD (sub-)cloud of linguistic resources, which covers various linguistic data bases, lexicons, corpora, terminology and metadata repositories. We give in some details an overview of the contributions made by the European H2020 projects "Prêt-à-LLOD" ('Ready-to-use Multilingual Linked Language Data for Knowledge Services across Sectors') and "ELEXIS" ('European Lexicographic Infrastructure') to the further development of the LLOD.

Keywords: language resources, standards, interoperability, Linguistic Linked Open Data (LLOD)

1. Background

1.1. Interoperability and Collaboration

After half a century of computational linguistics (Dostert, 1955), quantitative typology (Greenberg, 1960), empirical, corpus-based study of language (Francis and Kucera, 1964), and computational lexicography (Morris, 1969), researchers in computational linguistics, natural language processing (NLP) or information technology, as well as in digital humanities, are confronted with an immense wealth of linguistic resources, that are not only growing in number, but also in their heterogeneity. Accordingly, the limited interoperability between linguistic resources has been recognized as a major obstacle for data use and re-use within and across discipline boundaries, and represents one of the prime motivations for adopting Linked Data to our field. Interoperability involves two aspects (Ide and Pustejovsky, 2010):

How to access (read) a resource? (Structural interoperability)
Resources use comparable formalisms to represent and to access data (formats, protocols, query languages, etc.), so that they can be accessed in a uniform way and that their information can be integrated with each other.

How to interpret information from a resource?
(Conceptual interoperability)
Resources share a common vocabulary, so that linguistic information from one resource can be resolved against information from another resource, e.g., grammatical descriptions can be linked to a terminology repository.

With the rise of Semantic Web and Linked Data, new representation formalisms and novel technologies have become available, and different communities are becoming increasingly aware of the potential of these developments with respect to the challenges posited by the heterogeneity and multitude of linguistic resources available today.

Many of these approaches follow the **Linked (Open) Data Paradigm** (Berners-Lee, 2006), and this line of research, and its application to resources relevant for linguistics and/or Natural Language Processing (NLP) have been a major factor that led to the formation of the Open Linguistics Working Group[1] as a working group of Open Knowledge Foundation (OKFN).[2] The OWLG adopted OKFN's principles, definitions and infrastructure as far as they are relevant for linguistic data. The OKFN defines standards and develops tools that allow anyone to create, discover and share open data. The Open Definition of the OKFN states that "openness" refers to: "A piece of content or data [that] is open if anyone is free to use, reuse, and redistribute it – subject only, at most, to the requirement to attribute and share-alike."[3] One of its primary goals is thus to attain openness in linguistics. This includes:

1. Promoting the idea of open linguistic resources,

2. Developing the means for the representation of open data, and

3. Encouraging the exchange of ideas across different disciplines.

One of the earliest activities of the OWLG was to compile a list of potentially relevant language resources, and by the end of 2011, it developed the idea of a Linked Open Data (sub-)cloud of language resources. Subsequently, developing this Linguistic Linked Open Data (LLOD) cloud has become one of the main activities of the group.
The LLOD cloud is a result of a coordinated effort of OWLG participants, but also supported by several broad-scale projects, mostly funded by the EU. This includes early support projects such as *LOD2. Creating Knowledge out of Interlinked Data* (FP7, 2010-2014), an EU-funded project that brought together 15 European partners

---

[1]http://linguistics.okfn.org
[2]http://okfn.org/
[3]http://opendefinition.org

and one from South Korea, *MONNET. Multilingual Ontologies for Networked Knowledge* (FP7, 2010-2013), and *LIDER. Linked Data as an enabler of cross-media and multilingual content analytics for enterprises across Europe* (FP7, 2013-2015). A recently funded H2020 projet, *Prêt-à-LLOD. 'Ready-to-use Multilingual Linked Language Data for Knowledge Services across Sectors* is extending the line of development of LLOD, including also new industrial use cases. And the H2020 infrastructure project *ELEXIS.'European Lexicographic Infrastructure'* is having at its core the LLOD for the building of a dictionary matrix.

Along with these projects, a number of closely related W3C Community Groups emerged. The Ontology-Lexica Community (OntoLex) Group[4] was founded in September 2011, in parts as a continuation of the MONNET project (McCrae et al., 2012). OntoLex develops specifications for a lexicon-ontology model that can be used to provide rich linguistic grounding for domain ontologies. Rich linguistic grounding include the representation of morphological, syntactic properties of lexical entries as well as the syntax-semantics interface, i.e., the meaning of these lexical entries with respect to the ontology in question. The resulting OntoLex-Lemon vocabulary was published in 2016 as a W3C Community Report (Cimiano et al., 2016).[5]

In addition to its original application for ontology lexicalization, the OntoLex-Lemon model has also become the basis for a web of lexical linked data: a network of lexical and terminological resources that are linked according to the Linked Data Principles forming a large network of lexico-syntactic knowledge. This is reflected in the development of an accompanying OntoLex module for lexicography (OntoLex-Lexicog, (Bosque-Gil et al., 2019))[6] as well as the on-going development of modules for morphology (OntoLex-Morph, (Klimek et al., 2019)),[7] respectively frequency, attestation and corpus information (OntoLex-Frac).

Other notable W3C community groups include Linked Data for Language Technology (LD4LT) and Best Practices for Multilingual Linked Open Data (BPMLOD), both formed in 2013 in the context of the LIDER project. BPMLOD published a series of recommendations about using and creating linked language resources. LD4LT contributed to the development and dissemination of the NLP Interchange Format (NIF), an RDF vocabulary for linguistic annotations on the web, and continues its activities to this day. Another important community group is Open Annotation, a community that emerged in BioNLP with the goal to facilitate the annotation of web resources – albeit not specifically with linguistic annotation. The Open Annotation community report serves as the basis of the Web Annotation standard, published in 2017.

These W3C Community Groups differ from the Open Linguistics Working Group in their goals and their focus on specific aspects of, say, language resources or language technology. In particular, they aim to develop community reports on clearly delineated topics that can serve as a basis for future standardization efforts. At the moment, the OntoLex-Lemon vocabulary remains at the level of a community report, whereas Web Annotation has been published as a W3C recommendation. With the wider thematical scope and band-width that it provides, the OWLG serves as a platform to facilitate the flow of information between these W3C CGs, individual research projects and related efforts and thus serves an umbrella function.

1.2. Linked Data

The Linked Open Data paradigm postulates four rules for the publication and representation of Web resources: (1) Referred entities should be designated by using URIs, (2) these URIs should be resolvable over HTTP, (3) data should be represented by means of W3C standards (such as RDF), (4) and a resource should include links to other resources. These rules facilitate information integration, and thus, interoperability, in that they require that entities can be addressed in a globally unambiguous way (1), that they can be accessed (2) and interpreted (3), and that entities that are associated on a conceptual level are also physically associated with each other (4).

In the definition of Linked Data, the Resource Description Framework (RDF) receives special attention. RDF was designed to provide metadata about resources that are available either offline (e.g., books in a library) or online (e.g., eBooks in a store). RDF provides a generic data model based on labeled directed graphs, which can be serialized in different formats. Information is expressed in terms of *triples* - consisting of a *property* (relation, i.e., a labeled edge) that connects a *subject* (a resource, i.e., a labeled node) with its *object* (another resource, or a literal, e.g., a string). RDF resources (nodes)[8] are represented by *Uniform Resource Identifiers (URIs)*. They are thus globally unambiguous in the web of data. This allows resources hosted at different locations to refer to each other, and thereby to create a network of data collections whose elements are densely interwoven.

Several database implementations for RDF data are available, and these can be accessed using SPARQL (Harris and Seaborne, 2013), a standardized query language for RDF data. SPARQL uses a triple notation similar to RDF, only that properties and RDF resources can be replaced by variables. SPARQL is inspired by SQL, variables can be introduced in a separate `SELECT` block, and constraints on these variables are expressed in a `WHERE` block in a triple notation. SPARQL does not only support running queries against individual RDF data bases that are accessible over HTTP (so-called 'SPARQL end points'), but also, it allows

---

[4]`http://www.w3.org/community/ontolex`

[5]See also `https://www.w3.org/2016/05/ontolex/` and (McCrae et al., 2017).

[6]See also `https://www.w3.org/2019/09/lexicog/`.

[7]See also `https://www.w3.org/community/ontolex/wiki/Morphology`.

[8]The term 'resource' is ambiguous: *Linguistic* resources are structured collections of data which can be represented, for example, in RDF. In RDF, however, 'resource' is the conventional name of a node in the graph, because, historically, these nodes were meant to represent objects that are described by metadata. We use the terms 'node' or 'concept' whenever *RDF* resources are meant in ambiguous cases.

the user to combine information from multiple repositories (federation). RDF can thus not only be used to *establish* a network, or cloud, of data collections, but also, to *query* this network directly.

RDF has been applied for various purposes beyond its original field of application. In particular, it evolved into a generic format for knowledge representation. It was readily adopted by disciplines as different as biomedicine and bibliography, and eventually it became one of the building stones of the Semantic Web. Due to its application across discipline boundaries, RDF is maintained by a large and active community of users and developers, and it comes with a rich infrastructure of APIs, tools, databases, query languages, and multiple sub-languages that have been developed to define data structures that are more specialized than the graphs represented by RDF. These sub-languages can be used to create *reserved vocabularies* and *structural constraints* for RDF data. For example, the Web Ontology Language (OWL) defines the datatypes necessary for the representation of ontologies as an extension of RDF, i.e., *classes* (concepts), *instances* (individuals) and *properties* (relations).

The concept of Linked Data is closely coupled with the idea of openness (otherwise, the linking is only partially reproducible), and in 2010, the original definition of Linked Open Data has been extended with a 5 star rating system for data on the Web.[9] The first star is achieved by publishing data on the Web (in any format) under an open license, and the second, third and fourth star require machine-readable data, a non-proprietary format, and using standards like RDF, respectively. The fifth star is achieved by linking the data to other people's data to provide context. If (linguistic) resources are published in accordance with these rules, it is possible to follow links between existing resources to find other, related data and exploit network effects.

1.3. Linked (Open) Data for Language Resources

Publishing Linked Data allows resources to be globally and uniquely identified such that they can be retrieved through standard Web protocols. Moreover, resources can be easily linked to one another in a uniform fashion and thus become structurally interoperable. (Chiarcos et al., 2013) identified the five main benefits of Linked Data for Linguistics and NLP:

Conceptual Interoperability Semantic Web technologies allow to provide, to maintain and to share centralized, but freely accessible terminology repositories. Reference to such terminology repositories facilitates conceptual interoperability as different concepts used in the annotation are backed up by externally provided definitions, and these common definitions may be employed for comparison or information integration across heterogeneous resources.

Linking through URIs URIs provide globally unambiguous identifiers, and if resources are accessible over HTTP, it is possible to create resolvable references to URIs. Different resources developed by independent research groups can be connected into a cloud of resources.

Information Integration at Query Runtime (Federation) Along with HTTP-accessible repositories and resolvable URIs, it is possible to combine information from physically separated repositories in a single query at runtime: Resources can be uniquely identified and easily referenced from any other resource on the Web through URIs. Similar to hyperlinks in the HTML web, the web of data created by these links allows navigation along these connections, and thereby to freely integrate information from different resources in the cloud.

Dynamic Import When linguistic resources are interlinked by references to resolvable URIs instead of system-defined IDs (or static copies of parts from another resource), we always provide access to the most recent version of a resource. For community-maintained terminology repositories like the ISO TC37/SC4 Data Category Registry (Wright, 2004; Windhouwer and Wright, 2012), for example, new categories, definitions or examples can be introduced occasionally, and this information is available immediately to anyone whose resources refer to ISOcat URIs. In order to preserve link consistency among Linguistic Linked Open Data resources, however, it is strongly advised to apply a proper versioning system such that backward-compatibility can be preserved: Adding concepts or examples is unproblematic, but when concepts are deleted, renamed or redefined, a new version should be provided.

Ecosystem RDF as a data exchange framework is maintained by an interdisciplinary, large and active community, and it comes with a developed infrastructure that provides APIs, database implementations, technical support and validators for various RDF-based languages, e.g., reasoners for OWL. For developers of linguistic resources, this ecosystem can provide technological support or off-the-shelf implementations for common problems, e.g., the development of a database that is capable of support flexible, graph-based data structures as necessary for multi-layer corpora (Ide and Suderman, 2007).

To these, it may be added that the distributed approach of the Linked Data paradigm facilitates the distributed development of a web of resources and collaboration between researchers that provide and use this data and that employ a shared set of technologies. One consequence is the emergence of interdisciplinary efforts to create large and interconnected sets of resources in linguistics and beyond.

1.4. Linguistic Linked Open Data

Recent years have seen not only a number of approaches to provide linguistic data as Linked Data, but also the emergence of larger initiatives that aim at interconnecting these resources. Among these, the Open Linguistics

---

[9] `http://www.w3.org/DesignIssues/LinkedData.html`, paragraph 'Is your Linked Open Data 5 Star?'

Working Group (OWLG) of the Open Knowledge Foundation (OKFN) has spearheaded the creation of new data and the republishing of existing linguistic resources as part of the emerging Linguistic Linked Open Data (LLOD, Fig. 1) cloud.

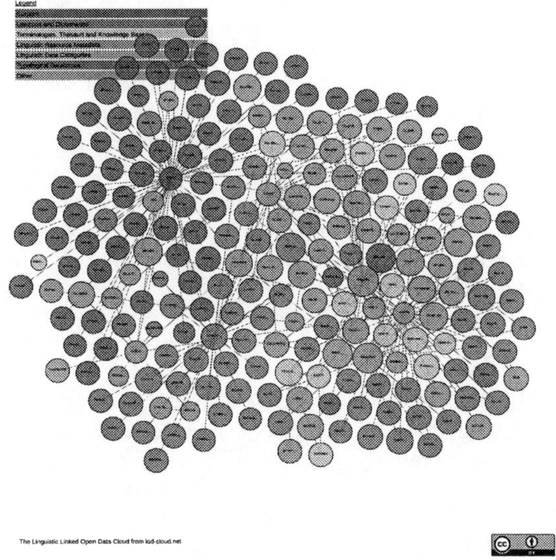

Figure 1: Linguistic Linked Open Data cloud as of March 2019.

With the increasing popularity of LLOD, 'linguistics' was recognized as a top-level category of the colored LOD cloud diagram in August 2014, with LLOD resources formerly being classified into other categories. In August 2018, a copy of the LLOD cloud diagram was incorporated into the LOD cloud diagram as a domain-specific addendum. Within the LOD cloud, Linguistic Linked Open Data is growing at a relatively high rate. While the annual growth of the LOD cloud (in terms of new resources added) in the last two years has been at 10.2% in average for the LOD cloud diagram, the LLOD cloud diagram has been growing at 19.3% per year, cf. Fig. 2.

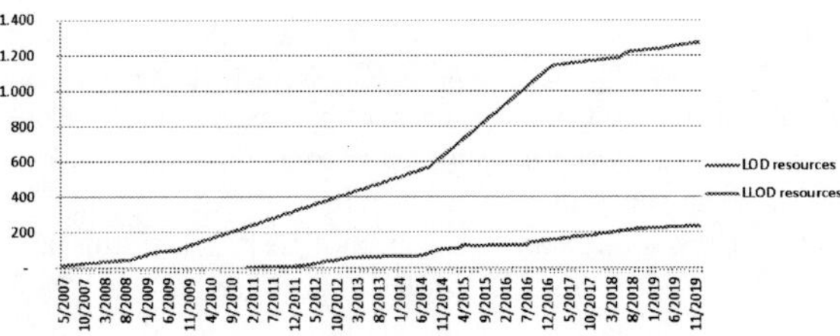

Figure 2: Number of resources in the LOD and LLOD cloud diagrams, 2007-2019, resp. 2011-2019

Aside from maintaining the LLOD cloud diagram, the OWLG aims to promote open linguistic resources by raising awareness and collecting metadata, and aims to facilitate wide-range community activities by hosting workshops, through their mailing list, and through publications. In doing so, they facilitate exchange between and among more specialized community groups, e.g., the W3C community groups such as the Ontology-Lexica Community Group (OntoLex),[10] the Linked Data for Technology Working Group (LD4LT)[11], or the Best Practices for Multilingual Linked Open Data Community Group (BPMLOD).[12] At the time of writing, the most vibrant of these W3C community groups is the OntoLex group, which is developing specifications for lexical data in a LOD context, and this correlates with the high popularity of the OntoLex vocabulary (Cimiano et al., 2016) among LLOD resources. Whereas specifications for lexical resources are relatively mature, as are term bases for language varieties (Nordhoff and Hammarström, 2011; de Melo, 2015) or linguistic terminology (Chiarcos, 2008; Chiarcos and Sukhareva, 2015), the process of developing widely applied data models for other types of language resources, e.g., corpora and data collections in general, is still on-going.

2. Current State and Future Directions

2.1. Usability and practicality of LLOD

It seems that two initial goals of the LLOD community have been achieved. First, the creation of a considerable amount of language resources in the interoperable RDF data format and the involvement of researchers from non-computational but language-focused disciplines like linguistics and philology. Second, these accomplishments revealed new challenges that need to be considered in the future. The growing number of Linked Data language resources opens new questions about interoperability, such as interlinking, ontology usage and the creation of new ontology standards. At the same time the practical needs of researchers unfamiliar with but willing to use the Linked Data framework demand to focus more intensely on the utilization of LLOD by developing appropriate tools to create and exploit the amount of existing language data.

2.2. Selected Developments since 2018

Since 2018, a number of important developments in the Linguistic Linked Open Data community took place. This includes a number of novel, large-scale projects building on LLOD technology and resources, e.g., the H2020 Research and Innovation Actions *ELEXIS. European Lexicographic Infrastructure* (2018-2022)[13], *Prêt-à-LLOD. Ready-to-use multilingual linked language data for knowledge services across sectors* (2019-2021)[14] and the ERC Consolidator Grant *LiLa. Linking Latin* (2018-2023, Marco Carlo Passarotti, Università Cattolica del Sacro Cuore).[15] Equally important is that the Open Linguistics Working Group and related initiatives are being complemented by the new Cost Action *Nexus Linguarum. European network for Web-centred linguistic data science.*[16]

---

[10] https://www.w3.org/community/ontolex
[11] https://www.w3.org/community/ld4lt/
[12] https://www.w3.org/community/bpmlod
[13] https://elex.is/.
[14] https://www.pret-a-llod.eu/.
[15] https://lila-erc.eu/.
[16] https://www.cost.eu/actions/CA18209/.

2.3. Prêt-à-LLOD

In this section we describe briefly the contributions of the Prêt-à-LLOD project to the further development of the Linguistic Linked Open Data infrastructure. Prêt-à-LLOD aims to achieve this by creating a new methodology for building data value chains applicable to a wide range of sectors and applications. This methodology is based around language resources and language technologies that can be integrated by means of semantic technologies.

This is realised by providing data *discovery* tools based on metadata aggregated from multiple sources, methodologies for describing the licenses of data and services, and tools to deduce the possible licenses of a resource produced after a complex pipeline. Related with this is the development of a *transformation* platform that maps data sets to the formats and schemas that can be consumed by the LLOD. Finally, the project is developing an ecosystem to support the linked data-aware language technologies, from basic tools such as taggers to full applications such as machine translation systems or chatbots, based on semantic technologies that have been developed for LLOD to provide interoperable pipelines.

One of the key approaches of the project is the application of state-of-the-art semantic *linking* technologies in order to provide semi-automatic integration of language services in the cloud. This is the method to implement approaches for ensuring interoperability and for porting LLOD data sets and services to other infrastructures, as well as the contribution of the projects to existing standards.

The sustainability of language technologies and resources is a major concern. Prêt-à-LLOD aims to solve this by providing services as data, that is, wrapping services in portable containers that can be shared as single files. Language data also eventually becomes valueless as the documentation and expertise for processing esoteric formats is lost, and the project thus apply the paradigm of data as services, where services can be embedded in multi-service workflows, that demonstrates the service's value and supports long-term maintenance through methods such as open source software. Furthermore, Prêt-à-LLOD is building tools to measure and analyse the validity, maintainability and licensing of the data and services, with the objective of increasing the quality and coverage of language resources and technologies by ensuring that services are easier to archive and reuse, and thus remain available for longer.

Prêt-à-LLOD is also concerned with the issue of detecting and "chaining" licensing conditions for the language resources and services, which can be combined in complex pipelines. So that in addition to the three basic methodologies concerned with delivery, transformation and linking, the project also deals with the automated execution of smart policies for language data transactions. In particular, part of this work is based on the ODRL specifications.[17]

Since all those steps need to be carefully designed and integrated in a workflow, Prêt-à-LLOD is therefore designing a protocol, based on semantic mark-up, that aims at enabling language services to be easily connected into multi-server workflows.

Sustainability of such an infrastructure can in the end only be warranted if it can prove its usability, in different academic and industrial scenarios. Prêt-à-LLOD involves four pilot projects, lead by industry partners, that are especially designed to demonstrate the relevance, transferability and applicability of the methods and techniques under development in the project to practical problems in the language technology industry and their solutions. While Prêt-à-LLOD workflows and methodologies cut across many potential application domains and sectors, the pilots showcase potentials in the context of the following sectors: technology companies, open government services, pharmaceutical industry, and finance. As overarching challenges, all pilots are addressing facets of *cross-language transfer* or *domain adaptation*, in varying degrees.

2.4. ELEXIS

The ELEXIS infrastructure (Krek et al., 2018) has its main aim, the creation of a virtuous cycle of lexicography that consists of the following steps:

1. The creation of digital-native (Gracia et al., 2017) lexicographic resources by lexicographers

2. The linking of these resources into a single dictionary matrix allowing sharing of information

3. The application of these linked dictionaries in natural language processing application

4. The development of tools utilizing natural language processing to help lexicographers develop and improve their dictionaries

As such, linguistic linked data is a key part of this architecture and provides the second step in this virtuous cycle. The project is developing new methods for linking dictionaries, in particular using the architecture of the Naisc system (McCrae and Buitelaar, 2018), which approaches the task of linking in the following steps: first the entries are grouped together and it is analyzed which senses may link taking into account any restrictions such as part-of-speech; at this stage entries with single senses are also linked. Secondly, the entries are examined and key textual facts such as the definition, translation or examples are extracted. Thirdly, textual similarity methods are used to estimate the similarity between the senses of each entry. Next, if there is a graph in the dictionary, such as in a wordnet, graph analytics are used to analyse similarity between senses. Then, machine learning based methods are used to combine all the features into a single probability that a sense is related. Finally, global constraints (Ahmadi et al., 2019) are applied to limit the number of senses and find the most likely overall matching.

The project has recently developed a new benchmark for this "monolingual word sense alignment" task (Ahmadi et al., 2020), which is available for 15 languages and enables evaluation of the approach. This system will then be made available as part of the ELEXIS infrastructure and offered to users through its dictionary matrix.

---

[17]ODRL stands for "Open Digital Rights Language" and is a W3C specification (see `https://www.w3.org/TR/odrl-model/`).

3. Summary and Outlook

Ten years after the formation of the OWLG, the situation of linked data in language technology and linguistics changed drastically. In 2012, when the first book dedicated solely to the topic was published (Chiarcos et al., 2012), the community was largely building on small-scale experiments and a bright vision of the future. Since then, providers of existing infrastructures and existing platforms are becoming increasingly involved in the process and the discussion, documented, e.g., in Pareja-Lora et al. (2019), and a clear set of community standards and conventions has emerged that facilitate creating and using Linguistic Linked Open Data.

In the ten years of existence so far, the OWLG has engaged in developing and advancing Linguistic Linked Open Data and provided an umbrella for numerous more specialized activities. A constantly pursued activity has been the organization of a long-standing series of international workshops, collocated with representative conferences, esp. the series of international workshops on Linked Data in Linguistics (LDL). The topics of LLOD have also been presented in Summer Schools and a series of Datathons.

In parallel, the LLOD cloud has grown considerably. Since 2014, linguistics is recognized as a top-level category of the LOD diagram, and since 2018, the LLOD diagram is also provided as an official 'sub-cloud' of the LOD diagram. As of March 2019, the diagram features 222 resources, i.e., it constitutes about a fifth (222/1239 resources) of the LOD cloud.

Recent changes to OWLG and LLOD infrastructures include the following:

- The LLOD cloud diagram was originally generated from DataHub.io. Since 2016, it had been generated from LingHub.org, initially populated from Datahub and a number of language resource metadata providers. The diagram version provided as part of the LOD cloud diagram uses the same mechanism as the LOD cloud diagram, i.e., an online form. An update of Datahub is currently under development and will represent the basis for future versions of both LOD and LLOD diagrams.

- The Open Knowledge Foundation has been restructuring their services. This includes the OWLG wiki and mailing list. In parts as a reaction to European GDPR, they have been discontinuing their mailing lists. After a long discussion, the Open Linguistics mailing list is now being continued as a Google Group. This is the result of a vote among the participants, and a compromise between stability and simplicity. Unfortunately, a number of providers that we would have preferred as hosts, could not offer a migration, again, in parts due to GDPR concerns. At the same time, we introduce and maintain the catgeory"Open Linguistic" at the Open Knowledge Forum.

- A GitHub organization for the OWLGdata and documentation was created.

- The website originally hosted by the Open KnowledgeFoundation, is now maintained via GitHub and hosted by NUI Galway.

On this basis, the community continues the work and welcome contributors. Upcoming events include the Fourth Summer Datathon on Linguistic Linked Open Data (SD-LLOD 2021) and the Third Conference on Language, Data and Knowledge (LDK-2021).

The general situation is that a remarkable amount of Linguistic Linked Open Data is already available and that this amount continues to grow steadily, so that in the longer perspective, we can expect more data providers to offer an L(O)D view on their data, and to support RDF serializations such as JSON-LD as interchange formats. However, further growth and popularity depends crucially on the development of applications that are capable of consuming this data in a linguist-friendly fashion, or to enrich local data with web resources.

At the time of writing, working with RDF normally requires a certain level of technical expertise, i.e., basic knowledge of SPARQL and at least one RDF format. The authors' personal experience in university courses shows that linguists *can* be trained to acquire both successfully. However, this not normally done, and unlikely to ever be part of the linguistics core curriculum. This may change once designated text books on Linked Open Data for NLP and linguistics are becoming available,[18] but for the time being, a priority for this effort and the community remains to provide concrete applications tailored to the needs of linguists, lexicographers, researchers in NLP and knowledge engineering.

Promising approaches in this direction do exist: Existing tools can be complemented with an RDF layer to facilitate their interoperability. Likewise, LLOD-native applications are possible, e.g., to use RDFa (RDF in attributes) (Herman et al., 2015) to complement an XML workflow with SPARQL-based semantic search by means of web services (Sabine Tittel and Chiarcos, 2018), to provide aggregation, enrichment and search routines for language resource metadata (McCrae and Cimiano, 2015; Chiarcos et al., 2016), to use RDF as a formalism for annotation integration and data management (Burchardt et al., 2008; Chiarcos et al., 2017), or to use RDF and SPARQL for manipulating and evaluating linguistic annotations (Chiarcos et al., 2018b; Chiarcos et al., 2018a).

While these applications demonstrate the potential of LOD technology in linguistics, they come with a considerable entry barrier and they address the advanced user of RDF technology rather than a typical linguist. Even though concrete applications to exist, a long way is still to go to achieve the level of user-friendliness expected by occasional users of this technology.

A notable exception in this regard is LexO (Bellandi et al., 2017), which is a graphical tool for the collaborative editing of lexical and ontological resources natively building on the OntoLex vocabulary and RDF, designed to conduct lexicographical work in a philological context (i.e., creating the *Dictionnaire des Termes Médico-botaniques de l'Ancien Occitan*). Other projects whose objective is to provide LLOD-based tools for specific areas of application have been recently approved, so that progress in this direction is to be expected within the next years.

---

[18]A first step being realised by (Cimiano et al., 2020).

4. Acknowledgements

This paper is supported by the Horizon 2020 research and innovation programme with the projects Prêt-à-LLOD (grant agreement no. 825182) and ELEXIS (grant agreeement no. 731015). It is also partially based upon work from COST Action CA18209 - NexusLinguarum "European network for Web-centred linguistic data science".
We also thank the anonymous reviewers for their helpful comments.

5. References

Ahmadi, S., Arcan, M., and McCrae, J. (2019). Lexical Sense Alignment using Weighted Bipartite b-Matching. In *Proceedings of the Poster Track of LDK 2019*, pages 12–16.

Ahmadi, S., McCrae, J. P., Nimb, S., Troelsgård, T., Olsen, S., Pedersen, B. S., Declerck, T., Wissik, T., Monachini, M., Bellandi, A., Khan, F., Pisani, I., Krek, S., Lipp, V., Váradi, T., Simon, L., Győrffy, A., Tiberius, C., Schoonheim, T., Moshe, Y. B., Rudich, M., Ahmad, R. A., Lonke, D., Kovalenko, K., Langemets, M., Kallas, J., Dereza, O., Fransen, T., Cillessen, D., Lindemann, D., Alonso, M., Salgado, A., Sancho, J. L., na Ruiz, R.-J. U., Simov, K., Osenova, P., Kancheva, Z., Radev, I., Stanković, R., Krstev, C., Lazić, B., Marković, A., Perdih, A., and Gabrovšek, D. (2020). A Multilingual Evaluation Dataset for Monolingual Word Sense Alignment. In *Proceedings of the 12th Language Resource and Evaluation Conference (LREC 2020)*.

Bellandi, A., Giovannetti, E., Piccini, S., and Weingart, A. (2017). Developing LexO: a collaborative editor of multilingual lexica and termino-ontological resources in the humanities. In *Proceedings of Language, Ontology, Terminology and Knowledge Structures Workshop (LOTKS 2017)*, Montpellier, France, September. Association for Computational Linguistics.

Berners-Lee, T. (2006). Design issues: Linked data. URL http://www.w3.org/DesignIssues/LinkedData.html (July 31, 2012).

Bosque-Gil, J., Lonke, D., Gracia, J., and Kernerman, I. (2019). Validating the OntoLex-lemon lexicography module with K Dictionaries' multilingual data. In *Electronic lexicography in the 21st century. Proceedings of the eLex 2019 conference.*, pages 726–746, Brno, Czech Republic, October. Lexical Computing CZ s.r.o.,.

Burchardt, A., Padó, S., Spohr, D., Frank, A., and Heid, U. (2008). Formalising Multi-layer Corpora in OWL/DL – Lexicon Modelling, Querying and Consistency Control. In *Proc. of the 3rd International Joint Conference on NLP (IJCNLP)*, pages 389–396, Hyderabad, India.

Chiarcos, C. and Sukhareva, M. (2015). OLiA - Ontologies of Linguistic Annotation. *Semantic Web Journal*, 518:379–386.

Christian Chiarcos, et al., editors. (2012). *Linked Data in Linguistics*. Springer Berlin Heidelberg.

Chiarcos, C., McCrae, J., Cimiano, P., and Fellbaum, C. (2013). Towards open data for linguistics: Linguistic linked data. In A. Oltramari, et al., editors, *New Trends of Research in Ontologies and Lexical Resources*. Springer, Heidelberg, Heidelberg, Germany.

Chiarcos, C., Fäth, C., Renner-Westermann, H., Abromeit, F., and Dimitrova, V. (2016). Lin|gu|is|tik: Building the Linguist's Pathway to Bibliographies, Libraries, Language Resources and Linked Open Data. In Nicoletta Calzolari (Conference Chair), et al., editors, *Proceedings of the Tenth International Conference on Language Resources and Evaluation (LREC 2016)*, Portorož, Slovenia, may. European Language Resources Association (ELRA).

Chiarcos, C., Ionov, M., Rind-Pawlowski, M., Fäth, C., Schreur, J. W., and Nevskaya, I. (2017). LLODifying Linguistic Glosses. In *International Conference on Language, Data and Knowledge*, pages 89–103, Cham. Springer, Springer.

Chiarcos, C., Khait, I., Pagé-Perron, É., Schenk, N., Fäth, C., Steuer, J., Mcgrath, W., and Wang, J. (2018a). Annotating a low-resource language with LLOD technology: Sumerian morphology and syntax. *Information*, 9(11):290.

Chiarcos, C., Kosmehl, B., Fäth, C., and Sukhareva, M. (2018b). Analyzing middle high german syntax with rdf and sparql. In *Proceedings of the Eleventh International Conference on Language Resources and Evaluation (LREC-2018)*, Miyazaki, Japan.

Chiarcos, C. (2008). An ontology of linguistic annotations. *LDV Forum*, 23(1):1–16. Foundations of Ontologies in Text Technology, Part II: Applications.

Cimiano, P., McCrae, J. P., and Buitelaar, P. (2016). Lexicon Model for Ontologies: Community Report. W3C community group final report, World Wide Web Consortium.

Cimiano, P., Chiarcos, C., McCrae, J. P., and Gracia, J. (2020). *Linguistic Linked Data - Representation, Generation and Applications*. Springer.

de Melo, G. (2015). Lexvo.org: Language-related information for the Linguistic Linked Data Cloud. *Semantic Web Journal*, 6(4):393–400, August.

Dostert, L. (1955). The Georgetown-IBM experiment. In W. Locke et al., editors, *Machine Translation of Languages*, pages 124–135. John Wiley & Sons, New York.

Francis, W. N. and Kucera, H. (1964). Brown Corpus manual. Technical report, Brown University, Providence, Rhode Island. revised edition 1979.

Gracia, J., Kernerman, I., and Bosque-Gil, J. (2017). Toward linked data-native dictionaries. In *Electronic Lexicography in the 21st Century: Lexicography from Scratch. Proceedings of the eLex 2017 conference*, pages 19–21.

Greenberg, J. (1960). A quantitative approach to the morphological typology of languages. *International Journal of American Linguistics*, 26:178–194.

Harris, S. and Seaborne, A. (2013). SPARQL 1.1 query language. W3C recommendation, World Wide Web Consortium.

Herman, I., Adida, B., Sporny, M., and Birbeck, M. (2015). RDFa 1.1 primer - third edition. W3C working group note, World Wide Web Consortium.

Ide, N. and Pustejovsky, J. (2010). What does interoperability mean, anyway? Toward an operational definition of interoperability. In *Proc. of the 2nd International Conference on Global Interoperability for Language Resources (ICGL*, Hong Kong, China.

Ide, N. and Suderman, K. (2007). GrAF: A graph-based format for linguistic annotations. In *1st Linguistic Annotation Workshop (LAW 2007)*, pages 1–8, Prague, Czech Republic.

Klimek, B., McCrae, J. P., Bosque-Gil, J., Ionov, M., Tauber, J. K., and Chiarcos, C. (2019). Challenges for the representation of morphology in ontology lexicons. In *Proceedings of eLex 2019. Electronic lexicography in the 21st century: Smart lexicography*.

Krek, S., Kosem, I., McCrae, J. P., Navigli, R., Pedersen, B. S., Tiberius, C., and Wissik, T. (2018). European lexicographic infrastructure (elexis). In *Proceedings of the XVIII EURALEX International Congress on Lexicography in Global Contexts*, pages 881–892.

McCrae, J. P. and Buitelaar, P. (2018). Linking Datasets Using Semantic Textual Similarity. *Cybernetics and Information Technologies*, 18(1):109–123.

McCrae, J. P. and Cimiano, P. (2015). Linghub: a Linked Data based portal supporting the discovery of language resources. In *Proc. of the 11th International Conference on Semantic Systems*.

McCrae, J., de Cea, G. A., Buitelaar, P., Cimiano, P., Declerck, T., Gómez-Pérez, A., Gracia, J., Hollink, L., Montiel-Ponsoda, E., Spohr, D., and Wunner, T. (2012). Interchanging lexical resources on the Semantic Web. *Language Resources and Evaluation*, 46(6):701–719.

McCrae, J. P., Buitelaar, P., and Cimiano, P. (2017). The OntoLex-Lemon Model: development and applications. In *Proc. of the 5th Biennial Conference on Electronic Lexicography (eLex)*.

W. Morris, editor. (1969). *The American Heritage Dictionary of the English Language*. Houghton Mifflin, New York.

Nordhoff, S. and Hammarström, H. (2011). Glottolog/Langdoc: Defining dialects, languages, and language families as collections of resources. In *Proceedings of the First International Workshop on Linked Science 2011*, Bonn, Germany.

Antonio Pareja-Lora, et al., editors. (2019). *Development of Linguistic Linked Open Data Resources for Collaborative Data-Intensive Research in the Language Sciences*. MIT Press.

Sabine Tittel, H. B.-S. and Chiarcos, C. (2018). Using RDFa to link text and dictionary data for medieval French. In *Proc. of the 6th Workshop on Linked Data in Linguistics (LDL-2018): Towards Linguistic Data Science*, Paris, France. European Language Resources Association (ELRA).

Windhouwer, M. and Wright, S. E. (2012). Linking to linguistic data categories in ISOcat. In *Linked Data in Linguistics*, pages 99–107. Springer.

Wright, S. (2004). A global data category registry for interoperable language resources. In *Proceedings of the Fourth Language Resources and Evaluation Conference (LREC 2004)*, pages 123–126, Lisboa, Portugal, May.

Proceedings of the 1st International Workshop on Language Technology Platforms (IWLTP 2020), pages 16–21
Language Resources and Evaluation Conference (LREC 2020), Marseille, 11–16 May 2020
© European Language Resources Association (ELRA), licensed under CC-BY-NC

Architecture of a Scalable, Secure and Resilient Translation Platform for Multilingual News Media

Susie Coleman◇, **Andrew Secker**◇, **Rachel Bawden**♣, **Barry Haddow**♣, **Alexandra Birch**♣
◇British Broadcasting Corporation, UK
♣School of Informatics, University of Edinburgh, UK
susie.coleman@bbc.co.uk, andrew.secker@bbc.co.uk, bhaddow@inf.ed.ac.uk, {rachel.bawden, a.birch}ed.ac.uk

Abstract

This paper presents an example architecture for a scalable, secure and resilient Machine Translation (MT) platform, using components available via Amazon Web Services (AWS). It is increasingly common for a single news organisation to publish and monitor news sources in multiple languages. A growth in news sources makes this increasingly challenging and time-consuming but MT can help automate some aspects of this process. Building a translation service provides a single integration point for news room tools that use translation technology allowing MT models to be integrated into a system once, rather than each time the translation technology is needed. By using a range of services provided by AWS, it is possible to architect a platform where multiple pre-existing technologies are combined to build a solution, as opposed to developing software from scratch for deployment on a single virtual machine. This increases the speed at which a platform can be developed and allows the use of well-maintained services. However, a single service also provides challenges. It is key to consider how the platform will scale when handling many users and how to ensure the platform is resilient.

Keywords: machine translation, AWS, platform, news media

1. Introduction

1.1. Media Context for NLP services

News does not only break in one language, and many modern large news media organisations seek to publish their material in multiple languages. These large news media organisations are, therefore, often working in a multilingual space. The BBC in the UK publishes news content in 40 languages and gathers news in over 100. The BBC distributes content on multiple platforms: radio, 24-hour TV and online video, audio and text content. The BBC's flagship Arabic and Persian services operate 24-hour TV news channels while other language services, including Kyrgyz, French, Russian, Ukrainian, Pashto, Burmese, Hausa and Tamil, also broadcast daily TV news bulletins via regional partner stations. All foreign language services publish news online. This is extremely important to promoting the reach of the news published by these world services, especially to under-served audiences.

Publication of news in multiple languages comes under the general category of *content creation*. With increasing language reach comes increasing demands on journalists' time. One way in which efficient use is made of journalistic endeavour is the republication of news originally authored in one language into another. An underused but key element to supporting journalists undertaking this task is Machine-Assisted Translation (MAT). With the appropriate user interfaces provided to support the translation step, a journalist is able to take a news story or script, in the case of an audio or video report, and quickly translate the original text using an automated technique. This translation is then manually edited to ensure it is in a state which is of sufficient quality. No matter how good the Machine Translation (MT), this will always be an important step for media organisations such as the BBC where quality is paramount; the reversioned content is usually prepared to be published in a different geographic region from where it originated, and therefore local knowledge, assumed geographical or cultural knowledge and colloquialisms must be expunged or explained in the translated copy.

The second application area, that of *news gathering* in multiple languages is supported via *media monitoring*, the (predominantly manual) monitoring of the world's media across video, audio, printed and online sources. In the current workflow, expert monitors and journalists have to perform a lot of manual work to keep up with broadcast and social media streams of data. Considering the huge growth in the number of streams of data that could potentially be monitored, the current processes fail to scale adequately. It is becoming imperative for technology to be used in this process to automate tasks, such as translation, in order to free monitors and journalists to perform more journalistic tasks that cannot be achieved with technology.

MT, the core of MAT, is an increasingly important technology for supporting communication in a globalised world and the use cases above illustrate how the News Media is an ideal candidate for promotion of efficiency through the use of MT.

However there exist significant gaps in the language pair coverage when considering supporting the BBC's multilingual news-gathering and dissemination operations. The European Union's Horizon 2020 research and innovation GoURMET project (Birch et al., 2019) aims to significantly improve the robustness and applicability of Neural MT (NMT) for low-resource language pairs and domains. Tangible outcomes of this process include the production of NMT models in 16 different language pairs. The BBC and Deutsche Welle (DW), the media partners on the project, will then use these in tools for journalists.

The outputs of the project will be field-tested at partners BBC and DW by inclusion in tools and prototypes (Secker et al., 2019b), and evaluation of the translation's utility in these real-world situations. A formal data-driven evaluation will also be undertaken (Secker et al., 2019a).

1.2. Related work

The SUMMA project[1] (Scalable Understanding of Multilingual MediA), ran from 2016 to 2019. The aim of SUMMA was to significantly improve media monitoring by creating a platform to automate the ingest and analysis of live news media. SUMMA integrated stream-based media processing tools (including speech recognition and machine translation) with deep language understanding capabilities (including named entity relation extraction and semantic parsing), and was implemented in use cases at the BBC and DW. Content was ingested in eight non-English languages plus English. All ingested content was translated into English for the purposes of analysis and as such, translation formed a key part of the process. SUMMA built evidence of the need for automated translation technologies to support news-gathering in modern media organisations, motivating GoURMET. The SUMMA platform was also built around micro-services but it was designed to be easy to install locally. It was deployable on the cloud but did not use native cloud scaling capacity as standard practices have evolved since.

The Elitr project[2], another EU project which is currently running, is building the European Live Translator platform (Franceschini et al., 2020). The aim of this project is to create an automatic translation and subtitling system for meetings and conferences. The platform used in Elitr builds on a platform developed by PerVoice[3], and also in an earlier EU project EU-Bridge[4]. The Elitr platform is optimised for real-time transcription and translation, and the transmission of audio and video data in addition to text. Due to the more demanding communication requirements, the Elitr platform has a custom data transmission protocol, and a C API which all components must implement.

1.3. Translation platform

In order to make the translation models available for use in such prototype tools, the BBC created a single platform in which they can be hosted, run and accessed. This single platform can then support numerous prototype tools, across multiple project partners, and with the correct provision around security and mediation of access by 3rd parties. The advantages of locating the translation technology in one place and then mediating access onto that via a service is this provides a single point for maintenance and updates. In contrast, if each prototype (tool, experience, etc.) has the translation technology integrated, an update to the translation technology (whether that be an improvement to the translation models themselves, a bug fix, a security improvement, etc.) must be undertaken numerous times.

There are a number of requirements for a translation platform that would not be present, or present in a different form, if the translation technology were built into each individual prototype or tool.

- **Scalability.** Since the platform now provides a single point of access, the platform must scale in response to the number of requests made from a variable number of tools and their users. Scaling must be automatic and reactive based on incoming request load.

- **Resilience.** With the platform now representing a single point of failure, it must be robust with automatic detection of failure and the ability to seamlessly move the servicing of incoming requests away from a failed process in a manner such that the end user sees no break in service.

- **Security.** As the translation service is accessed by multiple users, access must be secured to authorised parties and thus parties must identify themselves when submitting requests. It is also prudent to ensure that no one party can overload the platform with requests. While the service is required to scale, resources are not infinite and as such it is reasonable for the service to gracefully decline an unreasonable rate of requests from a single party in order to maintain a reasonable level of service for others.

- **Continuity**. It must be straightforward to apply updates to the service and these should not result in a noticeable break in responsiveness from the user's perspective.

- **Standard access.** External input and output to the translation modules occurs via a well defined API.

The effort required to create the above platform, successfully addressing the above considerations in the implementation, are enormous. Cloud computing platforms have developed around the need for institutions to create and maintain such platforms. Amazon Web Services (AWS) has emerged as a platform offering a diverse selection of cloud-based tools. Presented here is the architecture of the translation platform, implemented by the BBC on behalf of the GoURMET project and built entirely on the AWS platform. Whilst AWS is perhaps most known as a provider of Virtual Machines (VMs) via the EC2 product,[5] the development of a monolithic system for deployment on one or more VMs still requires considerable software development effort. In contrast the platform described herein combines a set of individual AWS products such that each manages a separate facet of the platform. Software development work is therefore minimised and limited to the setup of each AWS component and software engineering required to allow components to communicate.

The remainder of this paper describes the architecture of the platform. First the overall architecture of the platform is presented, then the implementation and customisation details of each major component are detailed. Finally, considerations around security, scalability of the platform and the deployment of MT models is covered.

---

[1] Funded by the European Union's Horizon 2020 research and innovation programme under grant agreement No 688139.

[2] Funded by the European Union's Horizon 2020 research and innovation programme under Grant Agreement No 825460

[3] http://www.pervoice.com/en/

[4] https://www.eu-bridge.eu/

[5] https://aws.amazon.com/ec2/

2. System Architecture of the Translation Platform

This platform is hosted on AWS and uses pre-existing services and components to create an architecture which is secure, robust and able to scale. By using the services that AWS offers it is possible to build and host a platform that combines existing components to build a solution rather than building the platform from scratch. This increases the speed of development and allows technology to be used that is already well tested and documented.

The other strength of AWS is the AWS Cloudformation[6] service which allows infrastructure to be defined using Cloudformation templates. A Cloudformation template is an example of infrastructure as code. By defining a template, a record of infrastructure is created that can be version controlled, provides visibility of the architecture and allows the system to be easily recreated from scratch.

There are multiple cloud services available that could have been used to implement this Architecture including Google Cloud Platform[7] and Microsoft Azure[8]. When choosing a platform cost, efficiency and reliability of services as well as the level of experience a development team has with a specific platform should all be considered. At the BBC AWS is the dominant provider of cloud computing services so when building a new service AWS is the default choice. As developers at the BBC are most familiar with AWS using it for new projects allows faster development times and more efficient debugging. However, it is still important to assess the feasibility of other platforms to ensure there is not a compelling reason to switch to an alternative.

The architecture required to fulfil a translation request is shown in Figure 1. A translation request will be initially handled by AWS API Gateway, which is the user facing part of the architecture. The request is then passed to an AWS Lambda, which acts as a bridge to a AWS Load Balancer, which will route traffic to the correct translation model running in AWS ECS (Elastic Container Service). The model in ECS will perform the translation and the response travels back up the stack to be served to a user by API Gateway. A more in depth explanation of the roles of the specific components is outlined in the following subsections as well as the user facing interface to the platform.

2.1. User Facing Interface

The platform is exposed via a RESTful API. The purpose of an API (Application Programmer Interface) is to expose a resource to developers to allow services and applications to make use of that resource (De, 2017). In the case of GoURMET, that resource is MT models. The goal of the API is to provide a consistent and logical interface that abstracts away from the specifics of how the MT models are implemented.

The API accepts and returns JSON objects, which is enforced by the Content Type HTTP Header. To translate text, a POST request is made to the API where the body of the request is a JSON object that specifies the source language,

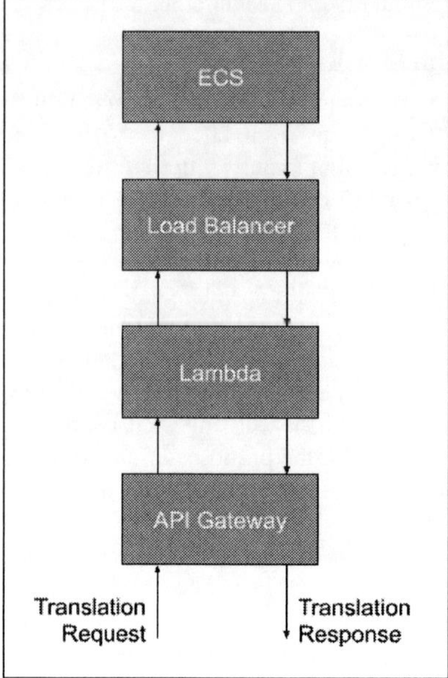

Figure 1: Architecture to fulfil a translation request

target language and text to translate. The text to translate must only use UTF-8 characters and can be multi-line text providing that it is escaped appropriately to still be valid JSON.

2.2. AWS API Gateway

API Gateway[9] is an AWS managed service for creating APIs. The service is used to manage exposure of the MT models to the public internet as outlined in the previous section. In this case, the API is a REST API where the interface is defined using Swagger.[10] As API Gateway is a managed service, it is easy to dynamically scale the API depending on traffic, and the service already implements multiple features for security, resilience and API life-cycle. This makes development of the user facing interface far quicker than starting from scratch.

2.3. AWS Lambda

AWS Lambda[11] offers serverless technology, which removes the need to maintain a server in order to run code. This makes it ideal for running short-lived tasks. A Lambda is created only when there is a need to execute the code and destroyed when that need no longer exists. This is good for both cost and dynamic scaling of services.

In the translation platform, the role of the Lambda is to route traffic from API Gateway to the Load Balancer.[12] This allows the Load Balancer to live within a private network and not be exposed to the public internet. This means

---

[6] https://aws.amazon.com/cloudformation/

[7] https://cloud.google.com/

[8] https://azure.microsoft.com

[9] https://aws.amazon.com/api-gateway/

[10] https://swagger.io/resources/open-api/

[11] https://aws.amazon.com/lambda/

[12] https://aws.amazon.com/elasticloadbalancing/

that traffic to the Load Balancer and, by extension, the MT models is controlled and managed via API Gateway.

2.4. AWS Load Balancer

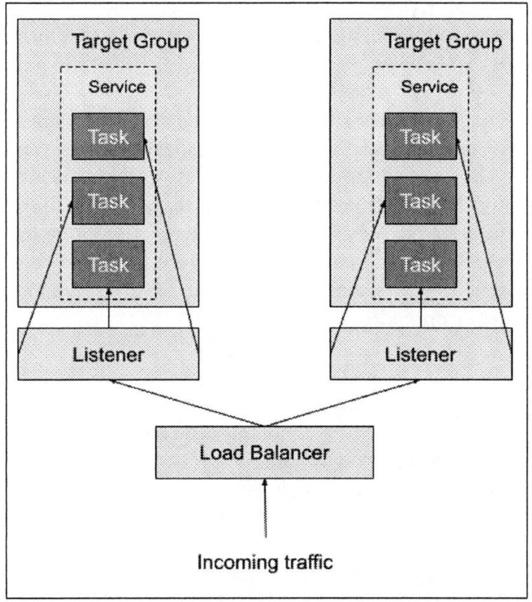

Figure 2: Routing traffic with a Load Balancer

The Load Balancer functions at the application layer of the OSI (Open Systems Interconnection) model. It listens for traffic on specific ports and will route traffic to a Target Group based on the port number as shown in Figure 2. The Target Group is made up of services that can receive the traffic. In this case, these are AWS ECS Tasks within an ECS Service. The Load Balancer will balance incoming traffic across all tasks within the Target Group.

2.5. AWS ECS - Elastic Container Service

The role of ECS[13] in the system is to run containers that contain the MT models.

All MT models are delivered as Docker images, which are definitions of how to create a container. This definition includes, but is not limited to, the operating system, programs installed, ports exposed, environment variables and file system. Containers provide an isolated environment for an application to run in, as defined in the Docker image. Multiple containers can run on a single physical machine to allow an efficient sharing of resources. ECS is a service to manage how containers run as well as the infrastructure they will run on.

The specific architecture of ECS is shown in Figure 3. An AWS Cluster has been created which defines the infrastructure the containers will run on. In this specific instance, AWS Fargate is used as it removes the requirement to manage EC2 instances. An AWS Task Definition has been created for each MT Docker image. The Task Definition defines the properties of a container. This includes but is not

---

[13]https://aws.amazon.com/ecs/

limited to which Docker image to use and where to pull the image from, how much CPU power and memory to allocate the container and any AWS IAM Roles[14] the container needs. Containers created using the Task Definitions are referred to as Tasks in AWS. The Tasks have been created within a Service. The Service maintains a specified number of instances of a Task and allows for the number of Tasks to be scaled up or down according to load on the system. The Service also health checks Tasks and destroys and replaces unhealthy ones.

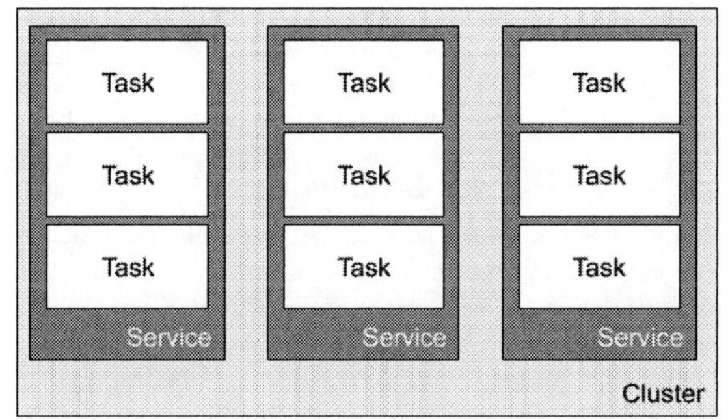

Figure 3: Architecture of an ECS Cluster

3. Security, Access Management and Request Rate Limiting

Security is important for any service available on the public internet, as the service is vulnerable to attacks from malicious users. In the case of an MT platform there is no sensitive information that could be exposed if an API key was to become compromised, therefore the biggest risks stem from DDoS (Distributed Denial of Service) attacks. A DDoS attack overwhelms a system with requests to stop it being able to handle legitimate requests. When using AWS, it is important to also consider the financial costs that can be caused by an insecure service. In this case, the scalable nature of the architecture would make it possible to require the services to use a large number of additional resources to handle malicious traffic increases, if the service is not properly secured.

The user facing API is secured:

- Using HTTPS: All traffic is served over HTTPS by default with API Gateway managing the certificate.

- Using API Keys

- Using Usage Plans: Usage plans are tied to specific API keys and add a throttling limit and quota limit.

- Sanitising Input: Ensure required request inputs are included and that the body matches the JSON schema and request model.

---

[14]https://docs.aws.amazon.com/IAM/latest/UserGuide/id_roles.html

- Limiting payload size: API Gateway has an upper payload limit of 10 MB[15]. This allows more than enough capacity to handle translation of news articles whilst setting an upper limit to prevent malicious attacks where the system is overloaded by requests with large payloads.

AWS's API Gateway service was one reason to favour AWS when building this platform. API Gateway provides all of the security features used to secure the API. This means that the in-depth knowledge needed to implement security features is not required as they do not need to be implemented from scratch. Furthermore, API Gateway is widely used in industry and is actively maintained which means that security flaws are detected early and patched quickly.

4. Scalability

It is important to have a service that can scale dynamically in response to changes in volume of traffic. There are two points of scalability in architecture shown in Figure 1.

The first is using ECS. A Service determines the number of instances created from a specific Task Definition that are running at any one time, and this allows the translation platform to scale up to accommodate more traffic. The Load Balancer will distribute the traffic amongst the growing number of Tasks available to fulfil the requests.

The other point of scalability is the Lambda. Serverless technology is designed to be flexible, as it is not the responsibility of the Lambda creator to define the hardware it will run on or to ensure sufficient compute resources are available for it to run. As a result, Lambdas can be automatically initiated as needed to handle increases in traffic without the need to predict traffic spikes and provision hardware to handle these. The API Gateway is able to handle large amounts of traffic hitting the translation platform and using Lambdas to fulfil these requests allows the system to handle these traffic increases.

The final consideration regarding scalability is the ability to automate this scaling. AWS provides Cloudwatch Alarms to monitor and automatically respond to changes in the system under monitoring. This allows the translation platform to alert in response to changes in traffic and use of resources. These alerts can be used to handle these changes without manual intervention.

5. Deploying MT Models

A key consideration for this system is how to provide flexibility for creativity in research to allow novel approaches to MT whilst still building a consistent production service. This was achieved by using Docker. A standard template project was agreed for producing a Docker image for each MT model. This template consisted of:

- A Dockerfile

- A simple Python Flask app with a root endpoint and translate endpoint

- An integration Python script

The integration script contains an `init` function that is called when a container is created from the Docker image and a `translate` function that is called whenever a translation is performed. It is the responsibility of anyone implementing an MT model to implement these two functions. This allowed a consistent interface to all translation models whilst still keeping the actual implementation of the model agnostic.

The Docker images created are hosted on AWS using the AWS Elastic Container Registry.[16] Docker images can be hosted as repositories on any service that provides a Docker registry. Registries provide a central place to store images and the ability to only allow authorised users access to those images. Repositories use tags to allow the images to be version controlled. When a Task is created in ECS, the image is pulled from ECR.

6. Summary

Modern large news media organisations exist in a multilingual environment. MT technologies can be used to promote efficiency in such organisations for both news-gathering and publication in multiple languages. In order to support multiple tools which require translation as a fundamental, a platform providing translation as a service is the preferred solution. This paper describes an architecture for the creation of such a platform using components provided by AWS. The requirements for such a platform were described and the tools available from AWS which realise the required functionality were detailed. The platform described herein will form the basis of a selection of tools and prototypes to be tested in the BBC and DW as well as supporting further formal evaluation of the underlying MT systems.

7. Acknowledgements

This work was supported by funding from the European Union's Horizon 2020 research and innovation programme under grant agreement No 825299 (GoURMET). It was also supported by the UK Engineering and Physical Sciences Research Council (EPSRC) fellowship grant EP/S001271/1 (MTStretch).

8. Bibliographical References

Birch, A., Haddow, B., Titov, I., Barone, A. V. M., Bawden, R., Sánchez-Martínez, F., Forcada, M. L., Esplà-Gomis, M., Sánchez-Cartagena, V., Pérez-Ortiz, J. A., Aziz, W., Secker, A., and van der Kreeft, P. (2019). Global under-resourced media translation (GoURMET). In *Proceedings of Machine Translation Summit XVII Volume 2: Translator, Project and User Tracks*, pages 122–122, Dublin, Ireland, August. European Association for Machine Translation.

De, B. (2017). *API Management: An Architect's Guide to Developing and Managing APIs for Your Organization.* Apress.

Franceschini, D., Canton, C., Simonini, I., Schweinfurth, A., Glott, A., Stüker, S., Nguyen, T.-S., Schneider, F., Ha, T.-L., Bojar, O., Sagar, S., Macháček, D., and Smrž, O. (2020). Removing European Language Barriers with

---

[15]https://docs.aws.amazon.com/apigateway/
latest/developerguide/limits.html

[16]https://aws.amazon.com/ecr/

Innovative Machine Translation Technology. In *Proceedings of the 1st International Workshop on Language Technology Platforms*.

Secker, A., Birch, A., van der Kreeft, P., and Sánchez-Martínez, F. (2019a). GoURMET deliverable D5.1 – evaluation plan.

Secker, A., Wall, J., van der Kreeft, P., and Coleman, S. (2019b). GoURMET deliverable D5.2 – use cases and requirements.

Proceedings of the 1st International Workshop on Language Technology Platforms (IWLTP 2020), pages 22–27
Language Resources and Evaluation Conference (LREC 2020), Marseille, 11–16 May 2020
© European Language Resources Association (ELRA), licensed under CC-BY-NC

CoBiLiRo: A Research Platform for Bimodal Corpora

Dan Cristea[1,2], Ionuț Pistol[1], Șerban Boghiu[1], Anca-Diana Bibiri[3], Daniela Gîfu[1,2], Andrei Scutelnicu[1,2], Mihaela Onofrei[1,2], Diana Trandabăț[1], George Bugeag[1]

[1]"Alexandru Ioan Cuza" University of Iași, Faculty of Computer Science (UAIC-FII)
[2]Institute of Computer Science, Romanian Academy, Iași Branch (ARFI-IIT)
[3]"Alexandru Ioan Cuza" University of Iași, Institute for Interdisciplinary Research, Social Sciences and Humanities Research Department (UAIC-ICI)
[1]16, Berthelot St., 700483 Iași, Romania,
[2] Dr. Theodor Codrescu St., 700481 Iași, Romania,
[3]54, Lascăr Catargi St., 700107, Iași, Romania

{danu.cristea, pistol.ionutcristian, serbanboghiu, anca.bibiri, daniela.gifu73, andreiscutelnicu, mihaela.plamada.onofrei,
diana.trandabat, bugeag.george}@gmail.com

Abstract

This paper describes the on-going work carried out within the CoBiLiRo (Bimodal Corpus for Romanian Language) research project, part of ReTeRom (Resources and Technologies for Developing Human-Machine Interfaces in Romanian). Data annotation finds increasing use in speech recognition and synthesis with the goal to support learning processes. In this context, a variety of different annotation systems for application to Speech and Text Processing environments have been presented. Even if many designs for the data annotations workflow have emerged, the process of handling metadata, to manage complex user-defined annotations, is not covered enough. We propose a design of the format aimed to serve as an annotation standard for bimodal resources, which facilitates searching, editing and statistical analysis operations over it. The design and implementation of an infrastructure that houses the resources are also presented. The goal is widening the dissemination of bimodal corpora for research valorisation and use in applications. Also, this study reports on the main operations of the web Platform which hosts the corpus and the automatic conversion flows that brings the submitted files at the format accepted by the Platform.

Keywords: bimodal corpus, annotation standard, web platform, speech and text processing, metadata of linguistic resources, CoBiLiRo, ReTeRom.

1. Introduction

In this paper we present CoBiLiRo, an environment intended to act as a hosting, editing and processing platform for large collections of parallel speech/text data. In actual use now for the data of the ReTeRom project, CoBiLiRo contains a collection of bimodal files on Romanian language. The researchers in the ReTeRom project belong to four natural language processing laboratories[1] in Romania that work on speech understanding, speech synthesis, text processing, alignment of speech - text resources and organisation of big repositories of language data for research and public use.

With the purpose to support future research on speech and text technologies dedicated to Romanian, we have done a careful inventory of existing bimodal resources at ReTeRom partners places and have acquired new donations from external providers. The Platform harmonizes the representations of these resources, their annotation and metadata formats, the final aim being to organise the existent and future resources and open large access to bimodal corpora for research valorisation and use in applications.

2. Similar Achievements

The reasons for keeping records of speech worldwide are very diverse. A brief enumeration should include: preservation of samples of dying languages, preservation of regional varieties of languages (e.g. the International corpus of English[2], which is an electronic corpus of regional varieties of English throughout the world: Great Britain, Ireland, New Zealand, Canada, Singapore, The Philippines), samples of language in evolution for diachronic comparative studies, interviews with famous people – for cultural heritage preservation. Since 2007, ELRA (European Language Resources Association) organises and distributes[3] a huge collection of language resources, in more than 70 languages and language varieties, among which many are speech or bimodal corpora (Mapelli et al., 2018). Famous speech corpora are: Santa Barbara Corpus of Spoken American English[4] (a large body of recordings of naturally occurring spoken interaction from all over the United States), Cambridge International Corpus[5] containing many other written and spoken corpora (Cambridge and Nottingham Corpus of Discourse in English (CANCODE), Cambridge and Nottingham Spoken Business English (CANBEC), Cambridge Cornell Corpus of Spoken North American English), The Buckeye Speech Corpus[6] (conversational speech on different themes), Bavarian Archive for Speech Signals Corpora (Siemens Synthesis Corpus)[7].

---

[1] "Mihai Drăgănescu" Research Institute for Artificial Intelligence of the Romanian Academy in Bucharest (RACAI), as ReTeRom Coordinator, Technical University of Cluj-Napoca (UTCN), Politehnica University of Bucharest (UPB) and "Alexandru Ioan Cuza" University of Iași (UAIC).

[2] http://ice-corpora.net/ice/index.html
[3] Via its operational body ELDA.
[4] https://www.linguistics.ucsb.edu/research/santa-barbara-corpus
[5] https://www.cambridge.org/elt/corpus/international_corpus.htm
[6] https://buckeyecorpus.osu.edu/
[7] https://www.phonetik.uni-muenchen.de/forschung/Bas/BasKorporaeng.html

Much less numerous are bimodal speech-text corpora[8] i.e. collections that keep voices and their transcribed text. Examples are: Turkish bimodal corpus (Polat and Oyucu, 2020), GermaParl: Corpus of Plenary Protocols of the German Bundestag (Blaette, 2017), The Spoken Dutch Corpus (representing contemporary standard Dutch as spoken by adults in The Netherlands and Flanders) (Oostdijk, 2000), C-ORAL-ROM – a multilingual corpus of spontaneous speech (around 1.200.000 words) representing four main Romance languages: French, Italian, Portuguese and Spanish (Cresti and Moneglia, 2005).

Platforms offering access to speech and bimodal resources are already available, perhaps the most significant ones due to their size and inclusion of Romanian language documents are the LRE Map and Clarin's VLO. Both of them include multiple resources of similar nature to those for which we designed and built the CoBiLiRo platform. More complex features are offered by the Virtual Language Observatory (VLO), which allows users to input search queries over the available resources using a custom designed syntax. Also, in VLO one can match resources with available processing tools, the interface indicating which of the available processing tools are compatible with the viewed resource. A functionality of this type is not implemented in CoBiLiRo, since our platform is designed specifically for aligned (speech-text) resources and includes special features allowing users to locate, filter and access such corpora. For example, none of the two platforms mentioned above allow users to search only male voices, only resources of a certain size or to process the available resources (annotate or convert them to a different format).

3. Architecture and Functionalities

3.1 Technologies and Architectural Patterns

ASP.NET Core is a high-performance, cross-platform, open-source framework used to develop the Cobiliro platform. The web application is hosted on premises in the "Alexandru Ioan Cuza" University of Iași, on a CentOS machine.

The Model-View-Controller (MVC) architecture is used in order to separate the platform into three main groups of components that can be easily extended and modified, each one having its own role:

- *Models*

Models are used to represent database tables and relationships between them. In order to manipulate the data, we use Entity Framework – an object relational mapper that provides a fast way of interacting with the databases and models. Model Validation techniques both server-side and client-side were used in order to ensure that the inserted data is consistent and reliable.

- *Views*

In order to provide a user-friendly interface, we decided to use jQuery and Razor syntax, which offers a way of creating server-side dynamic pages that receives and display data from the models.

- *Controllers*

Controllers handle the web application requests. The services are injected into controllers for achieving Inversion of Control between them and their dependencies. The dependency injection pattern implements inversion of control and assures a loosely coupled web application.

3.2 Security

The authentication, authorization, and role management of the application was implemented using the Identity Framework. This framework provides a powerful API that allows us to manage access control and security concerns regarding data privacy with respect to GDPR regulations[9]. Every password was hashed using the PBKDF2 algorithm[10] which is considered to be the safest encryption algorithm and also the most widely used by most applications.

In order to authenticate every HTTP request, we have attached a token (also known as a bearer token) to it. This assures that only allowed users access the shared content. ASP.NET framework also offers an easy mechanism that can facilitate protection for SQL Injection or Cross-Site-Request Forgery attacks.

3.3 Data Base

For persistent data storage we have used MariaDB, a free, open-source relational database. Pomelo Entity Framework is an Entity Framework provider that allows use of Entity Framework with a MySQL database.

3.4 REST API

Representational state transfer (REST) is a software architectural style that defines a set of constraints to be used for creating Web services. For example, for listening to a sound file, the files and their metadata should be sent as a byte array to the client-side application. The requests are going through our authorization and authentication filters. The serialization is done using the Javascript Object Notation (JSON) which is an open-standard file format.

3.5 External NLP Services - TEPROLIN

For the processing of texts that are uploaded as part of the bimodal resources, the Teprolin Web Service[11], developed by RACAI partner, is used. This service allows several operations to be applied to texts, such as:

- restoration of diacritics
- phonetic transcription of words
- converting numbers into their text spellings
- bordering into sentences
- tokenization
- POS-tagging
- lemmatization
- Named Entity Recognition
- NP-chunking

---

[8] Except for the very frequent sound and video, other bimodal corpora include speech and sign language, or sign language and text.

[9] https://gdpr-info.eu/
[10] https://en.wikipedia.org/wiki/PBKDF2
[11] http://89.38.230.23:5000/

- syntactic parsing, etc.

3.6 Functionalities

The Portal is opened to the following categories of users: *administrator*, *resource curator* (responsible for the monitoring and management of new resources), *donator* (a user that offers and uploads their resources, and which can do anything they want with their own resources, including deletion), and *ordinary user* (only for consultation, browsing, therefore having a passive role, or interested in doing theoretical or applied research with the Portal's resources). The access of ordinary users is restricted by IPR, each resource being paired with a specific IPR contract. The hierarchy of rights is: administrator > curator > donator > ordinary user.

The resources on the Platform can be interrogated by different criteria, matching keywords against the description field of the metadata and/or combining other different metadata values. Once found, a resource can be: consulted, by browsing its content with web GUIs, downloaded, deleted, upgraded/updated (delete + upload), or converted to a different format (see Section 4). The whole repository is backed-up periodically. Global statistics on the whole collection are automatically updated and can be consulted at the level of an ordinary user. Other functionalities offered by the Portal include: secured administration panel, responsive design (adapted for mobile devices), newsletter, contact forms with in and out email service for external users, forum of discussions and chat, RSS, Google Analytics.

4. Data Formats and Convertors

As part of the process of building the CoBiLiRo repository, we have contacted owners of speech/text resources open to the idea of offering them for research tasks. We have identified three types of original formats that pair speech and text components. This variety, well documented as a project delivery (Trandabăț, 2018), is as follows:

- PHS/LAB, a format which separates text, speech and alignment in different files;
- MULTEXT/TEI, a format described initially in the MULTEXT project and later used by various language resource builders;
- TEXTGRID, a format supported by a large community of European developers and used in a large set of existing resources.

The generous research and development goals that we envisage around the use of the CoBiLiRo platform, all shaped for the purpose of functioning as a sharing and distribution host of bimodal resources, imposes the adoption of a standard resting format for all hosted elements. Taken as an internal standard, this format will allow interchangeability of any types of resources and one-time implementation of a large spectrum of searching, editing and statistics functionalities. This format (Cristea et al., 2018) is inspired by the TEI-P5.10 standard (Sperberg-McQueen and Burnard, 2018), while also including elements from other proposals (Li and Yin, 2007). The TEI-P5 standard has been simplified in some respects and augmented in others to best accommodate the requirements of our bimodal corpora of speech and text data. To organise the functionality of the Platform around

this standard, input and output converters have been implemented to support in and out transfers. Central to this format, as will be seen below, is the idea of alignment between the speech and the text components.

The platform also includes an API able to automatically detect the format of the original uploaded resource and launch on it the proper convertor, in order to bring the input files to the standard format. The conversion process is performed on our servers without requiring any user input. Once converted to the standard format, the file can benefit from the Platform's search, editing and statistics capabilities. However, the original format is also preserved, at least for the reason that the conversion is not always lossless. At any time, the user has the option to download either the original format or the CoBiLiRo standard variant of a resource, the last one opening the door for enhanced integration with the Platform.

The CoBiLiRo format includes metadata, kept in a header, and content. The header records:

- source of the object stored,
- gender of speakers,
- identity of speakers (when they agreed to be nominated – as, for instance, in public speeches),
- voice's type (spontaneous or voice-in-reading),
- recording conditions (in lab, noisy environments, etc.),
- duration,
- type of speech files (mp3 or wav),
- speech-text alignment level (sentence, word),
- etc.

These pieces of information are stored in appropriate xml tags and attributes, within the teiHeader tag.

In the content part, segmentation of speech and its alignment with the text is marked. The most common levels of segmentation and alignment are the sentence and the lexical tokens. Since, in the voice files, sentences could sometimes be difficult to border, morphological units (such as words) and phonological elements (phonemes) constitute other possible segmentation elements. More higher layers of annotation could be added: on the speech signal – prosodic annotation (pitch, raise and decrease of the fundamental frequency), and on the textual component – sub-syntactic (nominal groups, clauses, etc.) and syntactic (parsing trees), performed with TEPROLIN services, as shown in Section 3.5.

The CoBiLiRo format allows for three types of segmentation and speech-text alignment, marked using `<unit>` tags. The first type, called "`file`", is adequate for resources held in multiple files. A `<unit>` tag includes child nodes: the `<speech>` child names the file containing the speech component and the `<text>` child points to the corresponding textual transcription file.

The second type of segmentation, called "`start-stop`" (see Figure 1), is adequate for resources that include only one speech file, which is segmented and aligned at temporal boundaries, the text being reproduced between each two such consecutive markers, given in seconds, with the `start` and `stop` attributes.

Finally, the third type, called "`file-start-stop`", represents a combination of the two types presented above.

```
<units>
  <unit>
    <speech speechFile="9C6c_86a.wav" />
    <subunit>
      <speech start="0" stop="0.1881085" />
      <text>"</text>
    </subunit>
    <subunit>
      <speech start="0.1881085" stop="0.2871186" />
      <text>\'1a"</text>
    </subunit>
    <subunit>
      <speech start="0.2871186" stop="0.33094275" />
      <text>n"</text>
    </subunit>
    <subunit>
      <speech start="0.33094275" stop="0.5378901" />
      <text>a::"</text>
    </subunit>
    <subunit>
      <speech start="0.5378901" stop="1.10175" />
      <text>"</text>
    </subunit>
  </unit>
</units>
```

Figure 1: An example of a start-stop segmentation and alignment marking (the `<text>` segments are specific characters, correctly decoded by the interface)

5. Data Acquisition, IPR, and Distribution

The audio components include television and radio programs, interviews, public speeches (as those delivered in Parliament or in public events), lectures, movies, theatre plays, read literary works, spontaneous short recordings collected on the street, and other types of speech recordings.

In this paper we classify speech recordings following three criteria. The first criterion takes into consideration the recording act:

- *spontaneous speech*, represented by: narrative voices, dialogs, MapTasks (validated technique in which two subjects work together to complete the task of navigating through a map by describing a route) (Bibiri *et al.*, 2012), appointment-tasks and meetings, "Wizard of Oz" simulations (interactions of human beings with computers for modelling real-life situations) (Bernsen *et al.*, 1998);
- *read speech*, as: chapters from books (or entire books, for instance *Mara*, by Ioan Slavici), news broadcasts, lists of words, number sequences, short sentences (as in the case of the RASC corpus[12]), etc.

The second classification criterion takes into consideration the source of the resource:

- acquired or originally recorded during previous national or international projects *for research purposes*;
- *ad-hoc acquisitions*, which are offered from generous contributors.

Finally, the third criterion considers the intention behind the creation of the resource:

- originally created with the purpose to *develop and improve speech technologies* for Romanian language (such as those created by consortium partners RACAI, UPB and UTCN),
- created for *linguistic, phonological and/or dialectal research* (in general, those created at UAIC).

To take one example, *read speech* resources, acquired for *research purpose* related to *dialectical investigations* offer the opportunity to analyse: various pronunciations in different dialects; the pronunciation specific to males and females; flapping across word boundaries in spontaneous speech; the effect of disfluencies on neighbouring words; duration of sounds at the end of an utterance (in accordance with the feelings expressed); the pronunciation of unstressed vowels (especially at the end of the words); sounds deletion; palatalization across word boundaries – Moldavian dialectal pronunciations, like: *g'ine* (for *bine*; EN: *good*); *k'atră* (for *piatră*; EN: *stone*), *hier* (for *fier*; EN: *iron*); or intonational patterns characterizing Romanian language.

At the moment of writing this paper, the following resources are hosted by the CoBiLiRo Platform. According to the above mentioned criteria, in the category of spontaneous speech corpora there are included: the CoRoLa[13] corpus, *the Reference Corpus for Contemporary Romanian* – supplied by ARFI-IIT and RACAI; the IIT corpus, containing radio debates and interviews – contributed by ARFI-IIT; the SoRoEs corpus, acquired in the project *Romanian and Spanish contrastive intonation analysis. A sociolinguistic approach* – contributed by UAIC-ICI; the Spontaneous Speech Corpus (SSC-train), Spontaneous Speech Corpus (SSC-eval) and Spontaneous Speech Corpus 2 (SSC-eval2) – all contributed by UPB. For read speech corpora, the following resources are uploaded: the Read Speech Corpus, including TV news and talk-shows – contributed by UPB; SWARA (*Mobile System for Rehabilitative Vocal Assistancee of Surgical Aphonia*); a large expressive Romanian speech corpus, reproducing the novel *Mara* written by Ioan Slavici in 1906, in an audiobook format, and Ro-GRID, short recordings with a fix format – all provided by UTCN. The lastly acquired resources consist of 74 hours or recordings, radio interviews, therefore spontaneous speech, ad-hoc acquisitions, offered to improve speech technologies: the "100 Years of Romania" corpus[14] , the "Guess Who's Coming to Dinner" corpus[15], and the "Conversations on culture and science" corpus[16]. All resources are bimodal, therefore including both audio files and transcripts, and the speech-to-text alignments are now being generated by the TADARAV[17] aligner (Georgescu et. *al.*, 2019). In total, the Portal includes now more than 520 hours of speech recordings and their transcriptions.

For all these resources we have agreed and signed with the donor's specific formulations of IPRs, which state also

---

[12] http://rasc.racai.ro/; https://speech.utcluj.ro/swarasc/

[13] http://corola.racai.ro/

[14] Contributed by prof. Gheorghe Iacob, "Alexandru Ioan Cuza" University of Iași.

[15] Contributed by Vasile Arhire, Romanian Public Television (TVR) Iași.

[16] Contributed by prof. Eugen Munteanu, in conversation with acad. Viorel Barbu.

[17] Same as CoBiLiRo, TADARAV is a component part of ReTeRom.

the distribution rules. The Platform offers more types of access: only consultation of titles (open to any user), access to samples of files, restricted and unrestricted download.

6.   CoBiLiRo as a Source of Applications and Student Work

Since the main purpose of building the CoBiLiRo Platform was to facilitate research and development of processing tools for Romanian spoken and written language, we already envisioned a list of projects, addressed to UAIC students in Computer Science that would make use of the resources and tools hosted by the Platform. Passed to a class of bachelor 3rd year students enrolled in the course *Techniques of Human Language Engineering* and to the master students in Computational Linguistics, some of these ideas are currently under design and development. We present few of them below.

"*The speaking dictionary*" refers to enhancing an electronic dictionary of the Romanian language, the Thesaurus Dictionary of the Romanian Language in Electronic Format - eDTLR (Cristea et *al.*, 2011; Pătrașcu et *al.*, 2016), with pronunciations for its entry words, as they have been discovered in the bimodal resources hosted by the Platform. This will be accomplished following these steps:

1.   All text components of bimodal corpora hosted by CoBiLiRo are lemmatised. Lemmatization (same as POS-tagging) follows the conversion process described in Section 4 of this paper.
2.   Resources are aligned at word level between the speech and the text components using the TADARAV aligner, and each alignment is accompanied by an estimated accuracy[18].
3.   For each dictionary entry we look for morphologically flexed forms of this lemma in the aligned textual documents. For many dictionary entries it is normal to find more matches. In this case, the specifications of the project require that the candidates be listed and uttered, in the descending order of their estimated accuracy, as long as the user keeps pushing a "Pronunciation" button.

Other project ideas involve adding speech components to previously developed applications. Here follow brief descriptions of three of them.

In "*My speaking diary*", the user can interact with an automatically built diary, by asking questions and listening to answers about the activities she/he has been involved in during the day. By using the device's GPS, the API running on the mobile device can log down the list of pairs <time, place> for the places the user has been located at all along the day. Then, by using a GIS[19], it can associate names to these locations and, using calendar entries and/or an ontology of locations, associate typical activities to these locations. Then, the application can use this information to answer questions such as "How much time did I spent at work today?", "How many times did I

go shopping last week?" etc. The generation of spoken answers will be done by using the CoBiLiRo bimodal repository and the technologies developed as part of the associated SINTERO project[20] (Stan and Giurgiu, 2018). Used by Alzheimer patients in incipient phases, the application can delay the boost of the illness.

The project "*I dialogue with the book I read*" will implement an idea uttered in a previous lab project (Cristea et al., 2015), in which we showed how semantic relations between characters of a book can be deciphered in a text. But, vocally interacting with a book content could be extremely attractive for a passionate or a young reader. In this project we want to allow a user that reads a novel from the screen of a device to ask an electronic assistant to bring her/him back to the page where, for instance, Vinicius met Ligia for the first time (from H. Sienkiewicz: *Quo Vadis*), or where Adam loses his father, as he is imprisoned by the police (from Tash Aw: *The map of the invisible world*), or where the kinship relationship between two characters has been explicitly uttered (were there are too many, as in *Forsyte Saga* of John Galsworthy).

As the GPS of the user's mobile seizes the instantaneous location where she/he is located while walking through a city, the application "*Reading while walking*" utters in the user's earphones passages of literature that mention that street, park or another place the user actually happens to be. Thus, traveling in a city is complemented with an enjoyable literary experience.

7.   Conclusions

CoBiLiRo, a very young accomplishment of the ReTeRom complex project, is a platform that aims to create a repository containing a vast collection of synchronised audio and textual resources, annotated on different levels on both the acoustic and the linguistic components. It will soon become the most significant speech & text repository for the Romanian language, addressing future developments of human-machine interfacing technologies.

After making a careful inventory of existing bimodal resources at partners, we continued to procure more and upload them on the Portal. Meanwhile, our partners in the ReTeRom project already use the material acquired there for speech-text alignment in view of further audio and linguistic experiments, out of which training speech-to-text and text-to-speech processes represent the principal objectives. Tools to harmonize the representation, the annotation and the metadata formats of all these resources are hosted on the Platform. It accounts also for a wide dissemination of the Romanian bimodal corpora, in benefit of research valorisation and usage in applications.

8.   Acknowledgements

This work was supported by a grant of the Ministry of Research and Innovation, Program PN-III-P1-1.2.-PCCDI, nr. 73/2018, as part of the ReTeRom project.

---

[18] Feature under development.
[19] Geographical Information System

[20] https://speech.utcluj.ro/sintero/, also a component part of ReTeRom.

9. Bibliographical References

Bernsen, N. O., Dybkær, L. and Dybkær, H. (1998). Wizard of Oz Simulation. In *Designing Interactive Speech Systems*. Springer, London, https:doi.org/10.1007/978-1-4471-08979_5, ISBN:978-3-540-76048-1.

Bibiri, A.-D., Turculeț, A. and Panaite Beldianu, O. (2012). The use of the MapTask technique in the projects: *Atlas Multimedia Prosodique de l'Espace Roman (AMPER-ROM)* and *Atlasul Multimedia Prozodic Român (AMPRom)*. In Iulian Boldea (Ed.), *Communication, context, interdisciplinarity. Studies and articles* – in Romanian, vol. II, Publishing house of „Petru Maior" University, Târgu-Mureș, 982-993, ISSN: 2069-3389.

Blaette, A. (2017). *GermaParl. Corpus of Plenary Protocols of the German Bundestag.* TEI files, https://github.com/PolMine/GermaParlTEI.

Cresti, E. and Moneglia, M. (Eds.). (2005). *C-ORAL-ROM: Integrated Reference Corpora for Spoken Romance Languages*, John Benjamins, Amsterdam/Philadelphia.

Koržinek, D., Marasek, K. Brocki, Ł. and Wołk, K. (2017). Polish read speech corpus for speech tools and services. *Selected papers from the CLARIN Annual Conference 2016.* Linköping Electronic Conference Proceedings 136: 54–62.

Cristea, D., Gîfu, D., Colhon, M., Diac, P., Bibiri, A-D., Mărănduc, C., and Scutelnicu, A. (2015) Quo Vadis: A Corpus of Entities and Relations. In: Language, Production, Cognition, and the Lexicon. Text, Speech and Language Technology, Part VI - Language Resources and Language Engineering, Nuria Gala, Reinhard Rapp and Gemma Bel-Enguix (eds.), Vol. 48, New York, USA, pp. 505-543.

Cristea, D., Scutelnicu, A., Pădurariu, C., Boghiu, Ş. (2018). Activity A1.3: Functional and architectural design of the infrastructure that will house the resources and the processing and accessing tools of the consortium; a prototype (in Romanian), internal research report, ReTeRom-CoBiLiRo, RACAI-UPB-UTCN-UAIC.

Cristea, D., Haja, G., Moruz, A., Răschip, M., Patraşcu, M.I. (2011). Partial statistics at the end of the eDTLR project - The Romanian Language Thesaurus in electronic format (in Romanian), in R. Zafiu, C. Uşurelu, H. Bogdan Oprea (eds.) Romanian language. Aspects of linguistic variation. Proceedings of the 10th Colloquium of the Romanian Language Department (Bucharest, 3-4 Dec. 2010), vol. I, Grammar and phonology, lexicon, semantics, terminologies, Romanian history, dialectology and philology, University of Bucharest Printing House, pp. 213-224, ISBN 978-606-16-0046-5.

Georgescu, A., Cucu, H. and Burileanu, C. (2019). Progress on automatic annotation of speech corpora using complementary ASR systems. In *Proceedings of the 42nd International Conference on Telecommunications and Signal Processing (TSP)*, Budapest, Hungary, pp. 571-574.

Li, Ai-jun and Zhi-gang, Yin (2007). Standardization of Speech Corpus. In *Data Science Journal*, vol. 6, supp, 18 November.

Mapelli, V., Arranz, V., Kamocki, P., Mazo, H., and Popescu, V. (2018). New Directions in ELRA Activities. In *Proceedings of LREC 2018*.

Oostdijk, N. (2000). The Spoken Dutch Corpus. Overview and first evaluation. In M. Gravilidou, G. Carayannis, S. Markantonatou, S. Piperidis & G. Stainhaouer (Eds.) *Proceedings of the Second International Conference on Language Resources and Evaluation- LREC-2000*, vol. II, pp. 887-894.

Patraşcu, M.-I., Clim, M.-R., Haja, G. and Tamba, E. (2016). Romanian Dictionaries. Projects of Digitization and Linked Data. In Diana Trandabăţ, Daniela Gîfu (Eds.) *Linguistic Linked Open Data.* 12th EUROLAN 2015 Summer School and RUMOUR 2015 Workshop, Sibiu, Romania, July 13–25, 2015. Revised Selected Papers, Springer, pp. 110-123.

Polat, H. and Oyucu, S. (2020). Building a Speech and Text Corpus of Turkish: Large Corpus Collection with Initial Speech Recognition Results. *Symmetry*, Volume 12 (2), 290.

Sperberg-McQueen, C.M. and Burnard, L. (2018). Original editors, revised and expanded under the supervision of the Technical Council of the TEI Consortium. TEI P5: Guidelines for Electronic Text Encoding and Interchange, version 3.3.0, last update: 31st January 2018, revision: f4d8439.

Stan, A. and Giurgiu, M. (2018). A Comparison Between Traditional Machine Learning Approaches And Deep Neural Networks For Text Processing In Romanian. In *Proceedings of the 13th International Conference on Linguistic Resources and Tools for Processing Romanian Language*, 22-23 Nov., Iaşi, Romania.

Trandabăţ, D. (2018). Activity A1.2. Inventory of available Romanian language data collections at partners or third-party coalitions. Internal research report, ReTeRom-CoBiLiRo, RACAI-UPB-UTCN-UAIC.

CLARIN: Distributed Language Resources and Technology in a European Infrastructure

Maria Eskevich[1], Franciska de Jong[1], Alexander König[1], Darja Fišer[2], Dieter Van Uytvanck[1], Tero Aalto[3], Lars Borin[4], Olga Gerassimenko[5], Jan Hajic[6], Henk van den Heuvel[7], Neeme Kahusk[5], Krista Liin[5], Martin Matthiesen[8], Stelios Piperidis[9], and Kadri Vider[5]

[1] CLARIN ERIC, Utrecht, The Netherlands ·[2] University of Ljubljana and Jožef Stefan, Ljubljana, Slovenia ·
[3] The Language Bank of Finland·[4] Språkbanken, University of Gothenburg, Sweden·[5] University of Tartu, Estonia·
[6] Charles University, Prague, Czech Republic ·[7] CLST, Radboud University, Nijmegen, The Netherlands ·
[8] CSC - IT Center for Science, Espoo, Finland ·[9] ILSP/Athena RC, Greece
clarin@clarin.eu

Abstract

CLARIN is a European Research Infrastructure providing access to digital language resources and tools from across Europe and beyond to researchers in the humanities and social sciences. This paper focuses on CLARIN as a platform for the sharing of language resources. It zooms in on the service offer for the aggregation of language repositories and the value proposition for a number of communities that benefit from the enhanced visibility of their data and services as a result of integration in CLARIN. The enhanced findability of language resources is serving the social sciences and humanities (SSH) community at large and supports research communities that aim to collaborate based on virtual collections for a specific domain. The paper also addresses the wider landscape of service platforms based on language technologies which has the potential of becoming a powerful set of interoperable facilities to a variety of communities of use.

Keywords: CLARIN, language resources, research infrastructure, repositories, interoperability

1. Introduction

CLARIN[1] is a European Research Infrastructure providing access to language resources and tools. It focuses on the widely acknowledged role of language as cultural and social data and the increased potential for comparative research of cultural and societal phenomena across the boundaries of languages. Since its establishment as a European Research Infrastructure Consortium (ERIC) in 2012, CLARIN has grown both in terms of number of members and observers (21 and 3 respectively in Spring 2020, see Figure 1.), and in terms of the variety of specific communities served (diverse subfields within the humanities and social science, such as literary studies, oral and social history, political studies, historical linguistics, developers of analysis systems based on machine learning, etc.). A strong focus on interoperability between the wide variety of resources ensures the steady and reliable development of the infrastructure, which is also reinforced by the polices for research infrastructures that have been established in alignment with the European Strategy Forum for Research Infrastructures (ESFRI)[2].

This paper is organised as follows: Section 2. describes the general principles that are to be followed to secure the interoperability for resources, and provides motivation for the CLARIN use case; and gives an overview of repository solutions that are being used within CLARIN; Section 3. provides a number of examples of data-driven communities that are brought together through the access to language resources that can be explored using approaches and methods of diverse academic fields; and Section 4. outlines the overall landscape of technical solutions CLARIN works in.

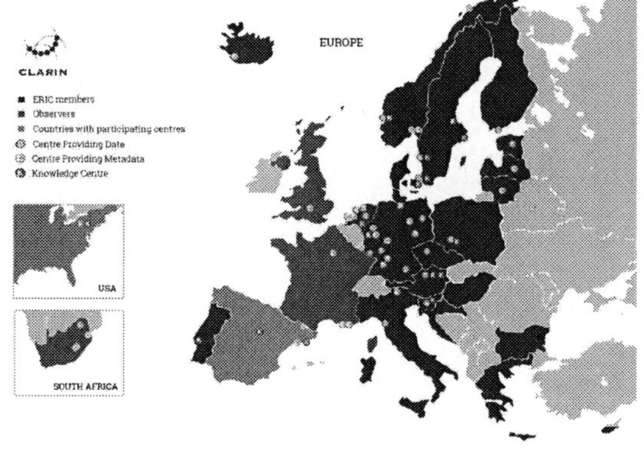

Figure 1: Map of CLARIN members, observers, and participating centres at the start of 2020.

2. CLARIN as a FAIR platform

The FAIR Guiding Principles for Data Management and Stewardship (Wilkinson et al., 2016) provide a universal framework for data management, based on the idea that research data should be **F**indable, **A**ccessible, **I**nteroperable and **R**eusable.

Overall, the FAIR principles are widely being promoted as part of the Open Science paradigm and are supposed to contribute to the ease of discovery and access of research data by researchers and the general public. Reuse of data is fostered by promoting the use of widely accepted standards both for the data itself and for the metadata describing it.

---

[1] https://www.clarin.eu
[2] https://www.esfri.eu/about

CLARIN is committed to promoting the FAIR data paradigm (de Jong et al., 2018). With the Virtual Language Observatory (VLO)[3] (see Section 2.2.) CLARIN provides a search engine that helps exploring over a million language resources from dozens of CLARIN Centres spread over all of Europe and beyond. Apart from a shared metadata paradigm that enables this kind of central discovery, technical interoperability is ensured by the technical specifications for CLARIN Centres (see Section 2.3.) and the accessibility of the data is managed with the help of a SAML-based Federated Identity[4] setup.

2.1. From FAIR to actionable

Both persistent identifiers (PIDs) and the FAIR guidelines have been existing for quite a while. Recent efforts in the context of the Research Data Alliance [5] have paved the way to enhance the already existing Handle infrastructure into an ecosystem for FAIR Digital Objects[6] (DOs) that fully supports machine-actionability: the capacity of computational systems to find, access, interoperate, and reuse data with none or minimal human intervention. The principle behind FAIR Digital Objects is to enrich Handles with a core of directly accessible metadata descriptions (the PID kernel information, which can have community-specific extensions). These metadata elements can be unambiguously interpreted with the help of a Data Type Registry, which contains the definitions of the elements. An important difference with the more extensive metadata provided outside the Digital Objects (as described in Section 2.2.) is the speed with which the information can be retrieved and the cross-community standardization.

While FAIR DOs are not yet in a production-ready state[7] it is clearly an initiative gaining a lot of traction (Hodson et al., 2018), with the potential to bring significant progress in the field of language resource processing and beyond.

2.2. Discoverability through the VLO and CMDI metadata

Within the concept of FAIR research data, the aspect of Findability is the most important one, because data that cannot be discovered by interested parties cannot be reused, no matter how well-designed and interoperable the data itself is. CLARIN has put this aspect front and centre by making it a hard requirement for their (B and C) centres to provide metadata about their collections in a well-defined format that is shared within all of CLARIN. A CLARIN centre has to provide its metadata in the CMDI-format (Broeder et al., 2012) via the OAI-PMH protocol[8]. All of these OAI endpoints are regularly checked for updates. Any new metadata elements are harvested and fed into the VLO, a facet-based search portal, where the collected metadata can be searched by interested users.

As the next step towards interoperability, a tool has been developed (Zinn, 2016) to provide guidance on which service is recommended for which data, known as the Language Resource Switchboard [9]. It acts as a simple forwarding application that, based on the URL of an input file and a few simple parameters (language, mimetype, task), allows the user to select relevant NLP web applications that can analyze the input provided.

2.3. CLARIN landscape of repositories

This section contains an overview of repositories used throughout the CLARIN infrastructure, and internal technical solutions to support the interoperability within the network of CLARIN centres. The CLARIN infrastructure backbone is a network of CLARIN Centres that provide access to language resources in a multitude of languages from European roots and beyond, in a variety of modalities and formats. Most prominent is the role of the service providing centres, called *B Centres*, which offer services to the CLARIN community, such as access to linguistic software or language data. There are also *C Centres* which allow the harvesting of metadata for the language resources and tools by the VLO, but do not offer any additional services. The most important difference between the two types of centres is that B centres have to follow precise technical specifications[10] and are regularly evaluated and certified. The certification procedure is led by CLARIN Central Assessment Committee.[11] One of the assessment criteria is that an application needs to be prepared for certification through the independent certification organisation CoreTrustSeal.[12]

The CLARIN network currently consists of 23 B and 22 C Centres. While C Centre status does not come with the expectation of running a research data repository, a lot of them actually do, resulting in a network of 41 centres with a repository. While the technical specifications (for B Centres, see above) have some requirements on what such a repository has to be able to do and the services it has to offer, the individual centres are free in their choice of the actual software they run and this results in a quite varied "repository landscape" within CLARIN.

Repository type	Number of centres
DSpace	14
Fedora	10
META-SHARE	4
Git	2
LAT	2
Dataverse	1
Custom	8
TOTAL	**41**

Table 1: Type of repositories used in CLARIN centers. This information is provided at registration stage.

---

[3]https://vlo.clarin.eu

[4]https://www.clarin.eu/node/3788

[5]https://www.rd-alliance.org/group/gede-group-european-data-experts-rda/wiki/gede-digital-object-topic-group

[6]https://fairdo.org/

[7]https://pti.iu.edu/centers/d2i/initiatives/rpid.html for a testbed implementation.

[8]https://www.openarchives.org/pmh/

---

[9]https://switchboard.clarin.eu

[10]http://hdl.handle.net/11372/DOC-78

[11]https://www.clarin.eu/governance/centre-assessment-procedure

[12]https://www.coretrustseal.org/

Looking at the current install base for repositories (see Table 1) two solutions appear to be prevalent, namely DSpace[13] (14 installations) and Fedora Commons[14] (10 installations). Both are general data management solutions that need some custom adaptions to be suitable for a CLARIN Centre, but while there are currently quite a number of different adaptions of Fedora Commons within the CLARIN community, most DSpace installations are using the modifications made by the CLARIN DSpace project[15]. The CLARIN DSpace project was started by LINDAT/CLARIAH-CZ, the Czech node of the CLARIN network based at the Charles University in Prague. But in the course of the last couple of years, as the DSpace repository has been installed at various CLARIN centres across the network, developers from those centres have started contributing to the project as well. CLARIN DSpace comes with very detailed installation instructions that include the various prerequisites and different software stacks that need to be installed for DSpace to work, for example, it bundles a handle server that is used to issue persistent identifiers to each new data submission and is also responsible for resolving those identifiers later on. Additionally, CLARIN DSpace is also available as a Docker project[16] which makes it easy for a new CLARIN centre to get started with their own repository. The project is working with Overlays[17] to make adaptions to the look and feel as easy as possible without having to touch the actual codebase. This means that the project can be customized to change the branding by each centre, while still being able to quickly update to new versions should they become available.

3. Enhanced multidisciplinarity through increased resource visibility

In order to target specific communities of researchers from the domains of humanities, social sciences and human language technologies, in 2017 CLARIN started an initiative called "Resource Families"[18], the goal of which is to collect and present in a uniform way prominent data types in the network of CLARIN consortia that display a high degree of maturity, are available for most EU languages, are a rich source of social and cultural data, and are as such highly relevant for research from a wide range of disciplines and methodological approaches in SSH as well as for cross-disciplinary and trans-national comparative research. (Fišer et al., 2018)

Currently, CLARIN Resource Families feature 10 families of corpora, 5 families of lexical resources, and 3 families of natural language processing (NLP) tools. The overviews are organized according to the types of data featuring in the resources and include listings sorted by language. The listings include the most important metadata and brief descriptions, such as resource size, text sources, time periods, annotations and licences, as well as links to download pages and concordancers, whenever available. Where applicable, overviews of other existing prominent language resources which have not yet been integrated in the infrastructure have also been provided. As a side project, overviews of related materials such as thematic CLARIN workshops and tutorials along with their accompanying VideoLectures recordings[19], as well as a list of key publications on the surveyed resources have also been generated [20].

The overviews serve as an entry point to the CLARIN infrastructure for individual researchers, lecturers and students from SSH, but have also proved to be a highly valuable instrument for further improvement of the infrastructure, either by improving the identified issues with the findability or documentation of the resources, or by working towards better interoperability of the resources (e.g. by developing common corpus encoding standards).

3.1. Parliamentary data

Parliamentary data is a major source of socially relevant content. It is available in ever larger quantities, is multilingual, accompanied by rich metadata, and has the distinguishing characteristic that it is spoken language produced in controlled circumstances which has traditionally been transcribed but is now increasingly released also in audio and video formats. All these factors require solutions related to structuring, synchronization, visualization, querying and analysis of parliamentary corpora. Furthermore, approaches to the exploitation of parliamentary corpora to their full extent also have to take into account the needs of researchers from vastly different SSH fields, such as political sciences, sociology, history, and psychology.

An inspiring and highly successful series of workshops focusing on parliamentary data, such as CLARIN+[21], ParlaCLARIN[22] and ParlaFormat[23] resulted in a comprehensive overview of a multitude of existing parliamentary resources worldwide,[24] a detailed needs analysis[25] as well as tangible first steps towards better harmonization, interoperability and comparability of the resources and tools relevant for the study of parliamentary debate[26].

In the context of H2020 cluster projects PARTHENOS[27]

---

[13] https://duraspace.org/dspace/

[14] https://duraspace.org/fedora/

[15] https://github.com/ufal/clarin-dspace

[16] https://gitlab.inf.unibz.it/commul/docker/clarin-dspace

[17] https://github.com/ufal/clarin-dspace/wiki/Overlays

[18] https://www.clarin.eu/resource-families/

[19] http://videolectures.net/clarin/

[20] https://www.clarin.eu/resource-families/parliamentary-corporapublications-on-the-parliamentary-corpora

[21] https://www.clarin.eu/event/2017/clarin-plus-workshop-working-parliamentary-records

[22] https://www.clarin.eu/ParlaCLARIN, https://www.clarin.eu/ParlaCLARIN-II

[23] https://www.clarin.eu/event/2019/parlaformat-workshop

[24] https://www.clarin.eu/resource-families/parliamentary-corpora

[25] https://office.clarin.eu/v/CE-2017-1091-Focus-group-UI-2017-03-27.pdf

[26] https://github.com/clarin-eric/parla-clarin

[27] https://training.parthenos-project.eu/sample-page/digital-humanities-research-questions-and-methods/researching-parliamentary-records-in-the-digital-humanities/, https://www.clarin.eu/event/2019/parthenos-workshop-cee-countries

and SSHOC[28], representatives from the CLARIN network have started to develop training materials for the community of researchers using CLARIN resources and tools using parliamentary data. They will be integrated in the SSH Open Marketplace that is planned to result from the collaborative efforts that the European research infrastructures for the social sciences and humanities have taken up as part of the SSHOC workplan.

3.2. DELAD

DELAD[29] (meaning 'shared' in Swedish) is an initiative to establish a digital archive of disordered speech and share this with interested researchers within CLARIN. The DELAD community consists of researchers involved in collecting and analysing Corpora of Disordered Speech (CDS), research data and infrastructure specialists, and legal experts. DELAD has chosen the CLARIN infrastructure as primary space for storing and sharing CDS. More specifically, DELAD has linked up with CLARIN's Knowledge Centre for Atypical Communication Expertise (ACE)[30] (Van den Heuvel et al., 2020b) for making CDS available through The Language Archive (TLA)[31] at the Max Planck Institute for Psycholinguistics in Nijmegen (being a CLARIN Data Centre) and CMU's Talkbank[32] (Clinical Banks). DELAD has organised four workshops over the years 2015-2019, the latter two of which were held under the umbrella of CLARIN ERIC. Topics addressed in these workshops were: Guidelines for collecting and sharing CDS (in the light of the General Data Protection (GDPR)[33]), levels of anonymisation, layered access, integration of CDS in the CLARIN infrastructure, formats, and relevant metadata. More information about DELAD and the application of the GDPR on CDS can be found in (Van den Heuvel et al., 2020a). The workshops are extremely fruitful since researchers from various disciplines (clinical researchers, speech and language scientists and technologists, infrastructural specialists and legal experts) can apply their own knowledge in a new context and learn about the practical challenges that their colleagues in other domains come across (e.g. clinical researchers facing ICT and legal issues).

3.3. Europeana

Part of the materials that has been aggregated in Europeana[34], Europe's platform for digital cultural heritage, consists of language data and is therefore of potential added value for researchers studying heritage data in spoken or textual form. This premise led to a joint project between CLARIN and Europeana that has been set up with an aim to bring the visibility of Europeana data through the VLO. CLARIN and Europeana do not share a common metadata model, and therefore a semantic and structural mapping had

to be defined, and a conversion implemented. CLARIN's ingestion pipeline was extended to retrieve a set of selected collections from Europeana and apply this conversion in the process.

Currently about 775 thousand Europeana records can be found in the VLO, with several times more records expected in the foreseeable future. About 10 thousand records are technically suitable for processing via the Language Resources Switchboard already. Relatively straightforward improvements to the metadata on the side of Europeana and/or its data providers could substantially increase this number.

4. CLARIN in the landscape of language technology platforms

CLARIN operates in the broader context of international initiatives that aim to support a diverse set of scenarios of use for services based on language technologies for a wide range of communities. As an initiative positioned in the wider European landscape of research infrastructures[35], CLARIN's service offer is strongly focusing on the needs of researchers. This mission comes with strong demands for both sustainability and interoperability. The Open Science agenda that by the various stakeholders is seen as a major driver for the investments, has added incentives for the support of multidisciplinary work and the integration of language data in interdisciplinary paradigms. (de Jong et al., 2018)

The value proposition put forward by CLARIN implies that an adequate level of alignment with other infrastructural initiatives is sought, and conversely: that there are several language technology platforms that reference the service offer of CLARIN and have adopted measures to ensure interoperability. In this section a number of these existing European initiatives are presented with the aim to articulate both the potential for collaboration and the complementarity of the services.

This work implies the incorporation and usage of previously developed technological components; and coordination of activities and clear distinction of audiences served and regulation of access between CLARIN serving primarily the research community and other initiatives and platforms that offer access to data and tools for industry.

4.1. META

META-SHARE[36] has been developed as the infrastructural arm of META-NET[37] and has served as a component of a language technology marketplace for researchers, developers, professionals and industrial players, catering for the full development cycle of language technology, from research to innovative products and services. It has been designed as a network of repositories that store language resources (data, tools and processing services) documented with high-quality metadata, aggregated in central inventories allowing for uniform search and access (Piperidis, 2012). Repositories can be local, set up and maintained

---

[28]https://www.sshopencloud.eu/news/using-corpora-implementing-validation-sshoc-masterclass

[29]http://delad.net

[30]https://ace.ruhosting.nl

[31] https://tla.mpi.nl/

[32]https://talkbank.org/

[33]https://gdpr-info.eu/

[34]https://www.europeana.eu/

[35]https://www.eric-forum.eu/the-eric-landscape/

[36]www.meta-share.eu

[37]www.meta-net.eu

by network members to store their own resources, or hosting (non-local) acting as storage and documentation facilities not only for their own resources, but also for resources developed in organisations not wishing to or not being able to set up their own repository, including donated and orphan resources. Every resource is primarily assigned to one of the network's repositories (master copy), and is formally described according to the META-SHARE metadata schema (Gavrilidou et al., 2012). The META-SHARE metadata schema has been mapped on a number of other schemas, including Dublin Core [38] and OLAC[39], the schema of the ELRA catalogue, and CLARINs CMDI. Metadata records are harvested and stored in the META-SHARE central inventory using a proprietary harvesting and synchronisation protocol, while lately an OAI-PMH bridge has been implemented as an additional harvesting protocol. While resources can be both open or with restricted access rights, free or for-a-fee, all metadata records are open, available under a Creative Commons Attribution 4.0 licence.

META-SHARE provides dedicated open-source software for setting up repositories[40], which has been used for technically setting up not only the network nodes themselves, but also for powering a number of CLARIN-related centres in a number of countries including Estonia, Finland, Greece, Portugal. While the provided solution could be readily used for setting up a language resource repository, a number of extensions were necessary to turn it into a solution satisfying the requirements set by CLARIN for establishing a CLARIN B-centre. Such extensions include: (i) assigning persistent identifiers to language resources, accommodated in and by the META-SHARE metadata schema through a dedicated metadata field, (ii) establishing an OAI-PMH bridge, implementations of which are provided, among others, by the META-SHARE nodes of Estonia and Greece, (iii) user authentication through Single Sign-On, an extension which has been implemented in variable ways by the CLARIN repositories which have opted for using the META-SHARE solution.

In the following subsections a number of META nodes for which interoperability with CLARIN has been realized are described.

4.1.1. CLARIN:EL and the Greek META-SHARE node

Prototype implementations for combining and extending data infrastructures, like META-SHARE, with linguistic processing services, have also been proposed (Piperidis et al., 2015). Such implementations aim to bring together language datasets and basic language processing services in a unified platform. The Greek META-SHARE node has been used for this prototype implementation and has been enhanced by providing a language processing mechanism for annotating content with appropriate NLP services that are documented with the appropriate metadata. Atomic services are combined into workflows modeled as an acyclic directed graph where each node corresponds to an NLP processing service (e.g. sentence splitting, part-of-speech tagging), running either locally or remotely. This implementation has been used for powering the language processing layer of the CLARIN:EL node (Piperidis et al., 2017), offering services and workflows for processing monolingual and bilingual content/resources in raw text, xces, tmx formats. From the legal framework point of view, a simple operational model has been adopted by which only openly licensed datasets can be processed by openly licensed services and workflows.

4.1.2. Language Bank of Finland

The Language Bank of Finland uses META-SHARE as its primary metadata repository. The software was deployed in 2012. Many of the Language Bank's services refer to META-SHARE directly, including the Language Bank Portal[41] and Language Bank Rights[42] the center's language resource access rights application and managing service.

The repository is populated and curated by the Language Bank's staff at the University of Helsinki and CSC – IT Center for Science. Each item has a persistent persistent identifier. URNs are mainly used as PIDs, but Handles are also supported with a 1:1 mapping[43]. PIDs to metadata records are used as the main way of referring to the language resources in other services and publications[44]. Where applicable, the resources also have PIDs for their access locations. The metadata is exported via a custom OAI-PMH bridge[45].

4.1.3. Center of Estonian Language Resources

The Center of Estonian Language Resources (CELR) uses META-SHARE as a register of language resources where metadata is stored[46]. In addition to the standard, META-SHARE node, Simple-SAML SSO, the OAI-PMH endpoint for VLO, and DataCite DOI as persistent identifier are used.

While META-SHARE provides file storage, an external data repository, ENTU[47], is used for storing the resources themselves, as it enables a better overview of the individual files. It also enables a better integration with other services, so that for a signed-in user the access permissions are managed for both download and further processing of the resource. The djangosaml2 module is implemented and connected to the local identity provider that serves as proxy, allowing access to the users of the CLARIN service provider federation.

Currently there are four resource types in META-SHARE to select. Sometimes other types are needed, for example because a specific CMDI profile is assumed, as in the case of workflow manager Weblicht[48]. A workaround has been developed by linking an external metadata file to the META-SHARE metadata field `metadataInfo/source`.

---

[38] http://dublincore.org/

[39] http://www.language-archives.org/

[40] https://github.com/metashare/META-SHARE

[41] https://www.kielipankki.fi/language-bank/

[42] https://lbr.csc.fi/

[43] Metadata curation: http://urn.fi/urn:nbn:fi:lb-201710212

[44] Citation instructions: https://www.kielipankki.fi/corpora/

[45] http://urn.fi/urn:nbn:fi:lb-201506011

[46] https://metashare.ut.ee

[47] https://entu.keeleressursid.ee

[48] https://weblicht.sfs.uni-tuebingen.de

For DOI allocation, a custom module was made using a central Handle server for Estonian resources. All data sets registered at CELR are findable at http://datacite.org by identifier ESTDOI.KEEL[49].

4.1.4. Swedish Language Bank

Språkbanken Text at the University of Gothenburg is one of the three divisions of the Swedish National Language Bank, and also a certified B centre of SWE-CLARIN, the Swedish node of CLARIN ERIC.

The centre's META-SHARE instance[50] predates the Swedish CLARIN membership, and was the result of its participation in the META-NET collaboration (2011–2013). With CLARIN membership, a strategic decision was taken to make META-SHARE the common language resource metadata format of SWE-CLARIN. Metadata editing is done primarily by SWE-CLARIN staff; with the present low volumes of metadata addition, this turns out to be the most time-effective solution. Metadata records are persistently identified using the Handle system.

4.2. European Language Grid

The European Language Grid (ELG) is a platform under development that aims to integrate a marketplace and community meeting point for Language Technology data, tools, services and developers, users and other stakeholders, with a specific focus on non-academic use cases, both commercial and non-commercial (Rehm et al., 2020). The envisaged platform is being developed as part of a European project[51], while an alpha release is expected to be open for the public as of March 2020. Eventually the platform may offer hundreds of services, technically scalable for large projects.

The ELG platform is consisting of three layers: (i) the base infrastructure operating on a managed Kubernetes cluster, (ii) the platform back end essentially implementing a repository back end containing metadata records of language resources, tools and services, as well as meta-information about language resources and technologies stakeholders, and (iii) the platform front end consisting of interfaces for different types of ELG users, including catalogue user interfaces, trial interfaces for functional services, registering/uploading interfaces for language resources and services providers. All components of the three layers are deployed as Docker containers on the Kubernetes cluster, with functional language technology services made available also through containerization and by being wrapped with the ELG LT service API.

The ELG catalogue will point to the tools contained either locally for developers and users to be able to incorporate them in their application, or simply use them for their language technology tasks. The catalogue will also contain or point to resources available in current LT repositories, such as ELRA/ELDA, META-SHARE(Piperidis, 2012), ELRC-SHARE(Piperidis et al., 2018) and other repositories. All entities are described in compliance with the ELG-SHARE metadata schema (Labropoulou et al., 2020). The schema builds upon, consolidates and updates previous activities, especially the META-SHARE schema and its profiles (Gavrilidou et al., 2012) taking into account recent developments in the (meta)data domains (e.g., FAIR, data and software citation recommendations , Open Science movement, etc.).

ELG has established a network of National Competence Centers led by country representatives who in many cases are also involved in national CLARIN consortia. It is to be expected that this will help facilitating the alignment of activities and the potential for interoperability between the platforms.

5. Concluding remarks

This paper presents the CLARIN research infrastructure as a platform for the sharing of distributed language resources in the context of the dynamics of the Open Science agenda and the inherent objective of giving sustainable access to FAIR data on the one hand, and on the other hand it positions CLARIN in the wider landscape of service platforms based on language technologies. The interoperability across platforms can be considered to bring added value for the further emergence of a seamless service offer to a variety of communities of use, both within and beyond academia.

Given that several complementary infrastructural initiatives have recently acquired public funding for the development of new services and/or deeper integration of language resources and technology into the ecosystem of digital infrastructures (e.g., EHRI[52], ELRC[53], ELEXIS[54] and Prêt-à-LLOD[55]) it is to be expected that further steps towards platform harmonization will be undertaken in the near future, and addressed in discussion fora such as the 1st International Workshop on Language Technology Platforms (IWLTP) workshop and other conversations organized in the context of networking and project events.

Bibliographical References

Broeder, D., Windhouwer, M., Van Uytvanck, D., Goosen, T., and Trippel, T. (2012). Cmdi: a component metadata infrastructure. In *Describing LRs with metadata: towards flexibility and interoperability in the documentation of LR workshop programme*, volume 1.

de Jong, F., Maegaard, B., De Smedt, K., Fišer, D., and Van Uytvanck, D. (2018). Clarin: towards fair and responsible data science using language resources. In *Proceedings of the Eleventh International Conference on Language Resources and Evaluation (LREC 2018)*, pages 3259–3264.

Fišer, D., Lenardič, J., and Erjavec, T. (2018). CLARIN's Key Resource Families. In Nicoletta Calzolari (Conference chair), et al., editors, *Proceedings of the Eleventh International Conference on Language Resources and Evaluation (LREC 2018)*, Miyazaki, Japan, May 7-12, 2018. European Language Resources Association (ELRA).

---

[49]https://search.datacite.org/works?query=estdoi.keel
[50]https://spraakbanken.gu.se/metashare/
[51]H2020 ICT Call 29a; https://european-language-grid.eu

[52]https://www.ehri-project.eu
[53]http://www.lr-coordination.eu
[54]https://elex.is
[55]https://www.pret-a-llod.eu

Gavrilidou, M., Labropoulou, P., Desipri, E., Piperidis, S., Papageorgiou, H., Monachini, M., Frontini, F., Declerck, T., Francopoulo, G., Arranz, V., and Mapelli, V. (2012). The META-SHARE metadata schema for the description of language resources. In *Proceedings of the Eighth International Conference on Language Resources and Evaluation (LREC'12)*, pages 1090–1097, Istanbul, Turkey, May. European Language Resources Association (ELRA).

Hodson, S., Jones, S., Collins, S., Genova, F., Harrower, N., Laaksonen, L., Mietchen, D., Petrauskaité, R., and Wittenburg, P. (2018). Turning FAIR into reality. Final report and action plan from the EC expert group on FAIR data. DOI:10.2777/1524.

Labropoulou, P., Gkirtzou, K., Gavriilidou, M., Deligiannis, M., Galanis, D., Piperidis, S., Rehm, G., Berger, M., Mapelli, V., Arranz, V., Choukri, K., Backfried, G., Pérez, J. M. G., and Silva, A. G. (2020). Making metadata fit for next generation language technology platforms: The metadata schema of the european language grid. In *Proceedings of the 12th International Conference on Language Resources and Evaluation (LREC'20)*, Marseille, France. European Language Resource Association (ELRA).

Piperidis, S., Galanis, D., Bakagianni, J., and Sofianopoulos, S. (2015). Combining and extending data infrastructures with linguistic annotation services. In *International Workshop on Worldwide Language Service Infrastructure*, pages 3–17. Springer.

Piperidis, S., Labropoulou, P., and Gavrilidou, M. (2017). clarin:el: a language resources documentation, sharing and processing infrastructure [in Greek]. In Thanasis Georgakopoulos, et al., editors, *Proceedings of the 12th International Conference on Greek Linguistics*, volume 2, page 851–869, Berlin, October. Edition Romiosini/CeMoG.

Piperidis, S., Labropoulou, P., Deligiannis, M., and Giagkou, M. (2018). Managing public sector data for multilingual applications development. In *Proceedings of the Eleventh International Conference on Language Resources and Evaluation (LREC 2018)*, Miyazaki, Japan, May. European Language Resources Association (ELRA).

Piperidis, S. (2012). The META-SHARE language resources sharing infrastructure: Principles, challenges, solutions. In *Proceedings of the Eighth International Conference on Language Resources and Evaluation (LREC'12)*, pages 36–42, Istanbul, Turkey, May. European Language Resources Association (ELRA).

Rehm, G., Marheinecke, K., Hegele, S., Piperidis, S., Bontcheva, K., Hajič, J., Choukri, K., Vasiljevs, A., Backfried, G., Prinz, C., Pérez, J. M. G., Meerten, L., Lukowicz, P., van Genabith, J., Lösch, A., Slusallek, P., Irgens, M., Gatellier, P., Köhler, J., Bars, L. L., Auksoriūtė, A., Bel, N., Branco, A., Budin, G., Daelemans, W., Smedt, K. D., Garabik, R., Gavriilidou, M., Gromann, D., Koeva, S., Krek, S., Krstev, C., Lindén, K., Magnini, B., Odijk, J., Ogrodniczuk, M., Ras, E., Rögnvaldsson, E., Rosner, M., Pedersen, B. S., Skadiņa, I., Tadić, M., Tufiş, D., Váradi, T., Vider, K., Way, A.,

and Yvon, F. (2020). The european language technology landscape in 2020: Language-centric and human-centric ai for cross-cultural communication in multilingual europe. In *Proceedings of the 12th International Conference on Language Resources and Evaluation (LREC'20)*, Marseille, France. European Language Resource Association (ELRA).

Van den Heuvel, H., Kelli, A., Klessa, K., and Salaasti, S. (2020a). Corpora of disordered speech in the light of the gdp: Two use cases from the delad initiative. In *Proceedings of the 12th International Conference on Language Resources and Evaluation (LREC'20)*, Marseille, France. European Language Resource Association (ELRA).

Van den Heuvel, H., Oostdijk, N., Rowland, C., and Trilsbeek, P. (2020b). The clarin knowledge centre for atypical communication expertise. In *Proceedings of the 12th International Conference on Language Resources and Evaluation (LREC'20)*, Marseille, France. European Language Resource Association (ELRA).

Wilkinson, M. D., Dumontier, M., Aalbersberg, I. J., Appleton, G., Axton, M., Baak, A., Blomberg, N., Boiten, J.-W., da Silva Santos, L. B., Bourne, P. E., et al. (2016). The fair guiding principles for scientific data management and stewardship. *Scientific data*, 3.

Zinn, C. (2016). The CLARIN Language Resource Switchboard. In *Abstracts of the CLARIN Annual Conference 2016*, Aix-en-Provence, France.

ELRI
A Decentralised Network of National Relay Stations to Collect, Prepare and Share Language Resources

Thierry Etchegoyhen,[1] Borja Anza Porras,[2] Andoni Azpeitia,[1] Eva Martínez Garcia,[3]
José Luis Fonseca,[4] Patricia Fonseca,[4] Paulo Vale,[4] Jane Dunne,[5] Federico Gaspari,[5]
Teresa Lynn,[5] Helen McHugh,[5] Andy Way,[5] Victoria Arranz,[6] Khalid Choukri,[6]
Hervé Pusset,[6] Alexandre Sicard,[6] Rui Neto,[7] Maite Melero,[8]
David Perez,[8] António Branco,[9] Ruben Branco,[9] Luís Gomes[9]

[1] Vicomtech, Spain - {tetchegoyhen, aazpeitia}@vicomtech.org
[2] Bexen Medical, Spain (Work done while at Vicomtech) - borja.anza@gmail.com
[3] CEIEC, Spain (Work done while at Vicomtech) - eva.martinez@ceiec.es
[4] AMA, Portugal - {jose.fonseca, patricia.fonseca, paulo.vale}@ama.pt
[5] DCU, Ireland - {jane.dunne, federico.gaspari, teresa.lynn, helen.mchugh, andy.way}@adaptcentre.ie
[6] ELDA, France - {arranz, choukri, herve, alexandre}@elda.org
[7] Linkare, Portugal - rneto@linkare.com
[8] SEAD, Spain - maite.melero@upf.edu, dperezf@minetad.es
[9] University of Lisboa, Portugal - {antonio.branco, ruben.branco, luis.gomes}@di.fc.ul.pt

Abstract

We describe the European Language Resource Infrastructure (ELRI), a decentralised network to help collect, prepare and share language resources. The infrastructure was developed within a project co-funded by the Connecting Europe Facility Programme of the European Union, and has been deployed in the four Member States participating in the project, namely France, Ireland, Portugal and Spain. ELRI provides sustainable and flexible means to collect and share language resources via National Relay Stations, to which members of public institutions can freely subscribe. The infrastructure includes fully automated data processing engines to facilitate the preparation, sharing and wider reuse of useful language resources that can help optimise human and automated translation services in the European Union.

Keywords: ELRI, Language Resources, European Infrastructure, Connecting Europe Facility

1. Introduction

The European Language Resource Infrastructure project[1] (ELRI) is an initiative funded within the Connecting Europe Facility (CEF) Programme[2], which started in October 2017 and ended in September 2019.[3] Its main goal has been the development of an infrastructure to help collect, process and share language resources (LR) in the European Union. Seven partners were involved in the project, representing four Member States (MS), namely France, Ireland, Portugal and Spain.

Quality multilingual language resources are of paramount importance to improve translation services, both human and automated, and thus support language equality in the European Union. The development of European Digital Service Infrastructures (DSI), in particular, is tied to the development of transversal services such as eTranslation[4], the automated translation service provided by the Directorate-General for Translation (DGT) to Public Administrations of the European Union. Such services can greatly benefit from language resources produced by public institutions on a daily basis across the European Union.

The ELRI initiative sought to support the collection of quality language resources, by mitigating obstacles iden-tified during the data collection efforts of companion initiatives such as the European Language Resource Coordination project[5] (ELRC). Among the main identified difficulties were the reluctance of data holders to make their data available due to perceived concerns related to Member State regulations and IPR issues, the lack of internal expertise or dedicated staff to take the steps needed to provide appropriately prepared language resources, and the lack of clear short-term incentives to share their resources.

ELRI has addressed some of these issues by providing a sustainable solution deployable at the Member State level, where data checking and processing take place prior to sharing the resources, at the Member State level or beyond, and users can benefit in the short term from fully prepared language resources that can improve their own translation processes, human or automated.

A key contribution of the ELRI project has been the development and deployment of National Relay Stations (NRS), which are web applications that facilitate the collection, preparation and sharing of language resources. Each NRS is available to members of public institutions in the corresponding Member State and its user interface is provided in the language(s) of the Member State, thus providing an environment for LR sharing that is in line with the linguistic specificities of the relevant Member State. National Relay Stations integrate fully automated processing of multilingual resources to reduce the time and effort required for the

---

[1] www.elri-project.eu
[2] https://ec.europa.eu/inea/en/connecting-europe-facility
[3] See (Etchegoyhen et al., 2019) for more details on the project.
[4] https://ec.europa.eu/cefdigital/wiki/display/CEFDIGITAL/eTranslation

---

[5] http://lr-coordination.eu/

manual reviewing and processing of file collections, whilst also providing stakeholders with fully prepared resources in the short term. This integrated processing notably allows the creation of translation memories from raw user data in the form of document collections in multiple languages and the automated cleanup of existing translation memories. ELRI also features a group-based sharing policy where users can select the group(s) with which they intend to share their resources, thus providing the means to share language resources according to the different sets of constraints that may be tied to specific resources.

A major outcome of this initiative was the provision of a sustainable infrastructure that will be maintained after the completion of the project itself, with a detailed governance plan to support the extension of the network to new Member States and EEA countries.

The remainder of this paper is organised as follows. In Section 2. we describe the core objectives and approach of the ELRI initiative. Section 3. presents the components of the infrastructure and Section 4. describes the LR validation process. In Section 5., we describe the activity of the network at the end of the project, including the community of stakeholders that was built and the initial resources that were collected during the 2-year project. Section 6. outlines the sustainability of the solution and the governance plan for countries willing to join the network after the conclusion of the ELRI project. Finally, Section 7. draws conclusions from the project.

2. Objectives and Benefits

The core objectives of ELRI can be summarised as follows:

- Build and deploy an infrastructure to help collect, prepare and share language resources that can in turn improve translation services in the European Union, both human and automated.

- Automate the creation of translation memories and other resources from raw data provided by public institutions and translation centres.

- Provide flexible means to share language resources at the national, European and Open Data levels.

- Prioritise resources that are relevant to Digital Service Infrastructures.

- Contribute to improve the EU automated translation services that are freely available to public institutions.

- Deploy ELRI in France, Ireland, Portugal and Spain, with a future extension to additional member states as a key objective beyond the current action.

- Provide a robust and sustainable infrastructure.

These objectives were aligned with the identified challenges regarding the collection of quality language resources, and aimed to provide the following benefits:

- The provision of flexible means of sharing resources establishes a clear process where compliance with the relevant restrictions can be established at every step.

- Raw language resources are converted automatically into a format useful for translation experts as well as machine translation infrastructures.

- Data sharing with ELRI provides broad compliance verification covering intellectual property rights and the Public Sector Information Directive.

- Language resources can be shared as deemed appropriate by stakeholders, with return benefits for providers as well as users of translation services.

- Data holders can benefit from the automatically prepared resources in the short term to help optimise their own translation processes.

- By sharing their resources, stakeholders can benefit from improved European translation services such as eTranslation and promote language equality for the languages of their Member States.

This set of benefits was at the core of the ELRI project and the infrastructure was designed to achieve these objectives.

3. ELRI Infrastructure

In this section, we provide a summary of the infrastructure developed within the project.

3.1. Architecture

ELRI is a decentralised network composed of National Relay Stations, i.e. the web applications designed to collect, prepare and share language resources. Figure 1 illustrates the currently deployed infrastructure, where Each Member State deploys an instance of a National Relay Station, localised into the language(s) of the Member State and comprising a Web application, data processing engines and a database of language resources.

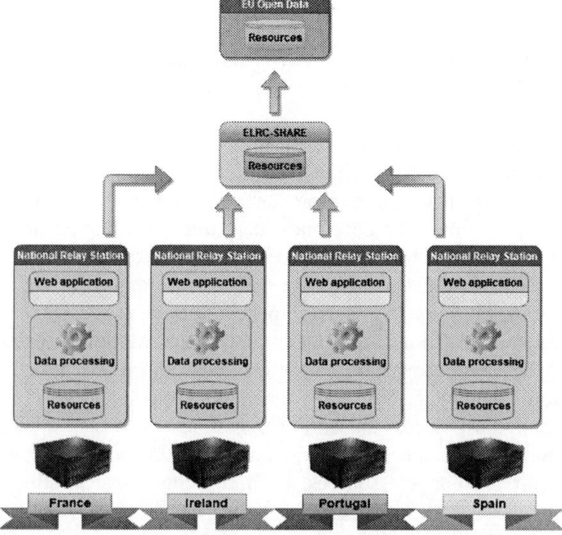

Figure 1: Overview of the ELRI network

The Web application serves as an interface where users of public institutions of the Member State can register and contribute their resources. The data uploaded by users of the NRS are processed by integrated engines, which perform sequences of processing steps to produce structured and clean language resources from raw data. These data processing pipelines, called toolchains, can notably create translation memories from raw document collections in multiple languages or clean existing translation memories. The processed resources are then available for review and validation, a task performed by designated personnel in each Member State.

Prepared resources that are deemed valid are then published in the NRS of the Member State, thus becoming directly available to the users who contributed them, as well as to the other users of the groups with which the data contributors are willing to share the resources. Resources that are shared with the European Commission are then transferred to the ELRC-SHARE repository[6], via API or manual transfer.[7] Additionally, resources that have been shared as Open Data are deposited to the EU Open Data Portal[8], via links to ELRC-SHARE. The communication between the principal components of a National Relay Station is illustrated in Figure 2.

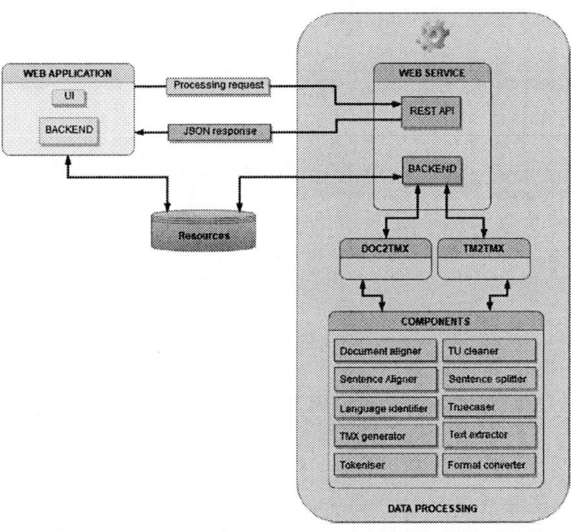

Figure 2: Communication between NRS components

The web application communicates with the data processing component via a web service, with requests sent via a REST API and responses provided as JSON objects. The initial user data as well as those generated by the data processing engines are stored in a shared repository, accessible to both the Web application and the data processing engines. The main components of the NRS software are provided as Docker containers, assembled via docker-compose, and comprise the web application itself, the data processing pipelines, an nginx web server, a solr search server, and a postgres relational database.[9]

The decentralised nature of the network provides robustness for a sustainable service, as eventual discontinuing of one of the NRS nodes would not impact the persistence of the service in the other Member States where it is deployed.

3.2. National Relay Stations

The Web application provides the necessary functionality for users to register, browse the catalogue of resources, download resources available to them and contribute their own resources. The application also handles all actions related to storage and retrieval of language resources, and interfaces with the automated data processing engines.

The application is a fork of the ELRC-SHARE software[10], itself based on the META-SHARE software[11]. The core functionality of the web application includes Web page navigation, user registration and access, data upload, user-provided information, interface with automated data processing functionality, metadata editing, data sharing under group-based policy, data download and email communication with users of the service. Even though modifications have been made to the look-and-feel of the ELRC-SHARE codebase, as well as fixes and adaptations of the user interface to match the requirements established for ELRI, the underlying infrastructure was preserved for the most part, and the metadata established for the resources stored by the system have notably been maintained as is. This ensures compatibility with the requirements of the Automated Translation services of the DGT. There are however three main differences between the original codebase and the ELRI Web application.

First, the application was localised into the language(s) of the four Member States that were represented in the project. The original English content was thus translated into French, Irish, Portuguese and Spanish. The main goal of the localisation process was to provide an environment suited for the users of the NRS in each Member State, also in line with the efforts towards language equality in the European Union. For Ireland, this requirement led to adding a language switch to the user interface, allowing NRS users of that Member State to switch at will between the Irish and English environments.

The second main difference is the integration of automated data processing, described in more detail in the next Section. To be able to process different types of data, the Web application was extended with a functionality to branch files to the appropriate data processing engine, according to file types, and to retrieve the results of data processing. The integration of automated data processing functionalities is one of the key features of the Web application in ELRI, one which allows to accelerate the preparation of language resources and their delivery to the users.

Finally, the third major difference is the inclusion of a group-sharing policy which provides flexible means to share data, acknowledging that sharing restrictions may need to vary for specific resources. Sharing via an NRS is

---

[6]https://elrc-share.eu/

[7]At the end of the project, manual transfer was still necessary, in part because information required for LR publication on ELRC-SHARE, such as LR documentation, could not be transferred at the time via its API.

[8]https://data.europa.eu/euodp/en/home

[9]Further documentation is available at: https://github.com/ELDAELRA/ELRI/tree/master/docker

[10]https://github.com/MiltosD/ELRC2

[11]https://github.com/metashare/META-SHARE

Figure 3: National Relay Stations in Ireland, Spain, France and Portugal (clockwise from the top left)

done on the basis of well-defined groups, where users can browse and download only those resources that are shared with a group that they belong to. There are three different groups to which users of an NRS belong by default:

- *NationalOrganisations*: This group includes all registered users of the NRS from a specific country and resources shared with this group are accessible to all registered users of the NRS based in that Member State.

- *NationalOrganisations+EuropeanCommission*: This group includes all registered users of the NRS and the European Commission, via the ELRC-SHARE repository, who may then utilise the shared resources to improve the eTranslation services.

- *OpenData*: This group includes all registered users of the NRS and all users of the free Open Data portal of the European Union.

These default groups are always available to data contributors and aim to cover the most frequent cases of resource sharing. If different sharing needs arise for specific resources, users may request the ad hoc creation of specific groups by contacting the designated staff running the NRS in the relevant Member State. The four localised National Relay Stations are shown in Figure 3.

3.3. Data Processing

As previously indicated, each National Relay Station includes data processing engines which can handle different types of content and file formats, including doc(x), odt, rtf, pdf, tmx, sdltm and plain text.[12] Figure 4 describes the main processing steps for the four major types of data handled by the engines.

The leftmost case in the figure describes the operations needed to handle documents containing translations in two or more languages. This is the most complex scenario and its main steps are summarised below.[13]

The contents of the input files in different formats are first extracted, followed by automated language identification which allows the different text files to be grouped by language.[14] Within each file, the text is then split into separate sentences, to allow further processes to apply. Each sentence is then pre-processed, which mainly includes tokenisation and truecasing; these operations are performed with scripts that are part of the Moses toolkit[15] (Koehn et al., 2007). All document pairs with content in different languages are then automatically aligned with the DOCAL document aligner (Etchegoyhen and Azpeitia, 2016). For all document pairs whose alignment score indicates that the documents are a translation of each other, sentence alignment is then performed on the content, retrieving translations at the sentence level.[16] From the aligned sentences a translation memory in TMX format 1.4b is then gener-

---

[12] Although processing (collections of) PDF files is possible, the recommendation is to process the editable source files when these are available, as some challenges remain with extracting text from PDF files, potentially resulting in smaller language resources generated from the original data.

[13] Unless otherwise specified, all components are Java components developed by Vicomtech and licensed to the Innovation and Networks Executive Agency (https://ec.europa.eu/inea/en) under conditions.

[14] Text extraction is performed with Apache Tika™ (https://tika.apache.org/).
Language identification is performed with the Cybozu language identification library (https://github.com/shuyo/language-detection/tree/master/src/com/cybozu/labs/langdetect).

[15] https://github.com/moses-smt/mosesdecoder

[16] Sentence alignment is performed with HunAlign (Varga et al., 2005): https://github.com/danielvarga/hunalign

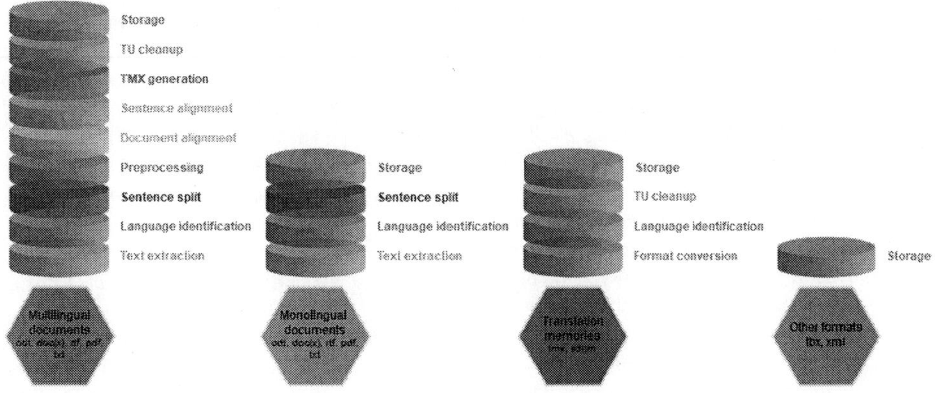

Figure 4: Main data processing scenarios

ated, with the identified sentence translations encapsulated in paired translation units. The entire translation memory is then cleaned up, removing the errors generated by erroneous alignments, filtering translation units that feature content mismatches indicated by marked length differences, unexpected languages or character sequences, for instance; duplicate translation units are also removed automatically. Finally, the clean translation memory is stored and indexed by the system.

The second case from the left is comparatively simpler, as it involves files with content in a single language. In this case, only a subset of the previously described processes apply, namely text extraction, language identification, sentence split and storage. Collections of monolingual files are thus transformed into a single file with one sentence per line. Although not as useful to human translators or automated translation as translation memories, domain-specific monolingual data can be helpful to train machine translation systems via several techniques and the ELRI processing engines are prepared to provide structured resources from strictly monolingual data.

The third case involves existing translation memories as input. In this case, the first step is format conversion, since the system handles translation memories in SDLTM format in addition to the TMX standard. Once converted to TMX, language identification is performed on the translation units as a second step. The translation memory then undergoes the previously described clean-up operations, generating a clean version of the initial translation memory.

Finally, a fourth case was added to the system, as terminology files in TBX format and resources in XML format can be stored and shared in a National Relay Station. In this case, no particular processing is performed, as terminological units cannot be filtered similarly to sentential translations and resources in unpredictable XML format cannot be processed without additional knowledge on the format.

The automated processing component of the NRS software is a Java application which integrates and connects the different components responsible for each processing step. Two major toolchains were designed and implemented: TM2TMX, which handles all processing related to existing translation memories, and DOC2TMX, which manages multilingual as well as monolingual input files.[17]

The overall process is performed with quality components, supporting an optimal creation of structured resources from raw data. For instance, the document alignment step, which is an essential part in multilingual scenarios, is performed with DOCAL, one of the top-performing tools for the task in terms of quality of the alignments and processing efficiency (Azpeitia and Etchegoyhen, 2019). The ability of the NRS software to ingest raw data in multiple file formats and generate structured resources in an automated manner is one of the main features of the ELRI infrastructure.

4. Quality Control and Validation

Language resources uploaded to a given NRS undergo a systematic validation process, summarised below.

The first step involves the contribution of a resource by registered users of the NRS, who upload their data and specify the desired level of sharing for each resource. Once uploaded, the data are then automatically processed via the integrated language processing engines, a process called Ingestion which results in prepared language resources. An important next step in the process is resource validation, which is performed by dedicated personnel on the basis of strict guidelines for quality control. If at any step an issue is detected, the process is put on hold until issues are eventually resolved with the user who contributed the data. An initial review is first performed to detect possible issues with the original data uploaded by the user. This might be the case, for instance, if the files significantly mix content in more than one language, or if the content underwent digital corruption at some point. Resources that pass initial review then undergo quality reviewing, which involves manual examination of samples of the processed data, to determine for instance the quality of the translation units in the case of translation memories generated by the automated language processing engines. Poor alignment quality, which may happen for instance with some input files in PDF format, would result in the resource not being validated and the user being notified of the issue.

---

[17]The second toolchain shares the initial processing steps in multilingual and monolingual scenarios, as can be seen in Figure 4; despite its name, the output of this toolchain for monolingual input data is a text file, not a TMX.

The third main step in the validation process involves the review of potential personal, confidential or sensitive information. Although users are required to warrant that the data they contribute does not infringe on any legislation, such as the GDPR[18], the ELRI validation process involves a specific step to help determine if the contributed data may nonetheless include such data. For this purpose, a specific tool was developed within the project to process the data under validation and generate a report on detected patterns of sensitive data and named entities.[19] Patterns include national identification numbers, passport numbers, words and phrases, in the relevant national language(s), indicating confidential material or typical formulations related to personal information, among others, that can be easily customised to country-specific needs and circumstances. The tool is meant only as an aid and no guarantee is given that it would fully or adequately capture sensitive or personal information in the data. However, it may help detect the presence of this type of data, in which case the validation process would be placed on hold until the matters are resolved, or eventually abandoned if no resolution is reached. The final step in the validation process involves reviewing the legal aspects associated with the resource. This includes a review of the licensing scheme selected by the user. By default, the user can select among the main types of licenses typically associated with the sharing of language resources, such as Creative Commons licenses[20]. Reviewers evaluate the selected license and check that the relevant information is available, such as attribution text and IPR holder information, as needed. Additionally, users may provide their own licenses for a given resource, in which case the legal validation will involve a specific examination of the user-provided licensing scheme prior to any further validation. The selected sharing group is also reviewed to set the appropriate metadata, for instance ensuring that resources shared as Open Data allow uses besides the DGT.

Finally, if no issues are detected during the validation process, the reviewer will sign off for publication of the resource, which will then be available for download for the data holder and all members of the selected sharing groups.

5. Network Activity

An important part of the ELRI project was dedicated to building communities of stakeholders across the four Member States involved in the initiative and beyond. In this section, we describe the main dissemination activities, the initial resource collection efforts which took place during the project, as well as key features that support the maintenance of the network and its eventual extension to new countries.

5.1. Stakeholders Communities

As a nationally deployable infrastructure, ELRI was meant to facilitate contacts and interactions with stakeholders, notably via the four institutions in charge of hosting an NRS in their respective Member States: the Administrative Mod-

ernisation Agency (AMA) in Portugal, Dublin City University in Ireland, the Evaluation and Language Resources Distribution Agency (ELDA) in France, and the Secretary of State for Digital Advancement (SEAD) in Spain. This key feature of the network proved to be an important factor in building strong communities of stakeholders across the board, to support the continuous collection and sharing of language resources.

Several events were organised during the project to disseminate the goals and benefits of the ELRI infrastructure, resulting in growing communities of users who viewed the approach based on localised National Relay Stations as an important component to handle their respective resources. A series of workshops was notably organised in all four Member States in spring 2019, to provide an open and practical forum on the use of the ELRI services for public institutions. These events drew large attendances overall, demonstrating the interest generated by the ELRI approach and opening the doors to public entities in the different Member States involved in the initiative. In addition to these dissemination events, a large number of direct contacts and interactions with stakeholders took place at the national level during the project, which helped raise awareness on the importance of language resources, digital advancement and optimised translation processes at the national and European levels.

As a result of these community building activities, the National Relay Stations have registered growing numbers of active users from different institutions of the Member States where they are deployed. Figure 5 shows the number of institutions and authorised users by the end of the ELRI project, in September 2019. With 71 participating institutions and 101 authorised users at the time, the National Relay Stations can be considered to have attracted the interest of public institutions in the Member States participating in the Action.[21]

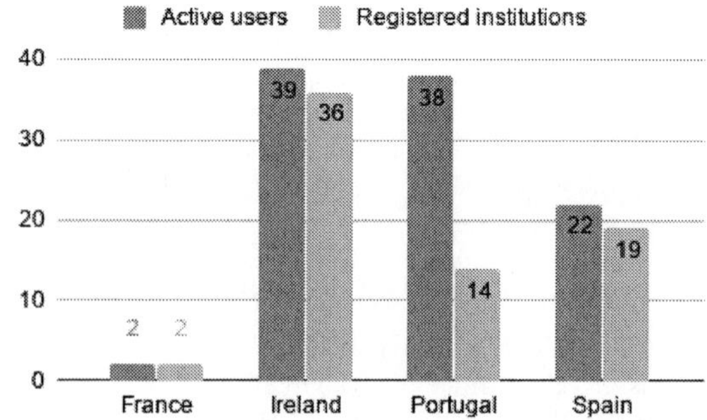

Figure 5: Registered institutions and active users (2019/09)

---

[18]https://gdpr-info.eu/

[19]Named entity recognition and classification are performed with the SpaCy toolkit: https://spacy.io/

[20]https://creativecommons.org/

[21]As a tentative basis of comparison to evaluate the significance of these numbers, (Lösch et al., 2018) indicates that "more than 58 public sector organisations across Europe had shared their language data with ELRC", at the end of the 2016-2017 project, which targeted all Member States of the Union and EEA countries.

5.2. Language Resource Collection

Registered users of the different National Relay Stations have contributed a number of initial resources, several of which have been fully validated and published on the corresponding NRS. Figure 6 shows the published resources in the four National Relay Stations as of September 2019.

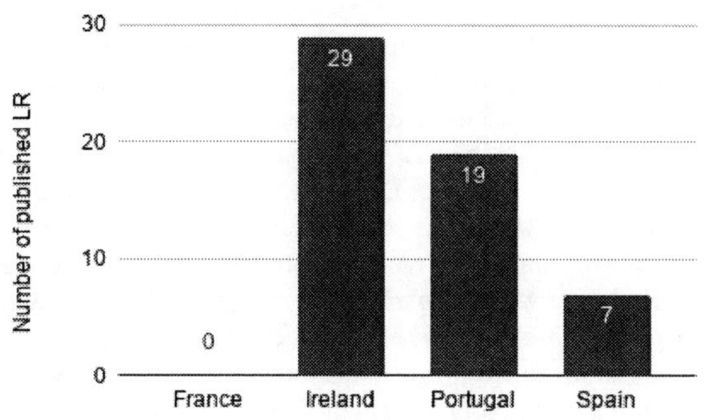

Figure 6: Number of published resources (2019/09)

The collection of resources had thus been initiated by the end of the project, with first sets of resources in all but one Member State. Regarding the French NRS, it should be pointed out that the national events addressing stakeholders took place at a later stage compared with other countries, and that several discussions are currently ongoing with institutions willing to participate and share data. Meetings have taken place for that purpose after completion of the project and initial resources are starting to be uploaded and processed via the French National Relay Station. The sustained National Relay Stations allow resource collection efforts to be adapted to the specific dynamics of the Member States and, in the case of France, ELRI will be available to support an increased sharing of resources over time.

Although the number of published resources is indicative of the initial activity for each NRS, resources vary in terms of content, with users uploading data of varying sizes. Figure 7 illustrates the number of translation units for published resources.

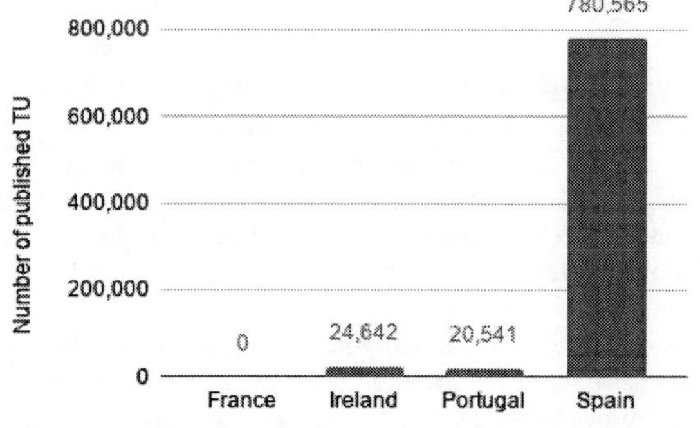

Figure 7: Number of published translation units (2019/09)

As shown in this figure, although the Spanish NRS has published a comparatively smaller number of resources than its Irish and Portuguese counterparts, several of the published resources in that Member State contain large amounts of content, with close to 800 thousand translation units. Although an important factor, the size of the resources, be it the number of translation units or the number of sentences for monolingual data, is only one indicator of the usefulness of a resource, as smaller resources may contain domain-specific information that is of equal importance for both human translators and for the training of accurate machine translation systems.

As previously described, the ELRI infrastructure provides the means to share resources beyond the national level. Figure 8 indicates the percentage of resources shared with the European Commission or as Open Data. Two main conclusions can be drawn from these figures. First, the fact that some resources remain at the Member State level indicates that there is some need for country-based repositories. Secondly, the fact that most LRs have been transmitted beyond the national level shows that ELRI stations can act as a relay in the global data collection effort. It is worth noting that resources that remain at the national level for the time being may be shared further in the future if the relevant data holders consider that the conditions are met for extended sharing of specific resources.

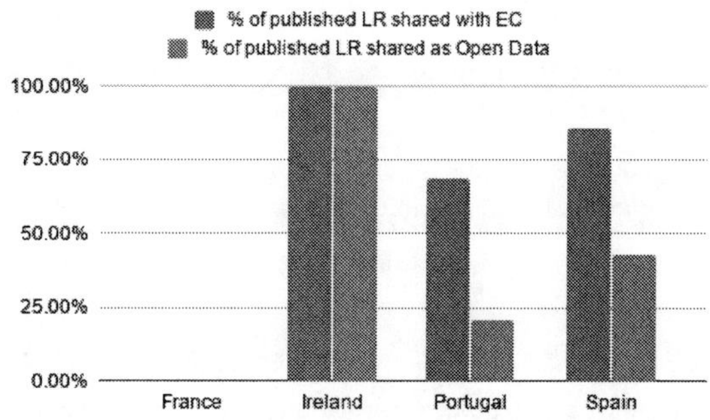

Figure 8: Percentage of published resources shared beyond Member States (2019/09)

Overall, 48 bilingual resources, amounting to 816,553 translation units, have been transferred beyond the national level during the initial resource collection phase in the last six months of the project.[22]

6. Sustainability and Expansion

A key objective of the ELRI project was the development of an infrastructure that would be sustainable beyond the lifetime of the EU-funded initiative. On technical and financial grounds, the outcome of the project is a solution that requires minimal management and associated resources, thus

---

[22]Although comparisons with other initiatives are difficult to establish, given the available information and differences in reporting methodology, indications regarding these numbers may be drawn from the results reported in (ELRC, 2017). Between 2016 and 2017, the authors report 225 collected resources, covering all official EU languages, plus Icelandic and both variants of Norwegian, out of which 138 were bi-/multi-lingual corpora. Information on the amount of translation units and on the proportion of resources gathered from direct crawling of public websites (an approach not undertaken in ELRI), are not available in the report, making further comparisons difficult.

providing a solid basis for its durable maintenance. The benefits provided by the ELRI infrastructure, from minimal management to integrated support for LR creation and management, play an important role in the decision of the different institutions in the different Member States to sustain its services after completion of the project, as has been the case since then with continued collection, preparation and sharing of LRs. Although the infrastructure provides the means to facilitate resource management, a sustained commitment by each institution in charge of an NRS is required to involve dedicated personnel for resource reviewing and publication. Future dedicated funding support for the National Relay Stations at the national or European level may help consolidate the sustainability investments already made by each institution.

As part of its activities, the ELRI project had also designed a structured plan that enables new countries to join the network and deploy its services with minimal efforts and costs. Managing an ELRI National Relay Station requires a Managing Body, with the following main characteristics and responsibilities:

- Be a public institution of the Member State/EEA country or an institution endorsed by a public body.

- Commit to maintain the NRS operations independently of associated project funding.

- Coordinate with the bodies in charge of similar projects and related initiatives.

- Oversee and execute the relevant activities to deploy, adapt and manage the NRS.

The candidacy of a Managing Body should be approved by the appropriate bodies, part of the governance structure, to be determined by the European Commission. This state of affairs is motivated by the fact that there should be only one National Relay Station per Member State/EEA country, to avoid conflicts and confusion on the part of end-users. Since the ELRI framework was developed within the Connecting Europe Facility programme, the integration of new countries should also be controlled to ensure the expected standards of representation and activity oversight.

The ELRI Advisory Board was established, with the seven entities who led the development of the infrastructure and whose role is to provide members of the network with their expertise on the infrastructure, including requirements, technical knowledge, best practices and overall experience in managing National Relay Stations. The Board is also meant to provide assistance to the European Commission in relation to new candidacies for countries willing to join the network, in an advisory capacity.

The inclusion of new countries is meant to be both facilitated and controlled. Thus, on the one hand, a detailed list of required activities and expected costs was prepared to assist potential new Managing Bodies, supported by the relevant documentation. On the other hand, the established governance structure, which requires approval by the relevant EU bodies, ensures that the deployment of an NRS in a new country would be controlled and in accordance with the established goals of the ELRI framework.

By the end of the project, several Member States and EEA countries had expressed their strong interest in deploying their own National Relay Station, and discussions are under way to follow through on this expansion of the network.

7. Conclusions

We have described the main achievements of the ELRI initiative, which has led to the development of a functional, tested and deployed infrastructure in all four Member States that participated in the CEF Action, namely France, Ireland, Portugal and Spain. The ELRI infrastructure is composed of independent National Relay Stations that facilitate the collection of language resources from public institutions joining the network, providing them with fully automated data processing services that allow the efficient creation of useful resources from raw data, such as translation memories from multilingual documents. The prepared resources can then be used to optimise translation services, provided either by professional human translators or by automated translation systems such as eTranslation.

ELRI services offer flexible means to share language resources and provide data holders, who dedicate time and effort to sharing their data, with prepared resources as an immediate benefit that has been a key feature of the initiative. Thus, the project aimed to benefit all stakeholders equally, as a means to build a community of interest and a positive dynamic around the sharing of quality language resources. Dissemination activities and direct contacts with stakeholders have led to positive feedback and strong interest in joining the ELRI network, from members of public institutions as well as representatives from new Member States willing to host their own National Relay Station.

The adopted bottom-up approach to LR collection, via National Relay Stations reserved for public institutions of a given country, is a unique feature of ELRI that provides a pragmatic solution to the actual difficulties in directly sharing resources outside the national realm. With a majority of collected resources having been shared beyond the national level, to repositories with wider access such as ELRC-SHARE, the ELRI network has demonstrated its potential to act as an effective relay for resource sharing, while also providing a framework adapted to needs and constraints of public institutions at the Member State level.

The collection and preparation of resources within the project was initiated in 2019 and led to the publication of an initial batch of resources in the independently deployed National Relay Stations. Overall, 71 institutions had registered to the network by the end of the project and contributed more than 800,000 translation units within the first months of activity. Although preliminary, and with different volumes collected in each country, the established community of users and dynamic are paving the way for continued and increased sharing of language resources across the board. As a sustainable solution, with National Relay Stations being maintained after the lifetime of the project, ELRI has provided additional building blocks to the global effort towards increased efficiency for translation services in the European Union.

8. Acknowledgements

The ELRI project was co-financed by the Connecting Europe Facility of the European Union, who we thank for their support. We would like to thank all stakeholders from public institutions in France, Ireland, Portugal and Spain who have participated in the data collection activities, for their time and effort in helping collect and share language resources. We also wish to thank the ELRC consortium and the Innovation and Networks Executive Agency for their assistance and support during the project, and the three anonymous IWLTP 2020 reviewers for the insightful comments.

9. Bibliographical References

Azpeitia, A. and Etchegoyhen, T. (2019). Efficient Document Alignment Across Scenarios. *Machine Translation*, 33:205–237.

ELRC. (2017). European language resource coordination: Final report. Technical report.

Etchegoyhen, T. and Azpeitia, A. (2016). A Portable Method for Parallel and Comparable Document Alignment. *Baltic Journal of Modern Computing*, 4(2):243–255. *Special Issue: Proceedings of EAMT 2016.*

Etchegoyhen, T., Gaspari, F., Dunne, J., McHugh, H., Vale, P., Fonseca, J. L., Fonseca, P., Melero, M., Branco, A., Gomes, L., Neto, R., Arranz, V., and Choukri, K. (2019). ELRI: Final Report. Technical report. `http://www.elri-project.eu/resources/` `D1.3_ELRI_Public_Final_Report.pdf`".

Koehn, P., Hoang, H., Birch, A., Callison-Burch, C., Federico, M., Bertoldi, N., Cowan, B., Shen, W., Moran, C., Zens, R., et al. (2007). Moses: Open source toolkit for statistical machine translation. In *Proceedings of the 45th Annual Meeting of the ACL*, pages 177–180. Association for Computational Linguistics.

Lösch, A., Mapelli, V., Piperidis, S., Vasiļjevs, A., Smal, L., Declerck, T., Schnur, E., Choukri, K., and Van Genabith, J. (2018). European language resource coordination: Collecting language resources for public sector multilingual information management. In *Proceedings of the Eleventh International Conference on Language Resources and Evaluation (LREC 2018)*, pages 1339–1343.

Varga, D., Németh, L., Halácsy, P., Kornai, A., Trón, V., and Nagy, V. (2005). Parallel corpora for medium density languages. In *Recent Advances in Natural Language Processing (RANLP 2005)*, pages 590–596.

Proceedings of the 1st International Workshop on Language Technology Platforms (IWLTP 2020), pages 44–49
Language Resources and Evaluation Conference (LREC 2020), Marseille, 11–16 May 2020
© European Language Resources Association (ELRA), licensed under CC-BY-NC

Removing European Language Barriers
with Innovative Machine Translation Technology

Dario Franceschini, Chiara Canton, Ivan Simonini (PerVoice),
Armin Schweinfurth, Adelheid Glott (alfatraining),
Sebastian Stüker, Thai-Son Nguyen, Felix Schneider, Thanh-Le Ha, Alex Waibel (KIT),
Barry Haddow, Philip Williams, Rico Sennrich (UEDIN)
Ondřej Bojar, Sangeet Sagar, Dominik Macháček, Otakar Smrž (CUNI),

PerVoice, Italy; `name.surname@pervoice.it`
alfatraining; `name.surname@alfatraining.de`
Karlsruhe Institute of Technology, Germany; `name.surname@kit.edu`
University of Edinburgh (UEDIN)
Charles University, MFF ÚFAL (CUNI); `surname@ufal.mff.cuni.cz`

Abstract

This paper presents our progress towards deploying a versatile communication platform in the task of highly multilingual live speech translation for conferences and remote meetings live subtitling. The platform has been designed with a focus on very low latency and high flexibility while allowing research prototypes of speech and text processing tools to be easily connected, regardless of where they physically run. We outline our architecture solution and also briefly compare it with the ELG platform. Technical details are provided on the most important components and we summarize the test deployment events we ran so far.

Keywords: automatic speech recognition, spoken language translation, machine translation, automatic minuting, live transcription, live translation

1. Introduction

While natural language processing (NLP) technologies like automatic speech recognition (ASR), machine translation (MT), spoken language translation[1] (SLT), natural language understanding (NLU), or automatic text summarization have recently seen tremendous improvements, and are provided to end users as services by large companies like Google, Microsoft or Facebook,[2] the output quality of applications is still insufficient for practical use in daily communication. The goal of the ELITR (European Live Translator) project[3] is to advance and combine different types of NLP technologies to create end-to-end systems that are usable in serious business communication. Specifically, the ELITR project targets the advancement and application of ASR and SLT in two challenging settings:

- Face-to-face conferences (interpreting official speeches and workshop-style discussions)

- Remote conferences (interpreting discussions held over a on-line platform)

In addition to addressing technological challenges in ASR, SLT, and MT, the project covers a large number of languages: ELITR tests its ASR technology in 6 EU languages. The subsequent MT technology is currently able to translate among all 24 official EU languages but

aims at supporting a larger set of language relevant for our user partner, the languages of members of European Organisation of Supreme Audit Institutions, EUROSAI.[4]

The paper is structured as follows: In Section 2., we describe the core of our systems, the processing platform, which is used in both face-to-face and remote meetings settings. In Section 3. we go through some of the differences between ELITR platform and the ELG Grid. In Section 4., we summarize the design decisions and status of the technologies connected to the platform. Section 5. describes our field tests and our first experience.

2. Processing Platform

The architecture of ELITR SLT systems builds upon the PerVoice Service Architecture, a proprietary software solution with roots supported also by several previous EU projects.

This architecture is composed of a central unit called the Mediator, and several modules for processing pipelines, called Workers, which can be easily provided by universities or research labs. These Workers are implemented as standalone programs that connect to the Mediator via TCP/IP. The communication protocol (or API) is prescribed and among other things requires each Worker to indicate the service it provides, for instance translation from a given source to a given target language. Typically, Workers are

---

[1] We interpret this term in the narrow sense: speech in one language to text in another language

[2] Microsoft Translator translates between 62 languages, with 22 handled by the novel neural approach, and recognizes speech in 11 languages. Two variants of Chinese and English can be included in a customized component.

[3] `http://elitr.eu/`

---

[4] EUROSAI languages are all EU languages and Albanian, Arabic, Armenian, Azerbaijani, Belorussian, Bosnian, Georgian, Hebrew, Icelandic, Kazakh, Luxembourgish, Macedonian, Moldovan, Montenegrin, Norwegian, Russian, Serbian, Turkish, and Ukrainian, over 40 languages in total.

simple wrappers of the partners' respective tools or research prototypes.

Clients connect to the Mediator, requesting a particular type of output and providing a source data stream, i.e. audio or text based on their use cases. The Mediator orchestrates the service provision by contacting the required Workers. PerVoice Service Architecture supports both batch and real-time processing.

2.1. Metadata: Fingerprint and Types

The first problem addressed by the PerVoice Service Architecture is the declaration of Services and service requests descriptions. For this purpose, so called *fingerprints* and *types* are used to specify the exact language and genre of a data stream. Fingerprints consist of a two-letter language code (ISO369-1) followed by an optional two-letter country code (ISO3166) and an optional additional string specifying other properties such as domain, type, version, or dialect (`ll[-LL[-dddd]]`). Types are: audio (audio containing speech), text (properly formatted textual data), unseg-text (unsegmented textual data such as ASR hypotheses).

Service descriptions and service requests are fully specified by their input and output fingerprints and types. For example, the ASR service which takes English audio as input and provides English unsegmented text adapted on news domain will be defined by "`en-GB-news:audio`" input fingerprint and "`en-GB-news:unseg-text`" output fingerprint. The service request of German translation of English audio will be defined by "`de-DE-news:audio`" input fingerprint and "`en-GB-news:text`" output fingerprint.

2.2. Workflow

When a Worker (the encapsulation of a service) connects to the Mediator (orchestration service) on a pre-shared IP address and port, it declares its list of service descriptions, i.e. the list of services it offers. As soon as the connection is established, the Worker waits until a new service request is received.

Several Workers can connect to the Mediator and offer the same service, which allows for a simple scaling of the system. As soon as the new service request has been accepted, the Worker waits for incoming packets from the Client's data stream to process, and performs specific actions depending on the message types (data to be processed, errors, reset of the connection). When the Client has sent all the data, the worker waits until all pending packets have been processed, terminates the connection with the Client and waits for a new Client to connect.

From the Client perspective, when a Client connects to the Mediator, it declares its service request by specifying which kind of data it will provide (output fingerprint and type) and which kind of data it would like to receive (input fingerprint and type). If the Mediator confirms that the mediation between output type and input request is possible, the Client starts sending and receiving data. When all data has been sent, the Client notifies it to the Mediator and waits until all the data has been processed by the Workers involved in its request. The Client can then disconnect from the Mediator.

2.3. Mediation

In order to accomplish a Client's request, a collection of Workers able to convert from the Client's output fingerprint and type to the requested input fingerprint and type must be present. For example, if a Client is sending an audio stream with the fingerprint `en-GB-news:audio` and requests `en-GB-news:unseg-text`, the Mediator must find one Worker or a concatenation of multiple Workers that are able to convert audio containing English into unsegmented English text, i.e. a speech recognition Worker in the example. The Mediator searches for the optimal path to provide a service using a best path algorithm that works on fingerprint names and types match.

In order to make sure that a mediation is still possible even if there are no workers available matching the requested stream types and fingerprints, back-up strategies have been implemented, which relax the perfect match on country and domain fingerprint's section.

2.4. MCloud Library

Through its light-weight API MCloud, the PerVoice Service Architecture defines a standard for services integration, allowing different partners integration and a flexible usage for different use cases. The Mediator supports parallel processing of service requests in a distributed architecture.

MCloud is a C library which implements the raw XML protocol used by the PerVoice Service Architecture and exposes a simplified API for the development of Clients and Workers. For convenience, the library integrates some high-level features like audio-encoding support and data package management. A .NET and a Java wrapper of the MCloud API are available in order to support the development of client desktop applications for the PerVoice Service Architecture.

3. Comparison of ELITR and ELG Platforms

Another EU project, European Language Grid (ELG)[5] also develops a common platform for natural language processing.

While starting from similar intentions, ELITR and ELG focus on different use cases. ELITR targets real-time business use cases—like face-to-face and remote video conferencing for selected events—ELG focuses on the creation of a shared European Language Technologies catalogue and marketplace for self-service usage of provided technologies. Both purposes and intentions are valuable but result in different technological approaches.

ELITR use cases include live video streaming and automatically transcribed and translated subtitles. For this reason the project preferred the low-latency solution provided by the PerVoice Service Architecture, which works in real-time and also enables the transparent concatenation of services (e.g., ASR output passed as input to translation Worker) based on "on-air" services. Real-time communication is provided by a fast protocol working over TCP/IP

---

[5]`https://www.european-language-grid.eu/`

sockets which ensures smaller latencies in contrast to approaches relying on external message brokers that introduce asynchronous interaction and delays.

The decentralized approach of the PerVoice Service Architecture allows companies to avoid sharing proprietary technologies. Furthermore, the actual service provider of a Worker component is secondary to the actual functionality being provided. ELG instead prefers the service categorization approach, creating a catalogue of services deployed in its infrastructure.

The ELITR solution could be deployed offline, should the use case require special security and data privacy measures—assuming that there are sufficient hardware resources and a partner agreement. The ELG grid instead is deployed only in cloud.

In general, we highlight the fact that language technologies can rely on different software architectures, and not all of them are suitable to be containerized. For example, a complex language processing solutions could run more than one process, making it harder to manage the container and debug problems, or they could have high resource requirements. Large virtual machine images become an issue when thousands of containers need to be deployed across a cluster. The PerVoice Service Architecture instead delegates service management to individual parties contributing services to the infrastructure, in order to exploit their specific training and knowledge of the technologies and systems for a better resource allocation and usage.

4. ELITR Technologies

With respect to the core language processing technology needed to realize the simultaneous translation service presented here we face several research questions that need to be addressed. Besides the obvious challenge of providing speech translation with sufficient performance, the special case of simultaneous speech translation for conferences, talks and lectures brings specific challenges with it. Two foremost challenges are a) that speech translation has to happen in real-time and with low latency in order to be simultaneous, and b) to cover and adapt to a large variety of domains as the topics of talks and conferences can be virtually arbitrary; therefore systems need to be either domain-independent (a still unsolved research question) or need to be able to adapt to the current domain, autonomously or with as little human supervision as possible.

Currently the systems for speech translation also undergo an architecture transformation from statistical models based on Bayes' rule towards all neural models that give better performance. In our scenario this transformation has to be done under the aspects of the need for low latency translation which leads to task specific considerations.

4.1. Architecture Consideration

Over the last years the basic technology of the components for speech translation has undergone radical transformations. While for decades systems for speech recognition and machine translation where based on Bayes' rule and made use of statistical methods such as Hidden Markov Models, Gaussian Mixture Models, N-Gram Models, and Phrase Based Translation Models, lately the use of neural networks has led to significantly improved performance. While first individual components, such as the acoustic model or the language models, of the systems were replaced, the latest improvements were gained from end-to-end systems that solve the problem of automatic speech recognition, machine translation etc. with a single neural network architecture, instead of solving the problem with several models given by Bayes' rule.

This single network architecture can go to the extreme of solving the whole problem of speech translation with one single neural network architecture.

4.1.1. Current SLT Architecture in ELITR

At this time, end-to-end speech translation systems do not yet outperform cascaded systems consisting of several components (Niehues et al., 2019). End-to-end speech recognition models (Nguyen et al., 2019; Pham et al., 2019) have been showing promising performance but have limit when being used in online conditions. Therefore, in ELITR we use a cascaded speech translation system consisting of:

- Automatic Speech Recognition System (ASR)

- Punctuation System (PUNCT)

- Machine Translation System (MT)

Automatic Speech Recognition   In our system, the ASR component is in charge of processing the audio stream sent from recording clients and output a stream of text transcript to the next component in the pipeline. We currently follow the HMM/ANN hybrid approach (Fügen et al., 2008; Niehues et al., 2018) to build up the ASR model. In this approach, ASR modeling is handled by two separate components: acoustic model (AM) and language model (LM). The task of AM is to model acoustic observations with regard to the labels of context dependent phonemes. As recent advances in the field of ASR, deep neural networks are used to leverage the modeling capacity of the AM on many hours of speech training data. Separately from AM, LM is trained solely on text data and it is used to provide the probabilities of word sequences. The AM and LM are then used in a dynamic decoding framework that is capable of online and low-latency inference. As one of the most important advantages of the hybrid approach, both AM and LM can be easily adapted for better performance if in-domain data is available for a particular application setup.

Punctuation System   The hypotheses from speech recognition contain no punctuation. As our machine translation system is trained on well-structured, written sentence-level texts, we use a separate component to insert punctuation and sentence boundaries into the ASR output. This component also adds correct capitalization to the otherwise lower-cased hypotheses.

Essentially, the punctuation system is a monolingual translation system, which translates the lower-cased, unsegmented outputs from the ASR components into well-formed texts prior to the translation system (Cho et al., 2015). We can employ any kind of translation approach and it is only required to train on a small amount of monolingual data. In our current punctuation system, for each language, we train a neural model on spoken texts, e.g the transcripts of TED talks. Using our compact representation described by Cho et al. (2017), we are able to add punctuation and correct capitalization in one go. Furthermore, this compact representation helps to reduce the vocabulary size of our neural-based monolingual system, thus, reducing the model size and making the training of such system faster.

Machine Translation System   With the ultimate goal of featuring a translation system for all EUROSAI languages, we opt for the multilingual approach (Ha et al., 2016; Ha et al., 2017; Johnson et al., 2017) where a single system is able to translate from and to multiple languages. This approach has many advantages:

- It leverages the large availability of multi-way, multilingual corpora in European languages such as the corpus of European Parliament documents and speeches' transcription (Europarl) (Koehn, 2005), the collection of legislative texts of the European Union (JRC-Acquis) (Steinberger et al., 2006) or the texts extracted from the document of European Constitution (EU-const) as well as the WIT^3 corpus extracted from TED talks (TED) (Cettolo et al., 2012).

- It uses the multilingual information to help improve the translation of the language pairs which are considered as low-resource languages in some domains. Our research has shown that our multilingual translation system maintains parity with the translation quality of systems trained on individual language pairs on the same small amount of data.

- In practice, having a small number of multilingual systems to cover all language pairs significantly reduces the development and deployment efforts compared with having one system for each pair.

Our multilingual systems are based on the neural sequence-to-sequence with attention framework (Bahdanau et al., 2014) and shares the internal representation across languages (Pham et al., 2017). At present, we have one many-to-many Transformer model (Vaswani et al., 2017) providing translation between all pairings of 36 languages, along with several specialized models focused on subsets of languages, in particular the project's primary languages of English, Czech, and German, see i.a. (Popel and Bojar, 2018; Popel et al., 2019).

The resulting multilingual models after training can be used immediately in deployment or can go through a language adaptation step. This language adaptation is simply continuing training the multilingual model on the data of a specific language pair for a few epochs in order to improve the individual translation performance. While we need to do this language adaptation for every single language pair in our system, it is a trivial job since we could automate the process with the same settings and it takes only a little of time and computing resources to reach decent performances.

4.2. Low-Latency Speech Translation

In order to realize low latency in automatic speech recognition we work with speculative output. The decoder in our speech recognition system realizes a Viterbi beam search. Due to the beam, partial hypotheses often have a stable part in which all alternative hypotheses have been pruned away by the beam further ahead in the search, and an unstable part that contains several competing hypotheses that fall within the beam.

Therefore it is possible to output the stable part, knowing that it will never change again as the search progresses. Previous experiments have shown that such a strategy would lead to a latency of about 6–8 seconds. A user study had shown that this considered too high a latency by the users. We therefore lowered the latency further by using speculative output, always putting out the current best hypothesis. Often this hypothesis will stay the most likely hypothesis, as the search progresses. In case it changes, we make use of an update mechanism that allows us to update the recent part of the hypothesis as necessary.

The punctuation component is set to generate the segmented, well-formed text whenever it receives any output, either unstable or stable, from the speech recognition system. And it passes its outputs along with the information of stability to the machine translation component.

Normally the machine translation component waits for the whole sentence before conducting the translation process. To reduce the latency, we force the component to directly and constantly produce outputs right after it receives outputs of the punctuation component. It might then fix the generated translation to be stable by its best hypothesis.

This brings down the average word-based latency, i.e. the time from which the last word of the sentence was spoken until the translation of that sentence is displayed and never changed again by the update mechanism, to under 5 seconds.

5.   Practical Tests

While each of the components (ASR, punctuation, MT) are tested and evaluated on their own, on their respective test sets, the whole complex setup also has to be evaluated.

We are still working on a tool which would allow for a rigorous evaluation of the performance considering multiple aspects like translation quality, delay or text updates which may damage the end user experience.

For the time being, we focus on running many 'field tests', deploying the technology at various occasions. Our experience in the two intended settings (face-to-face multilingual conferences and remote conferencing) is described in the respective sections below.

5.1.   Tests of Multi-Target Conference Speech Translation

Since the ELITR kick-off in January 2019, we carried out several tests and dry-runs to present our live-subtitling system. It first started with a Students Firms Fair in March 2019. During this event, we provided live subtitles on different languages that were spoken on the presentation stage, and we also collected a rather challenging speech test set (Macháček et al., 2019) which serves in the Non-native SLT task at IWSLT 2020.[6]

---

[6] `http://workshop2020.iwslt.org/doku.php?id=non_native_speech_translation`

Next, we had two officially planned events organized by the Supreme Audit Office of the Czech Republic (SAO) that were held in June 2019 and October 2019. In these events, the subtitles were delivered live to the participants through the presentation platform on their laptops. Apart from this, we also tested the input from interpreters into Czech and English respeakers. We also tried to show the live translation of the speaker in Czech, Hungarian, Spanish, German and Dutch from English. These translations were, however, unstable and inconvenient for users to interpret the context of the discussion. This event highlighted the required scope for improvement both in service functionalities and user experience. We made many critical observations from these two events and we gradually improved several aspects of the system for another dry-run in February 2020. Apart from the usual two-line subtitle view, we now present also a paragraph view of the transcript which contains more text in a history-style view. The subtitles were presented in English and translated into German, Czech, Russian, French, Hungarian, Polish, and Dutch.

5.2. Tests of Remote Conferencing

The functionality of live transcription has been succesfully tested in the field of labour market training by alfatraining, an educational provider using alfaview®.[7] A remote call participant with hearing impairment used the live transcript to follow the lessons and participate in discussions with a lecturer and other participants.

In another test, CUNI organized a call between two persons. One person followed only the transcript or translation, without listening. The second person was describing a word without saying it explicitly. We showed on multiple person pairs and languages that it is possible to guess the explained word both from transcripts and automatic translations of natural, spontaneous speech.

6. Conclusion

The PerVoice Service Architecture decouples clients and service providers by providing a simple protocol and an integration library, available for the major platforms, to connect both end-user application and service engines to it. It simplifies the creation of workflows among different service providers by providing automatic workflow creation solution.

Populated with state-of-the-art systems for automatic speech recognition and machine translation developed at KIT, UEDIN and CUNI, the architecture proves its applicability in challenging settings, as needed by the EU project ELITR.

Tests showed practical usability of our systems for face-to-face and remote conferences in real conditions. They also showed that the current and future main challenge is to improve speech recognition, especially for non-native dialects and out-of-vocabulary words.

Acknowledgement

This project has received funding from the European Union's Horizon 2020 Research and Innovation Programme under Grant Agreement No. 825460 (ELITR).

---

[7] https://alfaview.com

7. Bibliographical References

Bahdanau, D., Cho, K., and Bengio, Y. (2014). Neural Machine Translation by Jointly Learning to Align and Translate. *CoRR*, abs/1409.0473.

Cettolo, M., Girardi, C., and Federico, M. (2012). Wit³: Web inventory of transcribed and translated talks. In *Proceedings of the 16th Conference of the European Association for Machine Translation (EAMT)*, pages 261–268, Trento, Italy, May.

Cho, E., Niehues, J., Kilgour, K., and Waibel, A. (2015). Punctuation Insertion for Real-time Spoken Language Translation. In *Proceedings of the Eleventh International Workshop on Spoken Language Translation (IWSLT 2015)*, Da Nang, Vietnam.

Cho, E., Niehues, J., and Waibel, A. (2017). NMT-Based Segmentation and Punctuation Insertion for Real-Time Spoken Language Translation. *Proc. Interspeech 2017*, pages 2645–2649.

Fügen, C., Waibel, A., and Kolss, M. (2008). Simultaneous translation of lectures and speeches. *Springer Netherlands, Machine Translation, MTSN 2008, Springer, Netherland*, 21(4), 22. November.

Ha, T.-L., Niehues, J., and Waibel, A. (2016). Toward multilingual neural machine translation with universal encoder and decoder. *Proceedings of the 13th International Workshop on Spoken Language Translation (IWSLT 2016)*.

Ha, T.-L., Niehues, J., and Waibel, A. (2017). Effective Strategies in Zero-Shot Neural Machine Translation. *Proceedings of the 14th International Workshop on Spoken Language Translation (IWSLT 2017)*.

Johnson, M., Schuster, M., Le, Q. V., Krikun, M., Wu, Y., Chen, Z., Thorat, N., Viégas, F., Wattenberg, M., Corrado, G., Hughes, M., and Dean, J. (2017). Google's multilingual neural machine translation system: Enabling zero-shot translation. *Transactions of the Association for Computational Linguistics*, 5:339–351.

Koehn, P. (2005). Europarl: A parallel corpus for statistical machine translation. In *MT Summit 2005*.

Macháček, D., Kratochvíl, J., Vojtěchová, T., and Bojar, O. (2019). A speech test set of practice business presentations with additional relevant texts. In *Statistical Language and Speech Processing*, pages 151–161, Cham, Switzerland. Springer Nature Switzerland AG.

Nguyen, T.-S., Stueker, S., Niehues, J., and Waibel, A. (2019). Improving sequence-to-sequence speech recognition training with on-the-fly data augmentation. *arXiv preprint arXiv:1910.13296*.

Niehues, J., Pham, N.-Q., Ha, T.-L., Sperber, M., and Waibel, A. (2018). Low-latency neural speech translation. In *Interspeech 2018*, Hyderabad, India, Sept. 2 - 6.

Niehues, J., Cattoni, R., Stüker, S., Negri, M., Turchi, M., Ha, T., Salesky, E., Sanabria, R., Barrault, L., Specia, L., and Federico, M. (2019). The iwslt 2019 evaluation campaign. In *Proceedings of the 16th International Workshop on Spoken Language Translation (IWSLT 2019)*, Hong Kong, November.

Pham, N.-Q., Sperber, M., Salesky, E., Ha, T.-L., Niehues,

J., and Waibel, A. (2017). KIT's Multilingual Neural Machine Translation systems for IWSLT 2017. *Proceedings of the 14th International Workshop on Spoken Language Translation (IWSLT 2017)*.

Pham, N.-Q., Nguyen, T.-S., Niehues, J., Müller, M., and Waibel, A. (2019). Very deep self-attention networks for end-to-end speech recognition. *Proc. Interspeech 2019*, pages 66–70.

Popel, M. and Bojar, O. (2018). Training Tips for the Transformer Model. *The Prague Bulletin of Mathematical Linguistics*, 110(1):43–70.

Popel, M., Macháček, D., Auersperger, M., Bojar, O., and Pecina, P. (2019). English-Czech Systems in WMT19: Document-Level Transformer. In *Proceedings of the Fourth Conference on Machine Translation (Volume 2: Shared Task Papers, Day 1)*, pages 342–348, Florence, Italy, August. Association for Computational Linguistics.

Steinberger, R., Pouliquen, B., Widiger, A., Ignat, C., Erjavec, T., Tufiş, D., and Varga, D. (2006). The jrc-acquis: A multilingual aligned parallel corpus with 20+ languages. In *In Proceedings of the Fifth International Conference on Language Resources and Evaluation (LREC*, pages 2142–2147.

Vaswani, A., Shazeer, N., Parmar, N., Uszkoreit, J., Jones, L., Gomez, A. N., Kaiser, L. u., and Polosukhin, I. (2017). Attention is all you need. In I. Guyon, et al., editors, *Advances in Neural Information Processing Systems 30*, pages 5998–6008. Curran Associates, Inc.

Proceedings of the 1st International Workshop on Language Technology Platforms (IWLTP 2020), pages 50–53
Language Resources and Evaluation Conference (LREC 2020), Marseille, 11–16 May 2020
© European Language Resources Association (ELRA), licensed under CC-BY-NC

Eco.pangeamt: Industrializing neural MT

Mercedes García-Martínez, Manuel Herranz, Amando Estela, Ángela Franco, and Laurent Bié
Pangeanic / B.I Europa - PangeaMT Technologies Division
{m.garcia, m.herranz, a.estela, l.bie, a.franco}@pangeanic.com

Abstract

Eco is Pangeanic's customer portal for generic or specialized translation services (machine translation and post-editing, generic API MT and custom API MT). Users can request the processing (translation) of files in different formats. Moreover, a client user can manage the engines and models allowing their cloning and retraining.

Keywords: neural machine translation, customize translation, adaptive machine translation, NLP ecosystem

1. Introduction

Pangeanic is a language service provider (LSP) and language processing tool developer specialised in natural language processing and machine translation. It provides solutions to cognitive companies, institutions, translation professionals, and corporations. Pangeanic was the first company in the world to make use of the Moses statistical machine translation models in the translation industry (Yuste et al., 2010; Yuste et al., 2012). To this purpose, a platform to build models by the user was developed (PangeaMT's first platform[1]).

Eco.pangeamt[2] is a platform managing translation engines and an NLP ecosystem. It allows the access of three types of user profiles:

- Super Admin, is a reserved profile with which the translation infrastructure can be monitored and managed.

- Client, is an admin profile that allows the management of users and their access rights and statistics. Clients can check metrics and usage of their users, manage the access of the users to the different engines and process files. Moreover, Clients can also manage their models, they can clone models and train them from a baseline with new bilingual material, thus automating the task of engine specialization.

- User, this profile allows the processing of files and checking of information about usage and metrics of the API calls and processed files.

After logging in, the home page of the website shows the Dashboard with the charts about statistics and usage (see Figure 1).

The dashboard will be shown with information about the processes (translations) that have been carried out (processes per week, per month, total expenses, weekly, last processes, etc.).

The options (appearing in the left-side menu) are:

1. New Process: in this page Clients can process files and check their processes.

2. Services/Processes: in this page, Clients can check the files that are being processed and the ones already finished. Here, they will find all the information about them.

3. Profile: here, Clients can change their name, email, password and billing information.

4. Stats: here Clients can check their API stats, File stats and in the Details tab they can check the number of characters, words, segments, files and pages processed by their Users. The Range Date can be set to check the statistics of a particular period of time.

5. Corporate: in this tab Clients can manage their models and engines.

6. Users: where the list of created users is displayed. For a user it is possible to check which engines can be accessed and data about the usage. New users can be created with credentials for their access and with an APIKey that can be used in API or other applications access.

7. Subscriptions: in this page, Clients can check the assigned subscription and manage it.

User and Client profiles can directly translate text or send a file to be translated via the Eco platform. The system saves the files privately, only the file's owner has access to those files handling GDPR compliance. After processing, the translated file in its original format will be available to download. These features are described in services and processes (see Section 2.).

One of the main features of Eco.pangeamt is the possibility of adapting a neural machine translation (NMT) model to the user's own data in a friendly user interface. This feature is presented in Section 3. Finally, conclusions are explained in Section 4.

2. Services/Processes

The services and processes option allows Clients to process new files or translate paragraphs or sentences directly. In order to start a process, Clients have to choose the *Upload file* or *Translate text* option.

---

[1]https://www.gala-global.org/ondemand/pangeamt-platform-user-empowering-and-data-driven-domain-machine-translation
[2]https://eco.pangeamt.com/main

Figure 1: Example of dashboard for a client.

2.1. Processing a file

For processing a file the *Upload file* option is selected, the user selects the source language of the document or documents and the target language (into which language it is translated). To upload the files, the user clicks on the gray box or drags the files to the box (see Figure 2).

Once the files have been selected (the name of the selected files appears below the box) the user can click *Start upload* to upload them. A confirmation message will appear. A process must be carried out per language combination, i.e. if two files need to be translated from English to French, they can be uploaded together, if another file needs to be translated, for example from Japanese to Korean, another process must be carried out by pressing Send another. Clicking on *List of processes* will display the processes that are being carried out and those that have already been completed. In the Finished tab (see Figure 3), the details of the process are displayed: file name, process type, language combination and status.

In the Actions column, the option to download the translated file appears. Once it has been downloaded, next to the download button, the Trash icon appears; pressing it deletes the selected file from the list of completed files. In the Dashboard page, Clients can check that the process has been added to the list of last processes.

2.2. Translation of text

If *Translate text* is selected, users can enter text to translate in the box, the source and the target language have to be selected and pressing *Translate* the translated text will appear (see Figure 4) as the output of the selected engine.

3. Adapting an NMT model via Eco

One of Eco's most popular features is its model adaptation feature (Client role). A model can be trained with generic data (no specific domain). Usually, a generic model has been trained with a lot of data from several general domains. Users can use their clean data to adapt this generic model to a specific domain using specific Machine Learning routines. User material quickly specializes engines into for example technical, legal or science domains (see Figure 5).

A Client can clone or adapt models copying or cloning a model and specializing the model into a domain with the data it has previously acquired. Therefore, you can have a structure with father models (more generic models) and child models (specific models). Once the new model is created by cloning a father model, a Client can retrain the model with their own specific data.

By clicking on the Clone model icon, Clients can clone a model by entering the name and description and selecting the different options (see Figure 6).

Clients can also manage their models and engines. By clicking models on the corporate menu, Clients find all their models and data. Here, they can check all the information about these models: which models they can clone and train, the language pairs, description, the model's father, updates, when it was last saved, etc.

In the Engines section, Clients can verify their engines and check which ones are granted to their users. If the Grant all option is activated all users will have access to the engine.

3.1. Training models

Eco makes training models easy thanks to its user friendly interface. Clients just have to click on the *To Train* icon and upload a bilingual file with language declaration or ID. The allowed file formats are preferably .tmx although .csv and .af (aligned format) are also accepted. Training files must contain perfectly aligned and recognisable source and target segments. Clients can decide the weight or aggressivity of the training. This affects how data will be incorporated into the model and its impact on the engine. A series of ML techniques weigh the data, its length, its vocabulary, etc. Effects on the model are to train it heavily on specific data to ultra-specialise it on the field of application or to just add domain data without changing severely whilst keeping its more generic features. Eco has 3 selectable levels of aggressivity from less to more weighing, shallower or deeper learning: Conservative, Normal or Aggressive (see Figure 7). The time needed for training depends on the size of the file and the level of aggressivity. Training is available with GPU making it much faster.

After a training file has been sent, Clients can access the training page by clicking on the *Trainings* icon. This page shows the completed trainings, the requested ones and the failed trainings. If a training fails, the system notifies where the error is.

The effectiveness of model retraining allowing its specialization in specific data is well known and it has been shown (Domingo et al., 2019a; Domingo et al., 2019b).

Pangeanic has run many trials with the training feature. For that, we used a generic English to Spanish transla-

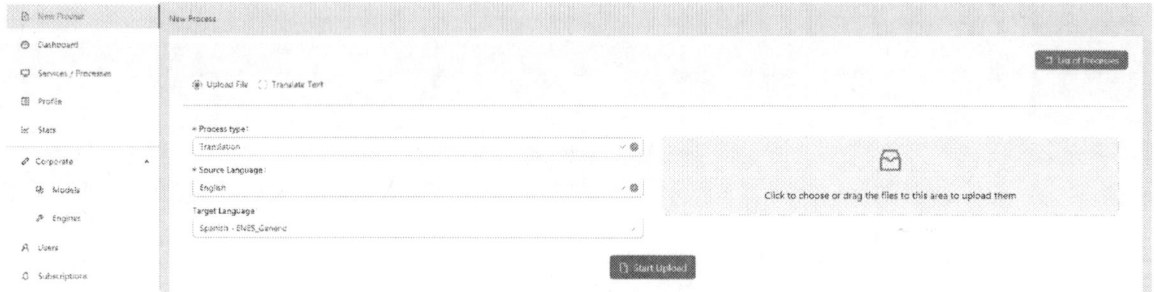

Figure 2: New process view for translating a file.

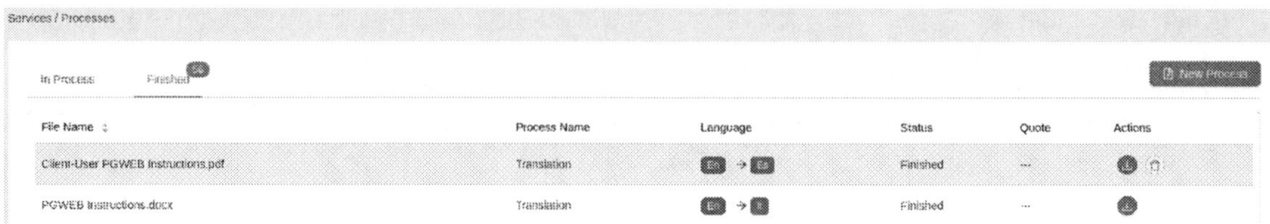

Figure 3: Finished process tab view.

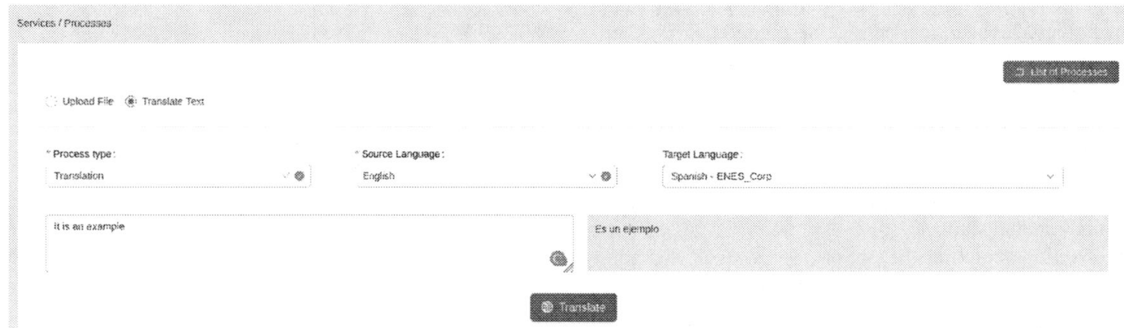

Figure 4: Translate text view.

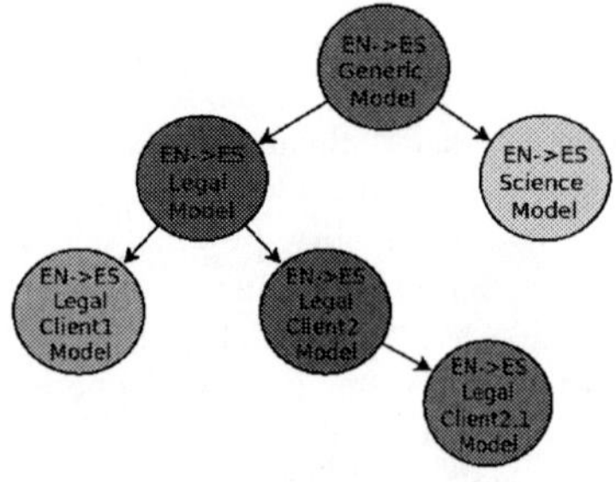

Figure 5: Example model cloning - each child specializes in an area with its own specific data.

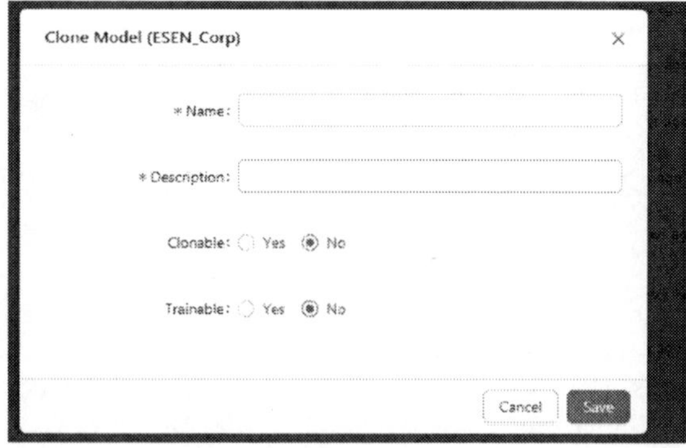

Figure 6: Clone a model view.

tion model trained with public corpora (filtered Paracrawl dataset[3]). We have retrained it with 2 different test files of

500 sentences from the DGT dataset[4].

---

[3]https://paracrawl.eu/

[4]https://ec.europa.eu/jrc/en/language-technologies/dgt-

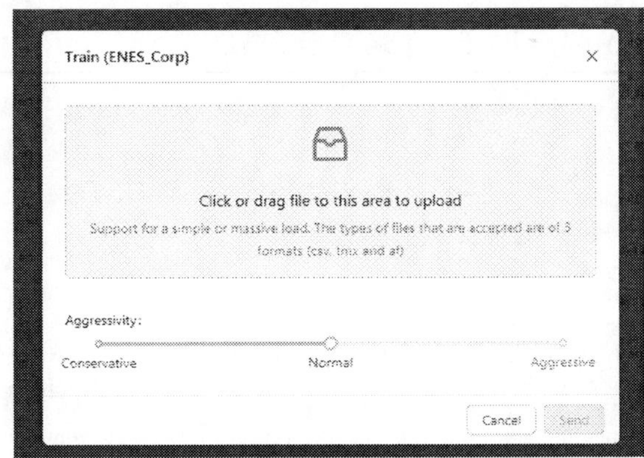

Figure 7: Training a model view where Client can chose the level of aggressivity.

The first test file (DGT test1) has been used to retrain the generic model. We used the 3 options of aggressivity and compared them with no training. We translated the 2 DGT test files (test1 and test2) and a generic test and we compared the results using the standard automatic translation metric BLEU score (Papineni et al., 2002). The results are shown in Table 3.1.

Training	Generic test	DGT test1	DGT test2
No train	66.29	38.25	38.01
Conservative	59.29	45.26	39.18
Normal	56.89	46.54	40.52
Aggressive	55.24	46.83	38.73

Table 1: Results in BLEU score using different types of trainings for the generic test and DGT test1 and test2 files.

Generic test results show a decrease in BLEU score when specializing in DGT domain, this is a normal behaviour because the model will translate better within the same domain. By contrast, the translation of DGT test1 file results show how BLEU score increases with the number of trainings as expected. Furthermore, when translating DGT test2 file, BLEU score improves using retraining. We expect this due to the fact that DGT test1 and test2 files are from the same domain. However, when translating DGT test2 file using aggressive training we obtain lower BLEU score than using conservative and normal training. This can be the case if the model has been adapted too much (overfitting) to data from DGT test1 file and translations to other files do not obtain the best results.

4. Conclusion

We have introduced Eco, Pangeanic's commercial translation platform describing its usage and different options. Eco incorporates a user friendly option for model adaptation. We have shown its effectiveness in a small set of experiments. This platform allows the translation of text

---

translation-memory

and documents as well as APIKey machine translation. The platform is hosted by Pangeanic but can be hosted by clients. Moreover, users are able to build their own models by cloning a generic model and can retrain those models with their own data and as many times as they wish to obtain specific results. Engines can be stored and recalled at a later date. These adapted models will adjust to their domain and generate translations with more quality for their purposes. As a result, machine translation output will be more accurate and productivity will increase due to a decrease in machine translation manual corrections.

For future work, in addition to machine translation more tasks will be added to this platform such as anonymization, summarization or sentiment analysis.

5. Acknowledgements

The research leading to these results has received funding from the Spanish Centre for Technological and Industrial Development (Centro para el Desarrollo Tecnológico Industrial) (CDTI) and the European Union through Programa Operativo de Crecimiento Inteligente (Project IDI-20170964).

6. References

Domingo, M., García-Martínez, M., Estela Pastor, A., Bié, L., Helle, A., Peris, Á., Casacuberta, F., and Herranz Pérez, M. (2019a). Demonstration of a neural machine translation system with online learning for translators. In *Proceedings of the 57th Annual Meeting of the Association for Computational Linguistics: System Demonstrations*, pages 70–74, Florence, Italy, July. Association for Computational Linguistics.

Domingo, M., García-Martínez, M., Peris, Á., Helle, A., Estela, A., Bié, L., Casacuberta, F., and Herranz, M. (2019b). Incremental adaptation of NMT for professional post-editors: A user study. In *Proceedings of the Machine Translation Summit*, pages 219–227.

Papineni, K., Roukos, S., Ward, T., and Zhu, W.-J. (2002). BLEU: a method for automatic evaluation of machine translation. In *Proceedings of the Annual Meeting of the Association for Computational Linguistics*, pages 311–318.

Yuste, E., Herranz, M., Lagarda, A.-L., Tarazón, L., Sánchez-Cortina, I., and Casacuberta, F. (2010). Pangeamt - putting open standards to work... well. In *Proceedings of the Association for Machine Translation in the Americas*, Denver, Colorado, USA.

Yuste, E., Herranz, M., Helle, A., Lagarda, A.-L., García-Martínez, M., Pla-Civera, J., Blasco, M., Morella, A., and Mallach, J. (2012). Pangeanic's do-it-yourself machine translation: User empowerment and user-driven mt processing. *Journal of the Asia-Pacific Association for Machine Translation*.

Proceedings of the 1st International Workshop on Language Technology Platforms (IWLTP 2020), pages 54–58
Language Resources and Evaluation Conference (LREC 2020), Marseille, 11–16 May 2020
© European Language Resources Association (ELRA), licensed under CC-BY-NC

The Kairntech Sherpa – An ML Platform and API for the Enrichment of (not only) Scientific Content

Stefan Geißler

Kairntech SAS

29 Chemin du vieux Chêne, 38240 F-Meylan, France

stefan.geissler@kairntech.com

Abstract

We present the Sherpa Platform and API that combines various ML and NLP approaches for the analysis and enrichment of textual content. The platform's design and implementation is guided by the goal to allow non-technical users to conduct their own experiments and training runs on their respective data, allowing to test, tune and deploy analysis models for production. Dedicated specific packages for subtasks such as document structure processing, document categorization, annotation with existing thesauri, disambiguation and linking, annotation with newly created entity recognizers and summarization – available as open source components in isolation – are combined into an end-user-facing, collaborative, scalable platform to support large-scale industrial document analysis. We see the Sherpa's setup as an answer to the observation that ML has reached a level of maturity that allows to attain useful results in many analysis scenarios today, but that in-depth technical competencies in the required fields of NLP and AI is often scarce; a setup that focusses on non-technical domain-expert end-users can help to bring required analysis functionalities closer to the day-to-day reality in business contexts.

Keywords: Natural Language Processing, Machine Learning, End-user software

1. Introduction

Machine Learning (ML) approaches have been able to go beyond the previous state of the art results in many different fields in the recent years and tasks in natural language processing (NLP) are no exception here. In scenarios such as machine translation, speech recognition, entity recognition, sentiment analysis, document categorization and many others, ML has proven to deliver the highest quality in many evaluations (Chollet, 2017).

At the same time ML comes with its own set of requirements such as the need for technical expertise in programming and data science as well as the necessity to prepare appropriate volumes of training data. Both these requirements can put a heavy burden on the application of ML in business contexts where data science expertise is scarce and costly and training data often not available in the right quality and formats. As Neven and Seva (2019) emphasize: "Manual annotation is still regarded as the bottleneck for many NLP experiments, given that it is a time-consuming manual process."

We present the Kairntech Sherpa, a web-based collaborative platform for ML that allows to address many NLP requirements and that at the same time can be operated by domain experts and end users with little or no technical data science expertise. Users can train, evaluate, tune and deploy ML models for subsequent use via an API in industrial document analysis scenarios.

2. Document Analysis Subtasks

NLP subtasks such as document structure recognition, entity recognition, document categorization, thesaurus-based indexing or summarization have not only been areas of active research for many years but they also have a firm place in business needs around the management, the digestion and distribution of text-based content in large industry organizations.

The Sherpa gives the user access to these functionalities; we go through each of these in the subsections below.

2.1 Document Categorization

Assigning a document to one or several of a predefined set of categories is a task that has its place in a wide range of document analysis scenarios; it also is a well-studied topic in the NLP field. The Sherpa offers users to either upload a precategorized corpus into the application or to upload uncategorized content and then add the categories manually and then to train a model. There is a broad range of categorization algorithms available in the public domain and while the display, the training and evaluation of document categorization is an important feature of the Sherpa API, the precise choice of the underlying algorithm may vary – at the time of the writing of this document categorization via the Python scikit-learn library[1] as well as approaches based on a deep learning library[2] are offered.

2.2 Thesaurus-based Indexing

Annotating ("indexing") document with a set of appropriate descriptors from a set of hierarchically structured terms is another well-established technique in information management, where automatic approaches have been studied and applied for many years and with great success. (Medelyan and Witten, 2006)

Automatic indexing needs to cope with a range of requirements beyond merely finding the occurrence of a string in the text: terms often occur with variations due to inflection, terms may be ambiguous (the same string can carry different meanings depending on the context), terms vary with respect to their importance from terms with only a peripheral role in the document to those that represent the core topic of a document. Finally, where terms are associated with background information, automatic indexing benefits from linking the occurrence of the term to this background information, thus enriching the document with information that is not originally part of the text but that is often of additional relevance to the reader. A typical example is the place (geo coordinates) of a location displayed on a map or background information for

---

[1] https://scikit-learn.org/stable/

[2] https://github.com/kermitt2/delft

a company (website, logo, etc) or a person (picture, address).

The Sherpa employs the "entity fishing" library[3] that uses more than 78 mio terms from Wikidata[4] to enrich content. Wikidata is a superset of many widely used domain-specific thesauri – the well-known MeSH[5] that is used for indexing medical content for instance, is a subset of Wikidata. While the approach can work in principle with Wikidata knowledge bases in any language, we have chosen to add by default the resources for only a selection of languages[6]. There is no technical reason for that decision, it is rather a matter of striking a balance between effort and disk space on one side and the demand from Sherpa use cases on the other.

Wikidata is constantly evolving and growing and we have put processes in place that allow the indexing approach inside Sherpa to keep up to date with this growth. While this is not yet fully automated (partly due to the considerable size and compilation requirements that are needed to turn Wikidata into the format deployed as part of the Sherpa), the application nevertheless benefits from regular updates prepared by the Kairntech development team.

2.3 Custom ML Annotators

Even with many pre-trained models and existing thesauri and term lists in the public domain or available within a given organization, often a given new task just requires setting up a new annotator from scratch in order to properly address a new requirement. Training a new annotator however can be costly: manipulating corpora and setting up and tuning sophisticated ML algorithms is a task that requires a certain level of precious data science expertise that may be scarce and even if that expertise is available, preparing a proper corpus often means conducting time-consuming corpus annotation efforts, which sometimes mean efforts of many days or more.

A prime focus in the design of the Sherpa was therefore making this process of annotating content as easy and effortless as possible.

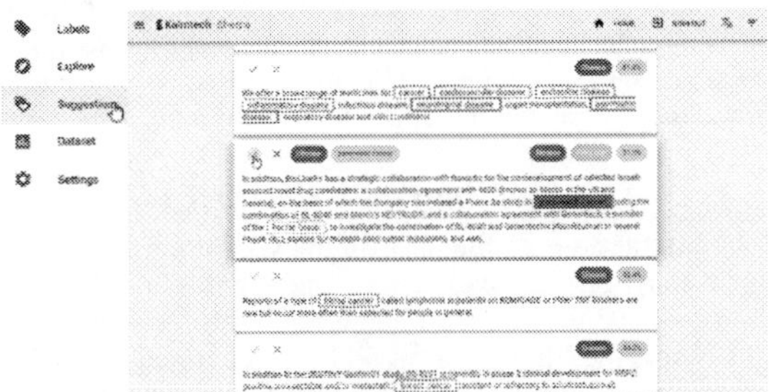

Figure 1: The Sherpa GUI presents the content as easy-to-consume snippets of text to be annotated by the user. Asking for new "suggestions" applies the current ML model which is continuously refined in the background.

Various implementation details support the manual annotators in proceeding with their tasks as quickly as possible: For instance the boundaries of the to-be-selected expressions are automatically extended to include the leftmost and rightmost word boundaries of the selection, respectively which frees the user from the burden of having to accurately hit these boundaries with the mouse herself. Also, after a given snippet is properly annotated (or when the user asks for new "suggestions") this new list is not presented in a random order (or just alphabetically) but instead an Active Learning scheme is applied (Settles, 2009) that ensures that the system focusses in particular on those examples that promise the highest learning progress. It has been observed that properly implemented Active Learning schemes can reduce the effort for manual

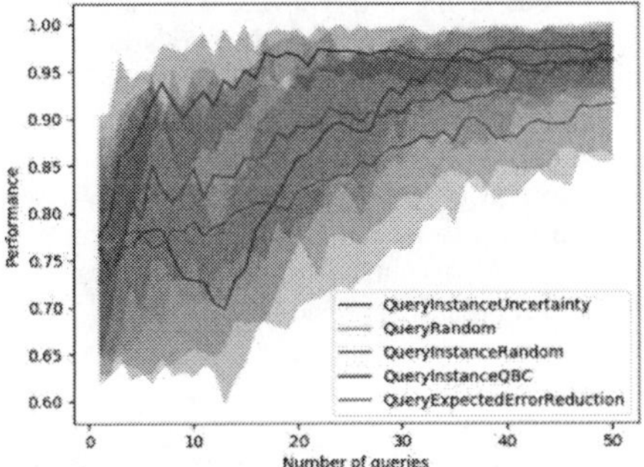

Figure 2: Chart showing how quickly training success on a categorization task improves in accuracy under different training example selection schemes.

annotation by up to 93% (Laws, 2013).

In the chart above we see different training sample selection schemes improving their performance on a categorization task, the well known "iris dataset"[7]: The naïve, random selection scheme (green line) rises comparably slow while one Active Learning approach ("QBC" – Query by committee, the red line) arrives at high accuracy level much more quickly. Translated into project efforts, this can mean drastic reduction of manual annotation efforts.

2.4 Document Structure Recognition

Many types of documents that are relevant in a business context today have a somewhat formal, fixed structure: Contracts, scientific papers, tech reports, invoices or patents typically have a fixed set of chapters and a type-specific way to present certain key metadata to the reader that is meant to facilitate reading and the digestion of the content. However, this information is often lost when the document is rendered into unstructured formats like the notorious PDF. For instance, in the process of writing a LaTeX[8] document, the information what a document's author or title is or what the names of the cited authors are is explicitly marked up; however this information is most of the time no longer present explicitly in the final PDF. The human reader can easily parse this PDF making use of visual clues like fonts and formatting but in order to be

---

[3] https://github.com/kermitt2/entity-fishing
[4] https://www.wikidata.org/
[5] https://www.nlm.nih.gov/mesh/meshhome.html
[6] German, English, French, Italian, Spanish and Dutch
[7] https://archive.ics.uci.edu/ml/datasets/Iris
[8] https://www.latex-project.org/

made available for subsequent document management processes this information must be recognized and extracted.

We use the Grobid[9] package to automate the processing and recognition of unstructured documents to reconstruct their structure and meta data for these tasks. The result of the processing of a document with Grobid is a TEI XML[10] document that makes information about the document's title, authors, their affiliations, the chapter structure, date, references and many others explicit.

Recognizing the structure of a document is again one of these tasks that appear easy for the human reader but that turn out to be hard to capture into explicit rules. Grobid therefore is based on a document-type-specific training corpus capturing text-based but also layout-based information and relying on an appropriate training corpus. The code and the accompanying models referenced above are set up to handle scientific documents; in order to handle another document type like, say, contracts, a new Grobid model would need to be generated. This adaptation of the Grobid component is currently not yet supported via the Sherpa GUI but must be carried out externally.

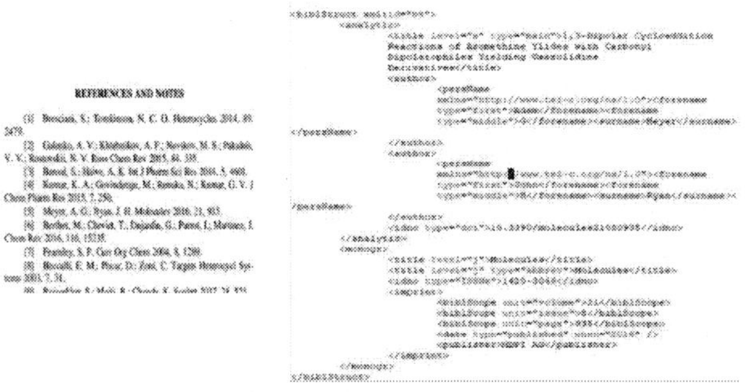

Figure 3: Example for document structure recognition.

The example in Figure 3 shows a part of the reference section of a scientific paper, first in the unstructured PDF, then as structured XML (TEI) after the processing by Grobid: each cited paper and each author is wrapped into the appropriate XML element. The author is optionally dereferenced, disambiguated and completed through a lookup in resources such as CrossRef[11].

Note, that while the Sherpa is a comparably recent development, Grobid in isolation has in fact already been deployed in production in quite a number of large scale installations such as ResearchGate, the European Patent Office EPO, the CERN, the INIST and others.

3. Tracking Quality

For some of subtasks listed above, the Sherpa offers different choices with respect to the used algorithm: For entity recognition / sequence labelling for instance users can decide between different options such as an implementation of Conditional Random Fields (CRF) or libraries implementing deep learning approaches (e.g.

Spacy[12], Delft[13] or Flair[14]). Different approaches may differ significantly in their behavior and appropriateness for a given task: A CRF is trained comparably fast while the results are often a few percent or more behind those of slower Deep Learning runs.

The Sherpa provides users with an overview of the development and the latest training successes of the various employed options. Users can also rely on the fast CRF approach to quickly refine a model that constantly presents new text snippets for manual annotation and once enough snippets have been annotated, launch a longer training run with the more resource-intensive Deep Learning libraries. This way of combining the various strengths and weaknesses of different ML approaches would normally require considerable technical ML expertise – we have chosen to offer that to also less or non-technical users as part of the Sherpa user interface.

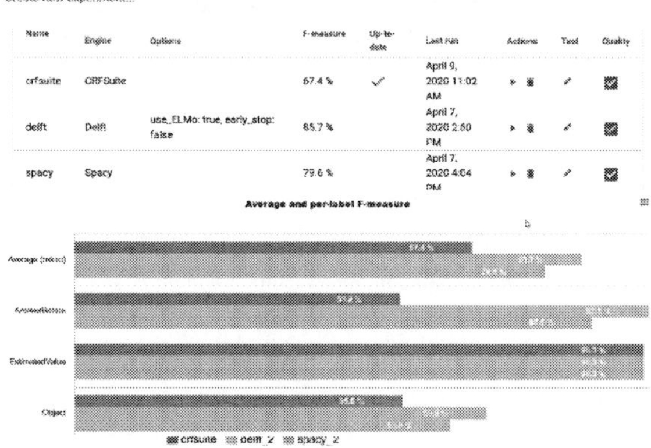

Figure 4: The Sherpa GUI provides the user with an overview about the respective quality reached by different algorithms launched on the same task.

Besides illustrating the fact that the Sherpa allows users to run and compare multiple experiments on the data of a project, the picture above also illustrates the quality delivered by the underlying Delft machine learning library. While a detailed evaluation of Delft is beyond the scope of this paper, the respective results and comparisons to other approaches can be studied at the Delft project page[2].

4. The Sherpa REST API

All the interactions of the user on the GUI are backed by a respective REST API call. That means that while the GUI is the preferred way to conduct an annotation campaign in the browser, the Sherpa can easily be integrated into third party environments via the API, either with the complete training, management and prediction use cases or for instance with only the prediction part.

The Sherpa API is available for inspection at https://sherpa.kairntech.com/swagger-ui/. Note that authentication is required in order to actually use it. While we are currently not in the position to make the API or the Sherpa (https://sherpa.kairntech.com/sherpa/signin) freely

---

9 https://github.com/kermitt2/grobid
10 https://tei-c.org/
11 https://www.crossref.org/
12 https://spacy.io/
13 https://github.com/kermitt2/delft
14 https://github.com/flairNLP/flair

accessible, we are always open to provide access for testing and evaluation on request[15].

5.   Collecting User Feedback

Since the Sherpa is in particular targeted towards end-users, collecting end-user feedback was an important item on our agenda early on.

We had invited professionals on two occasions to a "Hackathon" in July 2019 (20 users) and Oct 2019 (50 users), respectively, introduced them to the concepts and ideas behind the Sherpa and encouraged them to execute their own training experiments.

The key feedback we collected was that users support the claim by the Sherpa, that the annotation of text corpora – normally not the most cherished task of information professionals and related experts – is facilitated and supported favorably by the application. The way in which the GUI helps to minimize mouse movements and keystrokes when doing larger amounts of annotations was considered an important time-saver by users, many of which had previous experiences with training corpus preparation. The most important aspect for many however was the way in which users get constant, live feedback by the system as they go along. The fact that the Sherpa continuously uses the information created so far to refine and apply the model and was considered useful and motivating. One user told us "it even makes you want to annotate more" while another used the term "addictive".

The evidence above, however, remains anecdotal and needs to be complemented with more quantitative data and larger numbers of users as the adoption of the platform grows.

6.   Related Work

The booming popularity and continued success of ML-powered NLP led also to an increase in available NLP platforms that claim to wrap the complexities of ML underneath an end-user GUI. A comprehensive overview of the available systems is hard to achieve given the fast pace of developments in this field. Neves and Seva (2019) have presented such an overview together with an evaluation of the identified systems. They apply a set of criteria that may not be appropriate in industrial context: One of their criteria is that the studied system be available to them, another one that installation must be possible, again for them, in under 2h. These criteria can be defended in order to keep the effort in conducting a scientific study manageable, but they evidently limit the range of studied systems and are not entirely relevant in an industry context[16].

In their list, the authors identify several systems that follow a similar direction as the Sherpa, namely to combine easy corpus annotation directly with ML capabilities using the annotations to create and refine underlying ML models. Example here are Prodi.gy[17], tagtog[18] or LightTag[19].

Seen the list of existing text annotation environments above, the motivation for adding with the Kairntech Sherpa yet another one requires some explanation. Some tools like tagtog or webanno allow richer annotations like e.g. adding metadata on entities at the cost of making the application more complex for the kind of use case we had in mind. The guiding principles for the Sherpa were first of all speed of annotating content and the minimization of the mouse movements and buttons to press when stepping through corpus. Also, the direct integration with an underlying model that constantly learns as the user proceeds for user interaction was key. At any moment the user can request a new result to verify and curate, based always on the most recent model.

Verification is often much faster than adding annotations from scratch. Users find themselves quickly jumping in quick succession between adding annotations and applying the latest model to yet unannotated text. This not only speeds up annotation but moreover is perceived as rewarding by the users who see the automatically created results getting better as they proceed.

The perhaps broadest overlap of an existing tool with the process we felt we needed can be seen in the case of Spacy and its annotation extension Prodi.gy. While Spacy/Prodi.gy are exceptionally well designed pieces of software, some of the scenarios there rely on scripting in python. This however, while evidently greatly extending their reach, can be expected to intimidate the kind of users we have in mind for the Sherpa, i.e. domain experts with no experience or desire to dive into Python programming.

With an annotation process like this in mind and after inspecting existing tools, we concluded that none of them offered a workflow as the one we had in mind.

7.   On Commercial Software and Open Source

Several of the tools listed in the study above are available, at least partially, as open source systems. Not only tools coming from a predominantly academic background but also tools implemented by commercial players often come in limited, feature-reduced versions as open source, offering license-based options for larger, industrial installations.

The Kairntech Sherpa is also a commercial tool. Key components inside, however, are available without any restriction as open source, several of them implemented by members from the Kairntech development team, e.g. Delft, Grobid and Entity Fishing[20].

8.   Sample Sherpa Deployments

The range of functionalities listed above suggests that the Sherpa platform may address requirements from different industries and on different topics. We briefly describe two

---

[15] Enquiries can be addressed at info@kairntech.com

[16] For instance "availability" for a commercial client evidently does not mean the tool must be available free of charge on the internet.

[17] https://prodi.gy/

[18] http://www.tagtog.net/

[19] https://www.lighttag.io/

[20] Disclaimer : The key implementer behind the open source systems Delft, EntityFishing and Grobid is part of the Kairntech software development team.

use cases where the Sherpa has been selected by industrial users:

Inside the German Pharma company Boehringer Ingelheim, a dedicated group, the *Scientific Information Center*, is charged with the analysis and diffusion of scientific and market information to internal users. Boehringer has decided to deploy the Sherpa to support these processes[21]. Another scenario, relying largely on the Sherpa capacity for named entity recognition is addressed at Sealk.co whose mission is to scan large volumes of business news for information that is relevant for the topic of Mergers&Acquisitions.

9. Future Work

The Sherpa is ongoing development project and we plan to extend it continuously to cover more and more functionalities. Extending the analysis to the processing of relationships and integrating analysis results with Graph Databases is high on the agenda. A planned step for later in 2020 is the integration of the Sherpa into the ELG platform[22] allowing users to build their own analysis models on ELG content.

10. Conclusion

We have presented the Sherpa – a platform for the creation of ML training corpora, the training, evaluation and optimization as well as the deployment of the resulting models via a REST API. Technical subtleties of the use of ML approaches are "hidden" as much as possible underneath a simple user interface to allow non-technical users and domain experts to proceed using the system without the need for detailed ML background or any coding at all.

11. References

Chollet, F. (2017): Deep Learning with Python. Manning Publications.

Laws, Florian (2013) : "Effective active learning for complex natural language processing tasks.". Dissertation Univ of Stuttgart, http://dx.doi.org/10.18419/opus-3009

Medelyan, Olena, and Ian H. Witten (2006) : "Thesaurus based automatic keyphrase indexing." *Proceedings of the 6th ACM/IEEE-CS joint conference on Digital libraries.*

Neves, M. and Seva, J (2019): An extensive review of tools for manual annotation of documents. Briefings in Bioinformatics, https://doi.org/10.1093/bib/bbz130

Settles, Burr (2009) : *Active learning literature survey.* University of Wisconsin-Madison Department of Computer Sciences.

---

[21] https://www.kairntech.com/articles/dec2019.html

[22] https://www.european-language-grid.eu/

Proceedings of the 1st International Workshop on Language Technology Platforms (IWLTP 2020), pages 59–65
Language Resources and Evaluation Conference (LREC 2020), Marseille, 11–16 May 2020
© European Language Resources Association (ELRA), licensed under CC-BY-NC

Towards Standardization of Web Service Protocols for NLPaaS

Jin-Dong Kim[1], Nancy Ide[2], Keith Suderman[2]

[1]Database Center for Life Science (DBCLS), [2]Department of Computer Science, Vassar College
[1]Kashiwa, Chiba, Japan, [2]Poughkeepsie, New York, USA
jdkim@dbcls.rois.ac.jp, ide@cs.vassar.edu, suderman@cs.vassar.edu

Abstract

Several web services for various natural language processing (NLP) tasks ("NLP-as-a-service" or NLPaaS) have recently been made publicly available. However, despite their similar functionality these services often differ in the protocols they use, thus complicating the development of clients accessing them. A survey of currently available NLPaaS services suggests that it may be possible to identify a *minimal* application layer protocol that can be shared by NLPaaS services without sacrificing functionality or convenience, while at the same time simplifying the development of clients for these services. In this paper, we hope to raise awareness of the interoperability problems caused by the variety of existing web service protocols, and describe an effort to identify a set of best practices for NLPaaS protocol design. To that end, we survey and compare protocols used by NLPaaS services and suggest how these protocols may be further aligned to reduce variation.

Keywords: NLPaaS, web services, standards, synchronous protocols, asynchronous protocols

1. Introduction

There is considerable demand within both academia and industry for immediately available natural language processing (NLP) capabilities that can analyze and mine the vast amounts of textual data thar have become available in recent years. To answer this need, "NLP-as-a-service" (NLPaaS) web services are beginning to be developed, including Natural Language API of Google[1], Amazon Comprehend[2] and CLARIN-D NLP services[3], to name a few.

Every web service supports one or more protocols to remotely invoke its API (Application Programming Interface) in order to provide programmable access to its functionality. Among others, protocols which follow the REST (REpresentational State Transfer) architectural style (Fielding and Taylor, 2000) have become popular, due to its simplicity and flexibility. However, REST itself is a protocol design *style*, not a specific protocol, which leaves it to the implementer to decide how data objects are exchanged in client-server communication. This flexibility, while attractive to web service developers, has led to a lack of consistency in the protocols used by different NLPaaS services. As a result, those implementing clients for NLPaaS services that come from different developers often have to accommodate different communication protocols.

In this paper, we describe an effort to identify a minimal common protocol for NLPaaS based on best practices, with the aim of raising awareness of the interoperability problems caused by the variety of existing web service APIs and soliciting input for a standard set of NLPaaS service APIs. To that end, we survey and compare APIs used by NLPaaS services and provide a draft proposal intended to serve a basis for the eventual development of an NLPaaS API standard. We restrict the scope of NLP services to those that take texts as input and return the result of some NLP process as a result, as a starting point; however, we feel that an acceptable minimal common protocol for services

---

[1]https://cloud.google.com/natural-language/
[2]https://aws.amazon.com/comprehend/
[3]https://weblicht.sfs.uni-tuebingen.de

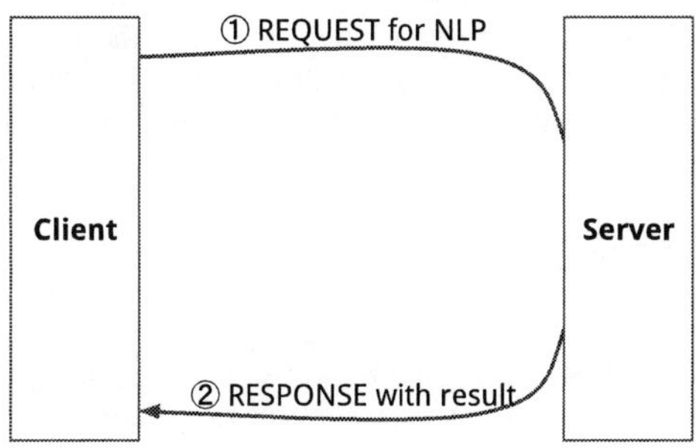

Figure 1: General synchronous protocol

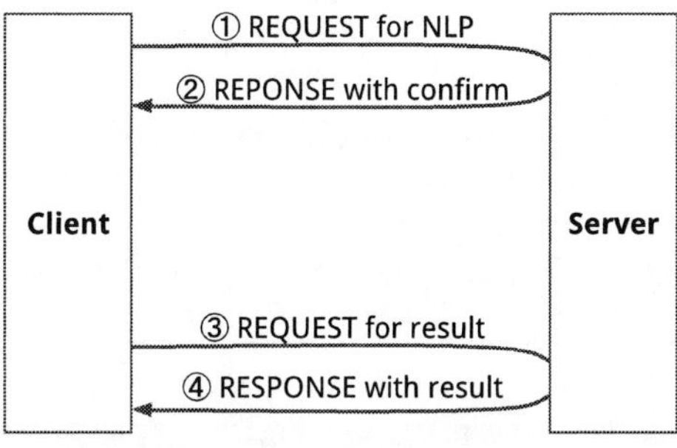

Figure 2: General asynchronous protocol

ingesting textual data could be generally applicable across web services performing a wider variety of tasks.

2. Synchronous and Asynchronous Protocols

There are two basic protocols for exchange of information among services and clients: *synchronous* protocols and *asynchronous* protocols,

Figure 1 illustrates a *synchronous protocol* exchange between a client and a server. The exchange is initiated by a request from the client to the server (typically, a GET or

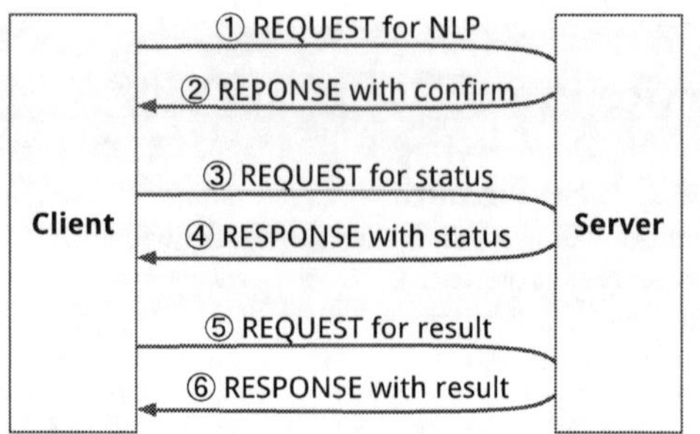

Figure 3: General asynchronous protocol with status checking

POST request) and completed by a response from the server to the client. Synchronous protocols block activity on the client as well as the server while the request is being processed; therefore, to avoid resource starvation in unexpected situations (network problems, errors, etc.), the request is typically subjected to a conservative timeout.[4] Therefore, when requests are expected to take an extended amount of time, e.g. in order to process a large amount of text or to execute a heavy task, the use of a synchronous protocol may be inappropriate.

Asynchronous protocols, illustrated in Figure 2, solves the timeout problem by separating the request from the delivery of the result, which is then handled by a separate connection. Services using asynchronous protocols are commonly coupled with an API that enables the client to check the status of the requested task, i.e., whether it is completed, still processing, or has encountered a problem. Figure 3 illustrates an asynchronous protocol with status checking.

3. Survey

This section presents our survey on the protocols used by existing NLPaaS services. For the purposes of comparison and to save space, only a selected subset of the services surveyed are included here. Note that due to the focus on NLP-related services, our survey is limited to services that take plain or annotated text as input and return a processing result as output. The result may be text or other forms of data (e.g., key-value pairs) resulting from the analysis. The subset of APIs we describe here is intended to include a variety of NLPaaS services available from different types of developers and serving a variety of audiences, including freely available services developed by academic and other non-commercial communities (CLARIN, CoreNLP, PubDictionaries), national services (PubTator, ETRI), and commercial services (Google).

Note that the focus of our survey is on the protocols used for sending and receiving data and does not consider the types of text analysis that the APIs provide (e.g., named entity recognition, sentiment analysis). For a comprehensive survey of the text analytic functions provided by different commercial services, see (Dale, 2020).

3.1. Synchronous Protocols

As described above, synchronous protocols involve a simple client-server conversation consisting of a request followed by the corresponding response. Differences among servers using synchronous protocols appear primarily in their conventions for specifying input and output.

Table 1 gives an overview of the synchronous protocol APIs for several NLPaaS services, including the CLARIN-D (Hinrichs et al., 2010) and CLARIN-PL (Piasecki, 2014) services from the European CLARIN project; ETRI NLP API Korean NLP[5], developed and maintained by the Electronics and Telecommunications Research Institute (ETRI); Google Natural Language API, a commercial service provided by Google; and PubDictionaries (Kim et al., 2019), a service provided by the Database Center for Life Science (DBCLS). We also include Stanford CoreNLP (Manning et al., 2014), which is one of the most widely used NLP toolsets that is also implemented as a NLPaaS web service.

3.1.1. Methods and Content types

Most NLPaaS services receive requests using the *POST* HTTP verb (Fielding et al., 1999) in order to accommodate the need to send a (relatively) large body of text for processing. Certain services, such as PubDictionaries, support requests using the *GET* method, in this case because the service processes primarily short, natural language queries. With the *POST* method, some services require the content type to be explicitly specified, while others assume that the content type is always text (CoreNLP) or JSON (ETRI). Again, PubDictionaries is somewhat more flexible, accepting data in various formats: the content type of a POST request may be either *multipart/form-data* (for key-value pairs), *application/json* (for a hash or an array), or *text/plain* (for plain text).

3.1.2. Parameters

NLPaaS services take several parameters, including a block of *text*, the NLP *task(s)* to be run, and *user information*(e.g., for access control)

Text Services utilize two different methods to pass text to the server: through a parameter on the GET request and as the payload of a POST request. In a GET request, the (short) text to be processed is given as the value of a parameter, whose name may differ among servers; *text* is commonly used, but more abstract names such as *content* may be used for services that can process multiple content types (e.g., HTML, XML). When using a POST request, the payload is typically either key-value pairs (*multipart/form-data*), JSON object (*application/json*), or the text itself (*text/plain*). In either of the first two cases, the key name *text* is commonly used to send a block of text to a service.

Process The protocols used by some services include specification of the NLP process or processes to be invoked. This is accomplished in various ways: Google provides a different URL for each different NLP service, and ETRI receives the specification through a parameter. CLARIN-D, CLARIN-PL, and CoreNLP allow specification of a sequence of NLP processes through a parameter; however,

---

[4]Many HTTP servers, e.g., Apache, NGINX, and Tomcat have a default request timeout of 60 seconds.

[5]http://aiopen.etri.re.kr/ (written in Korean)

Service	Method	Content type		Parameters		Identity
		Request	Response	Text	Process	
CLA-D	POST	multipart/form-data	n/s	*content*	*chain* (XML)	*apikey*
CLA-PL	POST	application/json	n/s	*text*	*lpmn*	*user* (email)
CoreNLP	POST	text (implicit)	multi	(payload)	*properties:annotators*	-
ETRI	POST	JSON (implicit)	application/json	*argument:text*	*argument:analysis_code*	*access_key*
Google	POST	application/json	application/json	*document:content*	(encoded in URL)	OAuth2
PubDict	GET|POST	multiple	application/json	*text*	(encoded in URL)	-

Table 1: APIs of synchronous protocols of several NLPaaS services. Note that "CLA" denotes CLARIN and "PubDict" denotes PubDictionaries. Items in italics are parameter names.

as indicated in Table 1, they use different parameter formats (XML for CLARIN-D, pipe ('|')-separated names of NLP processes for CLARIN-PL, and comma (',')-separated names of NLP processes for CoreNLP).

User Information   Some services require information concerning the user who is calling the service, e.g., for access control or billing. Services may obtain this information via a parameter of the request (e.g., *apikey* for CLARIN-D, *user* for CLARIN-PL, and *access_key* for ETRI), while others use standard authentication schemes (e.g., *OAuth2* for Google).

3.2.   Asynchronous Protocols

Asynchronous protocols are typically used when it is necessary to transmit large amounts of data–in the context of NL-PaaS services, a large body of text–in order to avoid the time-out problem outlined in Section 2.. Therefore, asynchronous requests typically use the HTTP *POST* method, which allows for sending texts of unlimited size using the naming and content specification conventions outlined above. The relevant differences among asynchronous protocols concern the methods used to pass information about a request and requests for metadata, e.g., status of the job. To illustrate these differences, three services are surveyed: *CLARIN-PL* (Piasecki, 2014), *PubDictionaries* (Kim et al., 2019) and *PubTator Central* (Wei et al., 2019).

The asynchronous protocols of PubTator Central and Pub-Dictionaries follow the overall request-response flow illustrated in Figure 2. However, they use different methods to pass necessary information in order for the client to follow the flow of execution. For example, when accepting a request such as

```
POST /annotate/submit/Gene ...(parameters)
```

PubTator Central responds with the status code 200 ("OK") together with a session number in the body of the response. The client is then supposed to compose the URL for retrieving the result using the session number and send a second request to the server, e.g.,

```
GET /annotate/retrieve/{SessionNumber}
```

In contrast, PubDictionaries returns the status code 303 ("See other") for a successfully received request, together with a *Location* HTTP header that specifies the URL for retrieving the result.

When a request for a result is submitted, PubTator responds with the status code 404 ("Not found") if the result is not ready, together with the warning message "[Warning : The

Result is not ready" in the body of the response. PubAnnotation responds instead with status code 503 ("Service unavailable"), along with a *Retry-After* HTTP header to provide a hint to the client as to when to try to retrieve the result again. In the case where the result is ready when requested, both services respond with 200 ("OK") together with the result in the body.

CLARIN-PL uses an asynchronous protocol following the request-response flow illustrated in Figure 3. Like PubTator Central, CLARIN-PL uses the body of the response to inform the client of the task ID, with which the client can compose the URL for checking the status of the task. Below is the synopsis of the initial request:

```
POST /nlprest2/base/startTask ...(parameters)
```

The response is a task ID in the body of the response, from which a request to check the status of the task can be composed:

```
GET /nlprest2/base/getStatus/{taskID}
```

The response to this request is a JSON object:

```
{
  "status":"DONE"|"ERROR"|"QUEUING",
  "value":"..."
}
```

The client will keep checking the status until the value of the *status* key is *DONE*. When completed, the *value* key will be filled with the result ID, from which the client can compose the URL and make a request for the result, e.g.,

```
GET /nlprest2/base/download/{resultsID}
```

3.3.   Summary

The differences outlined above for both synchronous and asynchronous protocols demonstrate the implementation options among services providing NLP processing. These differences complicate client development by requiring different means to handle sending requests and processing responses to different services. However, these variations are generally not due to systemic differences among services, but rather are in most cases simply a matter of arbitrary choice. It therefore seems possible to identify a set of conventions for client-server communication for NL-PaaS, thereby simplifying client development for both synchronous and asynchronous processes.

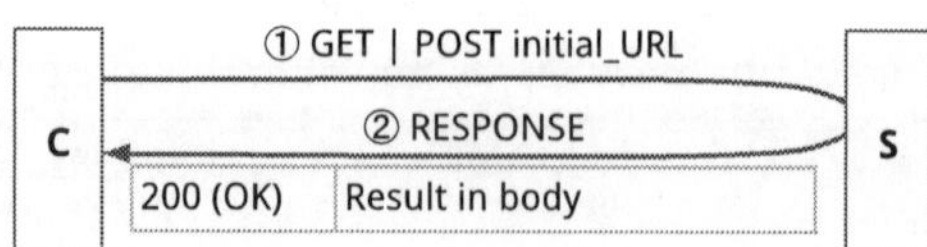

Figure 4: Synchronous protocol, proposal

4. A (Modest) Proposal

This section presents a preliminary proposal for protocols for NLPaaS services, based on the practices outlined in the previous sections. The aim is to provide a basis for continued discussion and development by members of the community at large.[6]

4.1. Criteria and Scope

The survey of differences among protocols used by NLPaaS services provides a basis for establishing the design criteria for protocol standardization.

The scope of this proposal includes:

- Request-response flow

- Request methods and headers

- The *text* parameter

- Response codes and headers

Note that the proposal does not cover input/output formats for the input text and the NLP processing results. There exist several standards for text and annotation formatting, and formatting can be dealt with in a separate layer from the protocols. Furthermore, input/output formats typically conform to the requirements of specific tools; a standard format would unnecessarily burden service developers with conversion to and from internal formats in order to be compliant. For the same reasons, we do not address user identification/authorization methods, nor do we consider parameters other than *text* since they are often tightly coupled with the functionality of a given service.

To illustrate how the proposed protocol might be used, we consider both a client-server communication environment and a server-server communication environment using *PUSH* notifications.

4.2. Synchronous protocol

Figure 4 illustrates the request and response flow of the proposed synchronous protocol. The initial request must be sent using the *POST* method. An NLPaaS service must receive a block of text through the request parameter *text*, which must be delivered either via the payload of *multipart/form-data* or as encoded in the URL. The following *cURL* command[8] illustrates this:

```
curl -F text="A␣sample␣text"
      URL_for_annotation
```

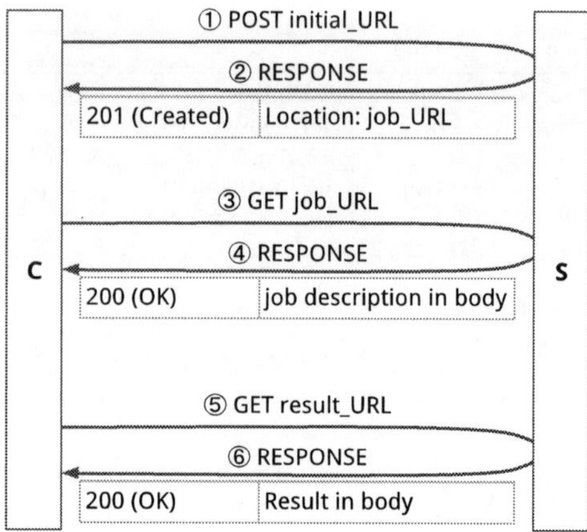

Figure 5: Asynchronous protocol

Note that specifying the request parameter *text* as a common channel for delivery of text does not prevent the service from receiving input through other channels, such as the *content* key[9]. When a request includes many parameters, and especially when it includes a structured parameter, it is common practice to include all the parameter settings in a single JSON object and send it through the payload of *application/json*; therefore, we recommend that services receive a payload of type *application/json*. Upon receiving a request, the service must execute its NLP process over the text, and, when successful, it must respond with status code 200 (OK) together with the result in the body. [10].

4.3. Asynchronous protocol with polling

Figure 5 illustrates our proposal for an asynchronous protocol for NLPaaS services, consisting of the following:

1. The initial request

   1-1. Must be sent using the *POST* method

   1-2. When successful, the response must include

       1-2-1. Status code *201 ("Created")*

       1-2-2. the *Location* header to specify the *job_URL*

       1-2-3. the description of the job, in the body

2. Second request

   2-1. Must be sent using the *GET* method

   2-2. The response must include

       2-2-1. Status code *200 ("OK")*

       2-2-2. the description of the job, in the body

3. Third request

   3-1. Must be sent using the *GET* method

---

[6]To conform to the formal specifications in RFC 2119[7], in our discussion we use the verb *must* when a given practice is required and *may* when a given practice is recommended.

[8]In the example *cURL* commands, parameters other than *text* are omitted.

[9]For example, Google uses the *content* key to receive documents as may plain-text or HTML. For Google to conform the standard, it may use *text* key to receive text, while retaining *content* to receive html.

[10]As discussed in Section 4.1., the format of the output is out of scope of this specification.

Attribute	Description	Format
submitted_at	Timestamp of submission	ISO 8601
started_at	Timestamp of execution	ISO 8601
finished_at	Timestamp of completion	ISO 8601
elapsed	Elapsed time	ISO 8601
ETR	Estimated time remaining	ISO 8601
result_location	Location of the result	URL
error_message	Error message	String
status	*IN_QUEUE* or *IN_PROGRESS* or *DONE* or *ERROR*	String

Table 2: Attributes for a job description.

3-2. The response must include

    3-2-1. Status code *200 ("OK")*

    3-2-2. the result, in the body

Initially, the client sends a request to a server to apply a certain NLP process to a block(s) of texts using the *POST* method (1-1). *POST* is used because the text may be very long, and, more importantly, POST is not a "safe" request[11] and therefore the response should not be cached. As for the synchronous protocol, the request parameter *text* must be used to send a block of text.

When the request is successfully accepted, the server must create a job to execute the desired NLP task and respond to the client with the status code *201* (1-2-1) together with a *Location* HTTP header (1-2-2), to indicate that the job is created and accessible via the URL specified by the header. The body of the response must contain the initial description of the job (1-2-3).

To describe a job, we propose the attributes listed in Table 2. At the time the NLP task terminates execution, the value of *finished_at* and either of *result_location* or *message* must be set. Among the attributes, *elapsed* and *status* are redundant, i.e., they can be calculated from other attributes as follows:

$$elapsed = \begin{cases} current\_time - started\_at & \text{if } finished\_at = \phi \\ finished\_at - started\_at & \text{otherwise} \end{cases}$$

$$status = \begin{cases} IN\_QUEUE & \text{if } started\_at = \phi \\ DONE & result\_URL \neq \phi \\ ERROR & message \neq \phi \\ IN\_PROGRESS & \text{otherwise} \end{cases}$$

However, because these attributes are frequently referenced they are included for convenience. The job description must be serialized into a response body of type *application/json*. This allows for structuring values, e.g., for status replies, it would be easier to define the ability to return multiple messages, possibly even with different "log levels" and with timestamps.

Once the job is created, it must be accessed using the *GET* method (2-1). Next, the service must respond with the status code 200 ("OK") and with the job description in the

---

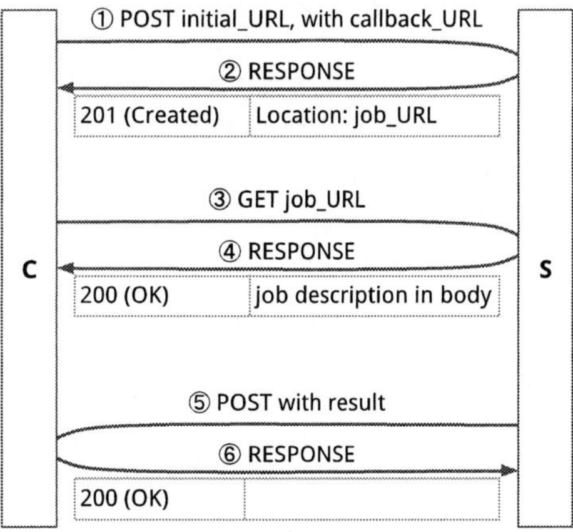

Figure 6: Asynchronous protocol with push notifications

body (2-2). Note that responding with the status code 200 to a *GET* request may results in caching the request somewhere between the client and the server, and it is therefore recommend to include the *Cache-Control: no-store* header. The client is expected to repeatedly access the job until it finds that the *status* is either *DONE* or *ERROR* (polling). During the loop, the value of *ETR* (Estimated Time Remaining) must provide the client with enough information to enable efficient scheduling of future requests. When the status is *DONE*, the job description includes the URL for result as the value of the *result_location* attribute. The client then accesses the result using the specified URL (3-1), after which the service must respond with status code 200 and include the result in the body (3-2).

After the result is retrieved the server may want to delete the job and the result, either immediately or after a specified period of time (e.g., 24 hours). While not required, it is generally recommended that the service explicitly state in the protocol and API documentation exactly when the job and the result will be deleted.

4.4. Asynchronous protocol with callback

The protocol with *polling* proposed in Section 4.3. is necessary when a service has no way to talk to a client except by responding to the client's requests. However, if the server can talk to the client at any time, the server can instead *push* messages to the client to report when new information becomes available rather than responding to periodic client requests, thus avoiding the crush of a potentially large number of clients polling continuously. To enable this scenario, the client registers a *callback* URL as a part of the job submission. When the server has new information available, it sends this information in the same format the client would use when issuing a polling GET request (with the obvious difference that the server is issuing a POST to the client). Figure 6 illustrates our proposal for an asynchronous protocol with push notifications.

The differences from the polling model are:

- The initial request includes the callback URL, for which we propose the parameter name

---

[11] An HTTP method is "safe" if it does not alter the state of the server.

callback_location;

- When the task is completed, the server immediately sends the result to the callback URL, using the POST method;

- When the client has successfully received the result, it responds with status code 200.

Because the server will send a notification when the task is completed (successful or not), the client does not need to repeatedly check the status of the job in order to know the timing required to retrieve the result. However, the API of the service from which a client may request the job description is still useful when it is necessary to estimate when the result will be received, and, even after the client receives the result, to see the metadata associated with the job, e.g., length of execution time.

5. Discussion

As stated in Section 1., the proposal presented in Section 4. is a first draft intended to serve a basis for further development. Here we explain the rationale for various design choices over possible alternatives.

5.1. Response code for the initial request

HTTP is not designed with explicit consideration of asynchronous protocols, and therefore no existing response status code exactly fits the asynchronous scenario. The draft proposal specifies that the server must issue status code 201 ("Created") in response to an initial request for asynchronous communication. However, among existing systems and in relevant articles, some advocate for using 202 ("Accepted") or 303 ("See other"). The rationale behind our choice of 201 is that the initial request can be defined as a request for the creation of an "NLP job", which can be immediately created upon submission of the request. A drawback of this choice is that it is not user friendly, i.e., it reflects an engineering perspective rather than the perspective of end users, who simply want the result of the job. If we view the initial request from the user's perspective, it may be more reasonable for the server to respond with 202 or 303. In the case of 202, the value of the accompanying *Location* header would be interpreted as the location of the result. In the case of 303, the value of the *Location* header would be interpreted as a location for a relevant resource (e.g., the job), not the requested resource itself (e.g., the result). Although we have suggested one code over other possibilities, this topic remains open for further discussion.

5.2. Response Code for Polling

For polling, the server needs to continuously inform the client of the status and the estimated time remaining (ETR) to complete the job. Some services follow the overall request-response flow illustrated in Figure 2 and use the the status code 404 ("Not found") or 503 ("Service unavailable"). Code 503, which is an indication of a transient problem, is typically accompanied with the *Retry-After* header, an HTTP-native way to tell the client to try again within an estimated wait time. We have avoided these two codes because they are broadly understood as error codes indicating

a problem with the request and/or the server. Ideally, there would exist a status code such as 309, standing for "Redirect to itself", that could be used together with *Retry-After*, but not with *Location*. With such a code the server could tell the client to make another request after a specified length of time because the request cannot be currently fulfilled.

5.3. Delivery of the result location

When the NLP task is complete and the result is ready to be served, the server responds to the request for polling with the status code 200 and the URL for the result in the *result_location* field of the response body. Some services use 303 with a *Location*, which is an HTTP-native means to inform the client of the location for the request; however, 303 was not chosen because it prevents the metadata of the job from being accessed after the job is completed.

5.4. Parameter passing

When a block of text is the single parameter of a POST request, a straightforward means to pass the parameter is to send it as payload of type "text/plain", possibly coupled with a specification of the character encoding (e.g., "text/plain; encoding=UTF-8"). However, NLPaaS services often require additional parameters, such as the specification of the NLP process to be applied. When the payload is used to pass a block of text, the only means to pass additional parameters is to encode them in the URL, which is often unwieldy. In this case, the standard practice is to send all the parameters as key-value pairs with the content-type header "multipart/form-data".

When a value of a key is a structured value (e.g., an array of NLP processes to make up a pipeline), it may be difficult or impossible to send them as key-value pairs. For this reason, we recommend sending all parameters as a JSON object, which is a common practice.

6. Conclusion

In this paper we survey a number of NLPaaS services in order to identify current common practice and, in so doing, establish a basis for development of a standard for NLPaaS protocols. We outline a draft proposal for such a standard drawing on our observations, and offer it to the community for future consideration.

We recognize that standardization is a major endeavor that necessarily involves gathering input from the community of users in order to reach a broad consensus. We have therefore set up a GitHub repository[12] containing the draft specification so that the community can be actively involved in furthering this effort.

7. Acknowledgements

Thanks to Richard Eckart de Castilho and Jan-Christoph Klie for their insightful comments. This work was supported in part by the Database Integration Coordination Program funded by National Bioscience Database Center (NBDC) of Japan Science and Technology Agency (JST) and U.S. National Science Foundation (NSF) grant 1811123.

---

[12]https://github.com/jdkim/NLPaaS-Protocol

8. Bibliographical References

Dale, R. (2020). *Text Analytics APIs: A Consumer Guide*. Language Technology Group, 3 edition.

Fielding, R. T. and Taylor, R. N. (2000). *Architectural Styles and the Design of Network-Based Software Architectures*. Ph.D. thesis, University of California, Irvine. AAI9980887.

Fielding, R., Gettys, J., Mogul, J., Frystyk, H., Masinter, L., Leach, P., and Berners-Lee, T. (1999). Hypertext Transfer Protocol – HTTP/1.1.

Hinrichs, E., Hinrichs, M., and Zastrow, T. (2010). WebLicht: Web-based LRT services for German. In *Proceedings of the ACL 2010 System Demonstrations*, pages 25–29, Uppsala, Sweden, July. Association for Computational Linguistics.

Kim, J.-D., Wang, Y., Fujiwara, T., Okuda, S., Callahan, T. J., and Cohen, K. B. (2019). Open Agile text mining for bioinformatics: the PubAnnotation ecosystem. *Bioinformatics*, 35(21):4372–4380, 04.

Manning, C., Surdeanu, M., Bauer, J., Finkel, J., Bethard, S., and McClosky, D. (2014). The Stanford CoreNLP natural language processing toolkit. In *Proceedings of 52nd Annual Meeting of the Association for Computational Linguistics: System Demonstrations*, pages 55–60, Baltimore, Maryland, June. Association for Computational Linguistics.

Piasecki, M. (2014). User-driven Language Technology Infrastructure -the Case of CLARIN-. In Jerneja Žganec Gros Tomaž Erjavec, editor, *Proceedings of the 17th International Multiconference Information Society - IS 2014*, volume G of *Language technologies*, pages 7–13. Institut Jožef Stefan.

Wei, C.-H., Allot, A., Leaman, R., and Lu, Z. (2019). PubTator central: automated concept annotation for biomedical full text articles. *Nucleic Acids Research*, 47(W1):W587–W593, 05.

Proceedings of the 1st International Workshop on Language Technology Platforms (IWLTP 2020), pages 66–72
Language Resources and Evaluation Conference (LREC 2020), Marseille, 11–16 May 2020
© European Language Resources Association (ELRA), licensed under CC-BY-NC

NTeALan Dictionaries Platforms: An Example Of Collaboration-Based Model

Elvis Mboning[1,2], Daniel Baleba[1], Jean Marc Bassahak[1],Ornella Wandji[1], Jules Assoumou[1,3]
NTeALan[1], ERTIM (INALCO)[2]
Tradex Makepe - Douala (Cameroon)[1] , 2 rue de Lille - Paris (France)[2]
elvis.mboning@inalco.fr[2], julesassoumou@yahoo.fr[1,3]
{levismboning, daniel.baleba, bassahak, ornella.wandji}@ntealan.org[1]

Abstract

Nowadays the scarcity and dispersion of open-source NLP resources and tools in and for African languages make it difficult for researchers to truly fit these languages into current algorithms of artificial intelligence, resulting in the stagnation of these numerous languages, as far as technological progress is concerned. Created in 2017, with the aim of building communities of voluntary contributors around African native and/or national languages, cultures, NLP technologies and artificial intelligence, the NTeALan association has set up a series of web collaborative platforms intended to allow the aforementioned communities to create and manage their own lexicographic and linguistic resources. This paper aims at presenting the first versions of three lexicographic platforms that we developed in and for African languages: the REST/GraphQL API for saving lexicographic resources, the dictionary management platform and the collaborative dictionary platform. We also describe the data representation format used for these resources. After experimenting with a few dictionaries and looking at users feedback, we are convinced that only collaboration-based approaches and platforms can effectively respond to challenges of producing quality resources in and for African native and/or national languages.

Keywords: African languages, NLP platforms, resources, XML serialisation, collaboration-based model, dictionaries, lexicography, open-source

1. Introduction

For several years now, artificial intelligence technologies, including those of NLP, have greatly contributed to the economic and scientific emergence of poorly endowed languages in northern countries, thanks to the availability of lexicographic and terminography resources in sufficient quantity. African languages benefit very little from these intelligent tools because of the scarcity of available structured data and collaborative platforms for building linguistic and cultural knowledge bases. In order to meet this need and complement the initiatives already present on the continent ((De Pauw et al., 2009), (Mboning, 2016), (Vydrin, Valentin and Rovenchak, Andrij and Maslinsky, Kirill, 2016), (Abate et al., 2018), (Mboning, Elvis and NTeALan contributors, 2017), (Mangeot and Enguehard, 2011), (De Schryver, 2010), Afrilex association (Ruthven, 2005)), and also those from other African, European and American research centers, NTeALan (New Technologies for African Languages), specialized in the development of NLP / NLU tools for teaching African languages and cultures, has set up a collaborative and open-source platform for building lexical resources for African native and/or national languages.

Our paper focuses on the description of NTeALan's architectures platform and its lexicographic data format (African linguistics and cultural resources), component of our collaborative language resource platform, which is an important starting point for the technological step forward of each African language. This platform is divided into three components: the open-source dictionary REST API (back-end), the dictionary management platform and the collaborative dictionary platform (fronts-end).

2. Context of the work

2.1. NTeALan project

Created in 2017[1] and managed by academics and the African Learned Society, NTeALan is an Association that works for the implementation of intelligent technological tools necessary for the development, promotion and teaching of African native and/or national languages. Our goals are to digitize, safeguard and promote these poorly endowed languages through digital tools and Artificial Intelligence. By doing so, we would like to encourage and help young Africans, who are willing to learn and/or teach their mother tongues, and build a new generation of Africans aware of the importance and challenges of appropriating the languages and cultures of the continent. Another purpose of NTeALan's work is to provide local researchers and companies with data which could help them improve the quality of their services and work, hence building open-source African languages resources is one of our core projects.

2.2. NTeALan approach: a collaboration-based model

Our approach is exclusively based on the collaboration model (Holtzblatt and Beyer, 2017). We want to allow African people to contribute to the development of their own mother tongues, under the supervision of specialists and academics of African languages. Our model involves setting up several communities: a community of speakers of these languages, a community of native specialists

---

[1]Namely by Elvis Mboning (NLP Research Engineer at IN-ALCO) and Jean Marc Bassahak (Contractor, Web designer and developer), who were later on joined by Jules Assoumou, Head of Department of Linguistics and African Literature at the University of Douala.

(guarantors of traditional, cultural and linguistic knowledge), a community of academics specialized in African linguistics technologies and a community of social and/or institutional and/or public partners. Grouped by languages, these communities work together with the same purpose: building as much linguistic and cultural resources as possible, required for research, education and technology needs.

The concept of community is not a trivial choice in our case. Indeed, African sociology is built on the community model, that is, a set of social groups and sub-groups sharing the same language, the same culture and the same geographic space. In such groups, solidarity is created and social actions emerge for the interest of all: this is the case with villages cultural associations and representations in urban cities, collaborative meetings and cultural events. This concept clearly shows the strong cultural link that unites each citizen with his community, even before that of his country. This is precisely the reason why we have chosen this approach and we apply it to all NTeALan internal projects, especially to the development of language resources, their platforms, as well as their data representation.

3. NTeALan language resources platforms

Our language resources platforms are divided into three parts: one independent architecture and two dependent architectures. The independent architecture serves not only the two other architectures but all NTeALan projects, as illustrated in figure 1.

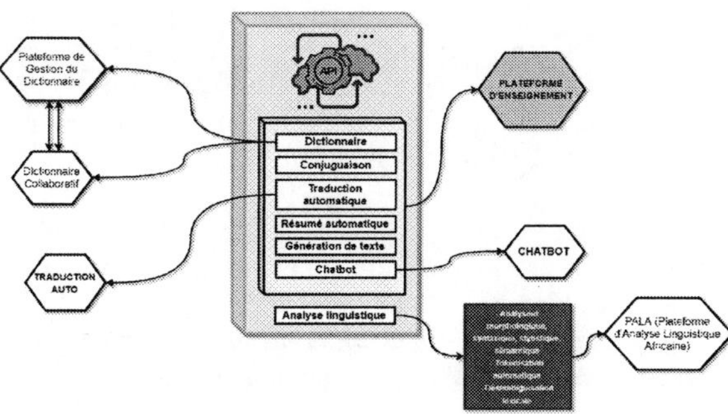

Figure 1: NTeALan REST/GraphQL APIs and services infrastructures

The three architectures are the fruit of two upstream processes depending on the input type (PDF files or images). The first process involves digitization and the second serialization:

- **digitization**: dictionaries in paper or digital format like PDF, TIFF, PNG by OCR (Optical Character Recognition) are digitized with Deep learning (Breuel, 2008); we annotate them to improve the OCR (see figure 2); each article constituents (featured word, translation, contextualization, conjugation, dialect variant, etc.) are automatically detected, extracted and xmlized in XND (NTeALan dictionary XML format) afterwards.

- **serialization**: dictionaries in an external format (toolbox, XML, TEI, LMF) are automatically serialized in XND format, using our internal NLP tools[2]. Reversed processes can also be done from XND to XML TEI, LMF, SIL Toobox.

In both cases, we start with a paper or digital dictionary and end up with a XML dictionary in XND format (see figure 6). The latter is the unique data entry format for our three architectures. It should be noted that the two processes described above are controlled by NTeALan linguists only. In future work, they will be opened to non-member contributors.

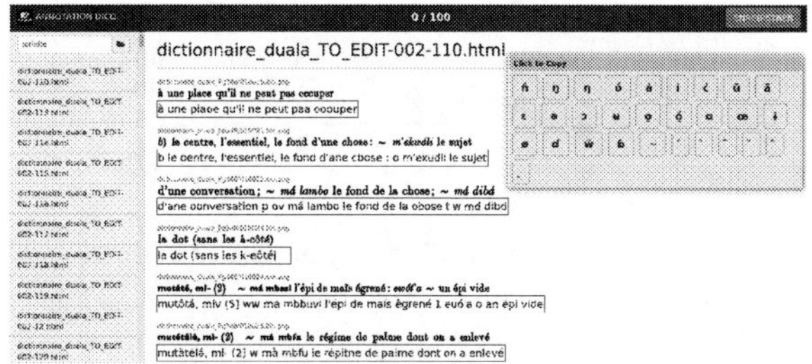

Figure 2: NTeALan dictionaries annotation platform based on the Ocropy tool and used to train Deep learning model for OCR. This platform is under license on Creative Commons BY-NC-SA 3.0 license: (`http://dico-edit.ntealan.net`)

Figure 2 shows an example of annotation (from the bilingual Duala-French dictionary) performed by NTeALan's members.

3.1. Independent architecture

The independent platform can also be called lexicographical resources management database. This architecture has two consultation interfaces : the web-based REST and the GraphQL APIs platform[3]. Built to be simple and accessible, this web application stores and distributes all lexicographic resources resulting from the collaborative work of NTeALan's communities members and external contributors.

The independent architecture uses our internal NLP tools to manage the XND file format in order to give users easy access to their contributions (see section 4.). The operations listed in table 3.1.1. are allowed in open access for each type of user.

3.1.1. Web-based REST API interface

This interface structures lexicographic resources into REST resources ranging from general to specific. It proceeds

---

[2]These include tokenizers, lemmatizers, text parsers and lexical disambiguation tools used for processing noisy lexicographic corpora.

[3]This architecture is close to the Kosh APIs for dictionaries `https://cceh.github.io/kosh/`, as well as the ELEXIS Dictionary Service `https://github.com/elexis-eu/dictionary-service`

from a dictionary in an African language to access its lexicographic components: *dictionaries > articles > entry > dialect_variant* or *dictionaries > articles > entry > translation > language* or *dictionaries > articles > entry > conjugation* (for more precision, see table 3.1.1.).

Actions	URL path (root is */dictionaries*)
get metadata of dictionary	/metadata/{dictionary_id}
get article	/articles/{dictionary_id}/{article_id}
get entry of article	/articles/{dictionary_id}/{article_id}?entry
get translation of article	/articles/{dictionary_id}/{article_id}?trans=en
get comments of article	/comments/{dictionary_id}/{article_id}

Table 1: Sample of a REST API structure for our lexicographic resources

The documentation[4] for this interface is accessible under the Creative Commons BY-NC-SA 3.0 license. The access privileges, for each type of user, is described in table 3.1.1.

Operations	NTeALan's users	Native communities	Scientific experts
manage dictionary	yes	no	yes
manage article	yes	yes	yes
data validation	no	yes	yes
cultural media	yes	yes	no
comments	yes	yes	yes

Table 2: User's privileges for each operation in NTeALan's REST API

3.1.2. Web-based GraphQL API interface

The resources available in our lexicographic database can also be consulted using a GraphQL query language associated to the system (through a GraphQL API interface)[5]. This API is also required for all data parallel to our lexicographic resources, namely the comments from dictionary users, the dictionary metadata and articles.

The GraphQL API interface uses the request system of the Python Graphene library, which render the exploration process of our resources data easier. An external GraphQL clients can also easily be linked to the GraphQL server to extract the information sought. Unlike the REST API, this interface cannot add, modify or delete data.

3.2. Dependent architectures

Dependent architectures are single web page platforms[6] which use the data stored in the common REST API database (Independent platform) and enriched by contributors. They can also perform the operations described in table 3.1.1. through their web interface.

3.2.1. Dictionaries management platform

As a web platform, the dictionaries management platform is a graphical management version of the REST API platform. It allows NTeALan members (users) to manage dictionaries, articles, users, users comments, access requests and cultural resources.

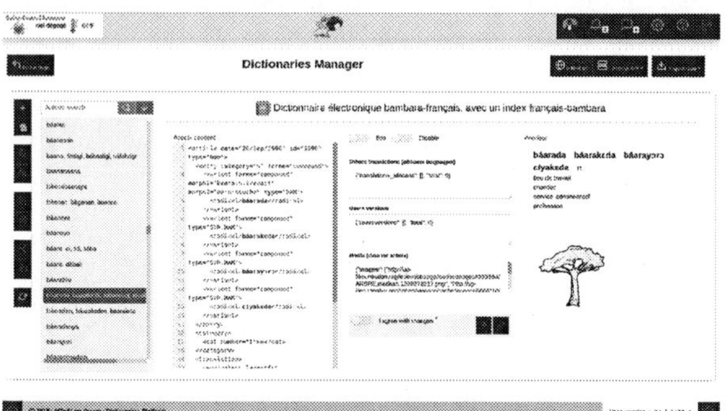

Figure 3: Dictionaries management platform for multi-modal and multilingual lexicographical resources for African languages. This platform is under NTeALan's license: (https://ntealan.net/dictionaries-platform)

Unlike the other above-mentioned platforms, this is not an open-source platform. It can be used strictly by NTeALan communities, as part of a direct collaboration between the linguistics team and other association members.

3.2.2. Collaborative dictionary platform

Collaborative dictionary platform[7] is also a web platform (see figure 4) which enhances the lexicographical resources from the REST API. It connects and gives native speakers and African languages experts (NTeALan communities as described in section 2.2.) the opportunity to build, in a collaborative approach, resources like lexicons[8], illustrations

---

[4] https://apis.ntealan.net/ntealan/dictionaries

[5] https://apis.ntealan.net/ntealan/graphql

[6] For these platforms, we have recourse to the latest front-end technologies (React Js and Angular Js), in priority the single web applications (SPA) for their simplicity, speed and robustness.

[7] This project was born following the research work of Elvis Mboning at the University of Douala and the University of Lille 3 (Master thesis): (Mboning, 2016) and (Mboning, 2017). We can also cite other related work in this field like: (Assoumou, 2010), (Mangeot and Enguehard, 2011), (Vydrin et al., 2016), (Maslinsky, 2014), (Nouvel et al., 2016), etc.

[8] To this aim, we built another platform to manage lexicographic resources: [https://ntealan.net/dictionaries-platform].

of cultural phenomena, sounds and videos (recording process) based on semantic information extracted from articles written in their native languages. These shared resources are stored and freely available for all contributors through our APIs.

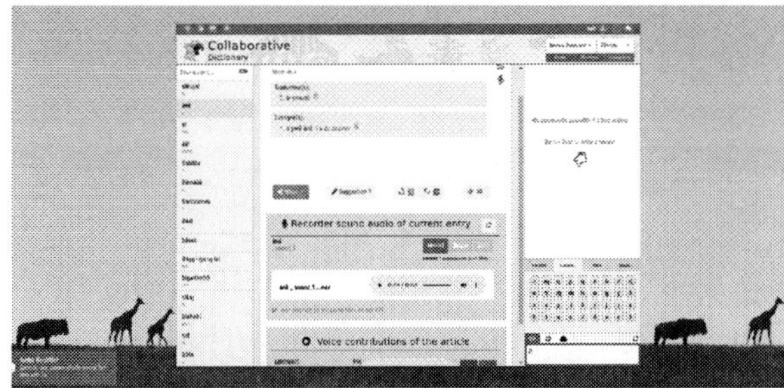

Figure 4: Collaborative dictionaries for sharing multimodal and multilingual lexicographical resources in African languages. This platform is under Creative Commons BY-NC-SA 3.0 license: (https://ntealan.net)

4. NTeALan language resources and representation

Most of our dictionaries resources are old bilingual dictionaries (from the work of linguists) found on the web as open-source or under Creative Commons BY-NC-SA 3.0 license. The links to the original sources and to the NTeALan's versions are provided on all our platforms from where they can also be consulted.

4.1. African language resource dictionaries

We currently host and share 7 dictionaries on our APIs. Although the number of articles entries to date is still relatively limited (from 0 to 11,500 entries), a growing community is participating daily in their filling. Table 4.1. shows the current statistics on the resources managed by our API.

Language resources	Entries	Entries contrib.	Media contrib.
Bambara-French	11487	1	1
Yemba-French	3031	2	90
Bassa-French	427	5	5
Duala-French	191	5	0
Ghomala-French	9	1	0
Ngiemboon-French	3	2	1
Fulfulde-French	0	0	0

Table 3: State of the art of NTeALan language resources currently saved in the REST API

Even if the current resources are insufficient and cover only 6 African languages, we are nevertheless satisfied with the

craze that is beginning to appear within the communities of users behind our platforms in just one year of existence. We would like to determine whether our different infrastructures fit with the resources produced, the load of connected users and their needs. Once we have completed the tests on the platform, the next steps will be generalizing the model to all others African languages.

4.2. Description of NTeALan's XML format

Each lexical resource management platform has its own model for structuring and presenting data, it is the case for (Mangeot, 2006), Kosh, ELEXIS Dictionary Service and (Benoit and Turcan, 2006). The XML format (mainly the TEI and LMF standards) is today a reference choice for structuring linguistic, lexicographic and terminographic data. We can also mention the TEI Lex-0 (Romary and Tasovac, 2018) and Lexicog (OntoLex Lemon Lexicography from W3C), which are frequently used to codify lexicographic resources. Unfortunately these standards are not often adapted to represent and describe some morpho-syntactic particularities of African languages. Indeed, several linguistic phenomena, such as the concept of nominal class, the notion of clicks and the management of the translation and localisation of dialect variants of the article entry, are not explicitly treated, despite all the needs expressed with regard to the matter[9].

By analyzing the structure of a Bantu language (Yemba spoken in West region in Cameroon), we decided to define a proprietary XML structuring model, whose structure was inspired by the 4 major families of African languages, namely: the Afro-Asian family, the Niger-Kordofan family, Nilo-Saharan family and the Koisan family. Three principles guided our choice: representation, simplification and extensibility:

- **representation**: with this principle, we describe the language data at the smallest morpho-syntactic level i.e. word components (prefix+root+suffix) and phrase components like class accord (1/2, 3/4, 5/7, etc.).

- **simplification**: here we choose XML tag names and international languages that are easily understandable for the research communities. Also, we chose to use a linear XML representation, with less parents and more children in the same parent node.

- **extensibility**: we give external contributors the possibility to extend our main XML structures by adding new nodes (children or parent nodes), depending on the element to be represented.

We design our *core-node* lexicographic data with a root node called <ntealan_dictionary>, which is divided into two subnodes: <ntealan_paratexte> and <ntealan_articles>. <ntealan_paratexte> describes the metadata around the version(s) of the document (context of the dictionaries production, source

---

[9]Note that it is nonetheless possible in these standards to add new formalisms (tags and attributes) in addition to existing classes.

description of the original authors and target description of the XML VERSION). `<ntealan_articles>` describes all the dictionary articles (`<article>`).

Each article has its own subnodes: `<entry>` (dialect variant currently processed), `<category>` (grammatical categor(y/ies) links to the dialect variants), `<translations>` (translations associated to the dialect), `<examples>` (contextualisation of dialect variants). Figure 5 illustrates this data representation.

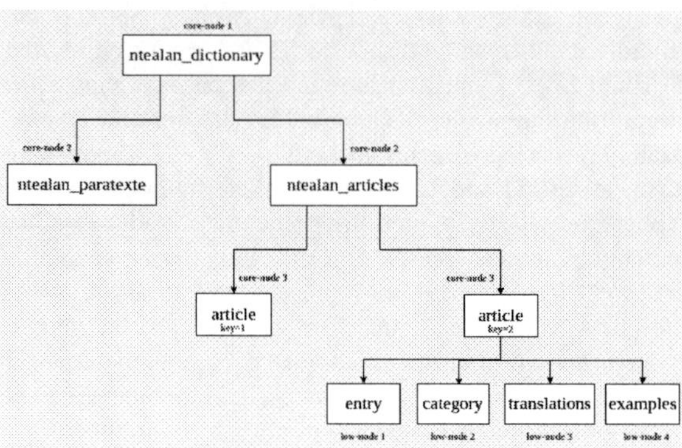

Figure 5: NTeALan dictionaries XML data model

The extension of the article structure by contributors is only possible in *low-node*, as shown in figures 5, 6 and 7, which means that the article model can be updated in each of its nodes, referred to by an id.

```
<article type="Nom">
 <entry forme="simple">
   <variant type="YN" forme="simple">
     <prefix>m</prefix>
     <radical>bā</radical>
   </variant>
   <variant type="YS" forme="simple">
     <radical>mba-nné</radical>
   </variant>
 </entry>
 <category>
   <cat number="1">n</cat>
 </category>
 <classe_d_accords>
   <cl_sing number="1">9</cl_sing>
   <cl_plur number="1">10</cl_plur>
 </classe_d_accords>
  <translations>
   <equivalent lang="fr" number="1">foureau</equivalent>
 </translations>
</article>
```

Figure 6: Sample of Xmlisation of noun article *mbā* extracted from the Yemba-French dictionary

Our XND format is not intended to be standardized to serve as a reference. On the contrary, it is used as intermediate format, required by our internal NLP tools and by well-known standardized formats. Indeed once the external formats are serialized in XND, we have the possibility to convert the data into other formats such as those of the TEI and LMF dictionaries. These features will be available at the

```
<article type="Verbe">
  <entry forme="simple">
    <variant type="YN" forme="simple">
      <prefix>le</prefix>
      <radical>baka</radical>
    </variant>
    <variant type="YS" forme="simple">
      <prefix>li</prefix>
      <radical>cu'o</radical>
    </variant>
  </entry>
  <category>
    <cat number="1">v</cat>
  </category>
  <conjugation>
    <conj_variant type="YN">
      <forme_conj type="2-F_infinitive">m̀báká</forme_conj>
      <forme_conj type="imperative">báká</forme_conj>
    </conj_variant>
    <conj_variant type="YS">
      <forme_conj type="2-F_infinitive">ncú'ó</forme_conj>
      <forme_conj type="imperative">cú'o</forme_conj>
    </conj_variant>
  </conjugation>
  <translations>
    <equivalent lang="fr" number="1" emprunt_En="pack">
      entasser, accumuler
    </equivalent>
  </translations>
</article>
```

Figure 7: Sample of Xmlisation of verb article *lebaka* extracted from the Yemba-French dictionary.

API level soon.

5. Problems encountered and further challenges

The implementation of these first platforms enabled us to take note of the type of challenges that can arise in such a project. We are currently focused on these issues, trying to improve and enrich our platforms.

5.1. Problems encountered

At the moment, we are facing two main difficulties with the NTeALan platforms:

- the first is the low number of contributors and the insufficient IT resources. The staff do not have all the specialists needed (in NLP, NLU, African languages) to reach the targeted goals and great ambitions. The current work is mainly carried out by 4 active members of the association. Regarding IT resources, we do not have enough robust IT infrastructures (servers, field tools) as required by our research work for African languages.

- the second is the lack of funding to carry out our research activities, more precisely for the development of NLP and NLU tools in and for African native languages. Our funding mainly comes from the contributions of the association members, which is not enough in the light of our current ambitions.

5.2. Further challenges

As already explained, our ambitions are great and will require more staff (language specialists) and financial resources. We would like to:

- Above all, encourage the greatest number of specialists in African languages and cultures from various African countries and in the world, to join our association. Together we are more powerful to meet the challenges.

- Find funding from private and public institutions, businessmen, companies, who can support our research work and the continuous development of our applications for the industrialization and teaching of poorly endowed African languages.

- Improve and enrich all our existing platforms and open them up more to the scientific community and to the speakers of these languages. We mainly focus on : the autonomous platform for teaching languages and cultures, the conversational assistant for language teaching and the virtual cultural museum for safeguarding of the African socio-cultural inheritance.

- Strengthen our partnerships with African social and cultural institutions, universities, research laboratories and companies specialized in our research areas. The aim is to enlarge our already existing communities of experts in linguistics, technological and cultural issues throughout the continent, so that we can keep on working hand in hand for the development of African native languages.

6. Conclusion

In this paper, we described three NTeALan lexicographic platforms and the XND data format used, and we showed how essential an association is nowadays, for the construction of quality linguistic and lexicographic resources and tools for poorly endowed African native and/or national languages. We lead, internally with our academic partners (the Language and African literature department of the University of Douala, the ERTIM team of the INALCO), numerous research activities in Artificial Intelligence, NLP and NLU, in order to contribute to the industrialization of African languages. It is obvious that a lot remains to be done, however the first results of our study have proven to be very useful for our applications (conversational agent NTeABot, learning platform, translation platform, etc.) and for the users as well. These results can be used by other researchers: they include data (in different common formats like XML TEI, TEI Lex-0, LMF, XND) and tools. We are convinced, as Tunde Opeibi (Tunde, 2012, p.289) already said, that "the linguistic diversity in Africa can still become the catalyst that will promote cultural, socio-economic, political, and technological development, as well as sustainable growth and good governance in Africa."

7. Acknowledgements

These platforms were developed by Elvis Mboning (REST API and Dictionaries Management platform), Daniel Baleba (Collaborative dictionaries) and Jean-Marc Bassahak (Web Design and interfaces). NTeALan's projects are actually supported by NTeALan Language Research, the Ministry of Post and Telecommunication of Cameroon, the Department of linguistics and African literature of the University of Douala (Cameroon), the Research teams ERTIM of INALCO (France) and Fractals system (France). We can also cite: Professor Jules Assoumou, Merci Christian Bonog Bilap, Marcel Tomi Banou, Ntomb David, Ntomb Nicolas, Théophile Kengne, Yves Bertrand Dissake, Juanita Fopa, Damien Nouvel and all our contributors.

8. Bibliographical References

Abate, S. T., Melese, M., Tachbelie, M. Y., Meshesha, M., Atinafu, S., Mulugeta, W., Assabie, Y., Abera, H., Ephrem, B., Abebe, T., Tsegaye, W., Lemma, A., Andargie, T., and Shifaw, S. (2018). Parallel Corpora for bi-lingual English-Ethiopian Languages Statistical Machine Translation. In *Proceedings of the 27th International Conference on Computational Linguistics*, pages 3102–3111, Santa Fe, New Mexico, USA, August. Association for Computational Linguistics.

Assoumou, J. (2010). *Enseignement oral des langues et cultures africaines à l'école primaire*. Éditions Clé, Yaoundé, Cameroun, 1st edition.

Benoit, J.-L. and Turcan, I. (2006). La TEI au service de la transmission documentaire ou de la valorisation des richesses patrimoniales : le cas difficile des dictionnaires anciens.

Breuel, T. M. (2008). The OCRopus open source OCR system. *Proc.SPIE*, 6815.

De Schryver, G.-M. (2010). State-of-the-Art Software to Support Intelligent Lexicography. *ResearchGate*, page 16.

Holtzblatt, K. and Beyer, H. (2017). 7 - Building Experience Models. pages 147–206, January.

Mangeot, M. and Enguehard, C. (2011). Informatisation de dictionnaires langues africaines-français. In *journées LTT 2011*, page 11.

Mangeot, M. (2006). Dictionary building with the jibiki platform. In Cristina Onesti Elisa Corino, Carla Marello, editor, *Proceedings of the 12th EURALEX International Congress*, pages 185–188, Torino, Italy, sep. Edizioni dell'Orso.

Maslinsky, K. (2014). *Daba: a model and tools for Manding corpora*.

Mboning, E. (2016). De l'analyse du dictionnaire yémba-français à la conception de sa DTD et de sa réédition sur support numérique. Mémoire Master 1, Université de Lille 3.

Mboning, E. (2017). Vers une métalexicographie outillée : conception d'un outil pour le métalexicographe et application aux dictionnaires Larousse de 1856 à 1966. Mémoire Master 2, Université de Lille 3.

Nouvel, D., Donandt, K., Auffret, D., Maslinsky, K., Chiarcos, C., and Vydrin, V. (2016). Resources and Experiments for a Bambara POS Tagger. *Intra Speech*, page 14.

Romary, L. and Tasovac, T. (2018). TEI Lex-0: A Target Format for TEI-Encoded Dictionaries and Lexical Resources. In *TEI Conference and Members' Meeting*, Tokyo, Japan, September.

Ruthven, R. (2005). The African Association for Lexicography: After Ten Years. *Lexikos journal*, page 9.

Tunde, O. (2012). Investigating the Language Situation in Africa. In *Language and Law*, Language rights, pages 272–293. Oxford Handbooks in Linguistics, Great Clarendon street.

Vydrin, V., Rovenchak, A., and Maslinsky, K. (2016). Maninka Reference Corpus: A Presentation. In *TALAf 2016 : Traitement automatique des langues africaines (écrit et parole). Atelier JEP-TALN-RECITAL 2016 - Paris le*, Paris, France, July.

9. Language Resource References

De Pauw, Guy and Waiganjo Wagacha, Peter and de Schryver, Gilles-Maurice. (2009). *The SAWA corpus: a parallel corpus English - Swahili*.

Mboning, Elvis and NTeALan contributors. (2017). *NTeALan lexicographic African language resources: an open-source REST API*. NTeALan Project, distributed via NTeALan, Bantu resources, 1.0.

Vydrin, Valentin and Rovenchak, Andrij and Maslinsky, Kirill. (2016). *Maninka Reference Corpus: A Presentation*. Speecon Project, distributed via ELRA, Madingue resources, 1.0, ISLRN 613-489-674-355-0.

Proceedings of the 1st International Workshop on Language Technology Platforms (IWLTP 2020), pages 73–80
Language Resources and Evaluation Conference (LREC 2020), Marseille, 11–16 May 2020
© European Language Resources Association (ELRA), licensed under CC-BY-NC

A Workflow Manager for Complex NLP and Content Curation Pipelines

Julián Moreno-Schneider, Peter Bourgonje, Florian Kintzel, Georg Rehm
Speech and Language Technology Lab, DFKI GmbH
Alt-Moabit 91c, 10557 Berlin, Germany
{julian.moreno_schneider, peter.bourgonje, florian.kintzel, georg.rehm}@dfki.de

Abstract

We present a workflow manager for the flexible creation and customisation of NLP processing pipelines. The workflow manager addresses challenges in interoperability across various different NLP tasks and hardware-based resource usage. Based on the four key principles of *generality*, *flexibility*, *scalability* and *efficiency*, we present the first version of the workflow manager by providing details on its custom definition language, explaining the communication components and the general system architecture and setup. We currently implement the system, which is grounded and motivated by real-world industry use cases in several innovation and transfer projects.

Keywords: LR Infrastructures and Architectures, Tools, Systems, Applications, Linked Data

1. Introduction

The last decades have seen a significant increase of digital data. To allow humans to understand and interact with this data, Natural Language Processing (NLP) tools targeted at specific tasks, such as Named Entity Recognition, Text Summarisation or Question Answering, are under constant development and improvement to be used together with other components in complex application scenarios. While several NLP tasks can be considered far from being solved and others increasingly maturing, one of the next challenges is the combination of different task-specific services based on modern micro-service architectures and service deployment paradigms.

Chaining tools together by combining their output requires not much more than simple interoperability regarding the annotation format used by the semantic enrichment services and individual NLP services. However, the notion of flexible workflows stretches, beyond annotation formats, to the flexible and efficient orchestration of NLP services. While a multitude of components and services is available, the next step, i. e., the management and integration into an infrastructural system, is not straightforward and proves challenging. This is problematic both for technology developers and users, as the whole is greater than the sum of its parts. Developers can add value to their tools by allowing the combination with other components. For users, the benefits of combining annotations obtained from NER with those obtained by coreference resolution, for example, are obvious. There have been several attempts, both commercial and open source, to address interoperability and service orchestration for scenarios that include the processing of document collections, achieving comparatively good results for specific use cases, tasks and domains (see Section 2 for an overview).

Recently, new opportunities have been generated by the popularity of containerisation technologies (such as Docker[1]), that enable the deployment of services and tools independently from the environment in which they were developed. While integration benefits from this approach by enabling easy ingestion of services, the methodology comes with several challenges that need to be addressed, including, crucially, container management. This is not just about keeping services alive on different nodes, which can be done using tools such as Kubernetes[2] or Openshift[3]. The key challenge remains allowing the organisation and interconnectivity of services in terms of their functionality, ensuring that they work together in an efficient and coordinated way.

The work presented in this paper is carried out under the umbrella of the QURATOR project[4], in which a consortium of ten partners (ranging from research to industry) works on challenges encountered by the industry partners in their own specific sectors. The central use case addressed in the project is that of *content curation* in the areas of, among others, journalism, museum exhibitions and public archives (Rehm et al., 2020b; Bourgonje et al., 2016). In QURATOR, we develop a platform that allows users to curate large amounts of heterogeneous multimedia content (including text, image, audio, video). The content is collected, converted, aggregated, summarised and eventually presented in a way that allows the user to produce, for example, an investigative journalism article on a contemporary subject, content for the catalogue of a museum exhibition, or a comprehensive description of the life of a public figure, based on the contents of publicly available archive data on this person. To achieve this, we work with various combinations of different state-of-the-art NLP tools for NER, Sentiment Analysis, Text Summarisation, and several others, which we develop further and integrate into our platform. The interoperability and customisation of workflows, i. e., distributed processing pipelines, are a central technical challenge in the development of our platform.

The key contribution of this paper is the presentation of a novel workflow management system aimed at the sector-specific content curation processes mentioned above. Technically, the approach focuses on the management of containerised services and tools. The system design is optimised and aligned with regard to four different dimensions

---

[1] https://www.docker.com

[2] https://kubernetes.io
[3] https://www.openshift.com
[4] https://qurator.ai

or requirements: (i) *generality*, to work with a diverse range of containerised services and tools, independent of the (programming) language or framework they are written in; (ii) *flexibility*, to allow services or tools – which may be running on different machines – to connect with one another in any order (to the extent that this makes sense, semantically); (iii) *scalability*, to allow the inclusion of additional services and tools; and (iv) *efficiency*, by avoiding unnecessary overhead in data storage as well as processing time. The rest of the paper is structured as follows. Section 2 describes approaches similar to ours that support the specification of workflows for processing document collections. Section 3 provides an overview of the proposed system and lists requirements regarding the services to be included in workflows. Section 4 presents the workflow specification language. Section 5 outlines the general architecture and the following subsections provide more detail on individual components. Finally, Section 6 concludes the article and sketches directions for future work.

2. Related Work

The orchestration and operationalisation of the processing of large amounts of content through a series of tools has been studied and tested in the field of NLP (and others) from many different angles for decades. There is a sizable amount of tools, systems, frameworks and initiatives that address the issue but their off-the-shelf applicability to concrete use cases and heterogeneous sets of services is still an enormous challenges.

One of the most well known industry-driven workflow definition languages is Business Process Model and Notation (BPMN, and its re-definition BPMN V2.0) (OMG, 2011). Many tools support BPMN, some of them open source (Comidor, Processmaker, Activiti, Bonita BPM or Camunda), others commercial (Signavio Workflow Accelerator, Comindware, Flokzu or Bizagi). There are also other business process management systems, not all of which are based on BPMN, such as WorkflowGen[5], ezFlow[6], Pipefy[7], Avaza[8] or Proces.io[9]. Their main disadvantage with regard to our use case is that they primarily aim at modelling actual business processes at companies, including support to represent human-centric tasks (i.e., foreseen human interaction tasks). This focus on support deviates from our use case, in which a human user interacts with the content, but not necessarily with other humans.

Another class of relevant software are frameworks for container management, focusing on parallelisation management, scalability and clustering. Examples are Kubernetes, Openshift, Rancher[10] and Openstack[11]. We use Kubernetes for cluster management. However, because this does *not* cover (NLP) task orchestration or address interoperability, with our workflow manager we go beyond the typical Kubernetes use case.

On the other hand, there are numerous frameworks and tool kits that focus more on workflow management and the flexible definition of processing pipelines (and less on the technical, hardware related implementations like Kubernetes, Openshift and Rancher). Examples are Apache Kafka[12], a distributed streaming platform; Apache Commons[13]; Apache NIFI[14]; Apache Airflow[15]; Kylo[16]; and Apache Taverna[17]. With our workflow manager, we attempt to cover these workflow-focused features, but, crucially, combine them with the more technical details for cluster management and scalability.

Specifically targeted at NLP, some popular systems are GATE (Cunningham et al., 2011) and UIMA (Ferrucci and Lally, 2004), and, more recently (but covering a narrower range of tasks), SpaCy[18]. While the data representation format is based on a standard format for some of these (GATE for example supports exporting data in XML), we attempt to extend beyond this and use the NLP Interchange Format (NIF) (Hellmann et al., 2013). Using NIF ensures interoperability for different NLP tasks while at the same time addressing storage and scalability needs. Since NIF is based on RDF triples, the resulting annotations can be included in a triple store to allow for efficient storage and querying. In addition, the above-mentioned systems are designed to run on single systems. Our workflow manager is designed to combine output from different micro-services that address different NLP services, potentially running on different machines. In addition to the above, CLARIN (Hinrichs and Krauwer, 2014) provides an infrastructure for natural language research data and tools. The focus, however, is on sharing resources and not on building NLP pipelines or workflows. A more exhaustive and complete overview of related work can be found in (Rehm et al., 2020a).

3. System Overview

The objective of the QURATOR project is to facilitate the execution of complex tasks in the area of content curation. The human experts performing these tasks typically have limited technical skills and are expected to analyse, aggregate, summarise and re-arrange the information contained in the content collections they work with. The Curation Workflow Manager aims to support these users, by allowing them to flexibly and intuitively define just the workflow they need. Ultimately, the aim is to make this as intuitive as using a single call to a single system. The single system will be the Workflow Manager, and the single call will be the request to process the document collection using a specific workflow. The workflow includes all the needed services (i.e., which services, such as NER, summarisation, topic modeling, clustering, etc. to include, and which parameters, such as language or domain, to set). The order of the services, and which can be parallelised, can be specified, as well as which data needs to be stored internally

---

[5]https://www.workflowgen.com
[6]http://www.ezflow.it
[7]https://www.pipefy.com
[8]https://www.avaza.com
[9]http://proces.io
[10]https://rancher.com
[11]https://www.openstack.org

[12]https://kafka.apache.org
[13]http://commons.apache.org/sandbox/commons-pipeline/
[14]https://nifi.apache.org
[15]https://airflow.apache.org
[16]https://kylo.io
[17]https://taverna.incubator.apache.org
[18]https://spacy.io

(for immediate processing) or externally. Afterwards, the processed content collection is meant to be presented in a GUI, featuring the relevant data visualisation components, given the original document collection and the result of the individual semantic enrichment processes that have run.

While from a user's perspective, this high level description may sound similar to comparable systems like GATE (Section 2), the following description provides an idea of the intended deployment scale and ambition of the workflow manager. Though developed in the context of the QURA-TOR project, we plan to implement the workflow manager also in the technical platform architecture developed in the project European Language Grid.[19]. The main objective of the project ELG is to create the primary platform for Language Technology in Europe (Rehm et al., 2020a). Release 1 alpha of the European Language Grid platform was made available in March 2020 and provides access to more than 150 services including NER, concept identification, dependency parsing, ASR and TTS.

3.1. Service Requirements

Since we want to allow for the inclusion of as many different services as possible in a workflow, yet at the same time have to ensure that they work together seamlessly, we specified a few core dimensions along which to classify services, to establish whether or not they can be included. First (i), we check whether a service is dockerised or not. Then (ii), we check the execution procedure, i. e., is it a fully automated service, or is human intervention or interaction included, or even at the very core (such as, for example, in annotation editors). Furthermore, we check (iii) where the service is located, i. e., is it included in the Docker cluster or is it a service hosted externally? Finally (iv), we check how the service is communicating, i. e., is it accessible through a REST API or a command-line interface? If a given service is (i) dockerised (or otherwise containerised), (ii) does not need human intervention, (iii) is stored inside our Docker cluster and (iv) has a REST API interface through which it can be accessed, we conclude that the service can be included in our workflow.[20]

4. Curation Workflow Definition Language

To facilitate the definition of workflows for users with limited technical knowledge (i. e., little to no programming experience), we opted for the widely used JSON format to specify workflows, considering that the specification of actual workflows will be carried out using a corresponding graphical user interface.

We specified a JSON-based Curation Workflow Definition Language (CWDL). It currently supports the inclusion of services with REST API access (Richardson et al., 2013) (i. e., services must be accessible through HTTP calls), and allows users to specify whether these services should be executed in a synchronous or asynchronous way. The execution in a sequential or parallel fashion can also be specified.

---

[19]https://www.european-language-grid.eu

[20]As part of future work we will investigate if and how these core dimensions can be included in the metadata scheme that governs all metadata entries for all services in order to automate this process as much as possible (Labropoulou et al., 2020).

A workflow relies on three main components: *controllers*, *tasks* and *templates*. The *controllers* element relates to a service to be included. This element communicates basic identity information (`controllerName`, `serviceId`, `controllerId`), queue information (`nameInput{Normal|Priority}`) and connection information (`connection`) to the micro-services it is calling. The `connection` element contains information needed to communicate with the service (via REST API), including `method`, `endpoint_url`, `parameters`, `headers` and `body`. Listing 1 shows an example.

The next element, *task*, sends messages to and from a controller through the messaging control system. The `taskId` and `controllerId` fields contain identifying information on the two. Listing 2 illustrates this using an example.

```
1  {
2    "controllerName": "NER Controller",
3    "serviceId": "NER",
4    "controllerId": "NERController",
5    "queues": {
6      "nameInputNormal": "NER_input_normal",
7      "nameInputPriority": "NER_input_prio"
8    },
9    "connection": {
10     "connection_type": "restapi",
11     "method": "POST",
12     "endpoint_url": "http://<host>/path/",
13     "parameters": [
14       {"name": "language","type": "parameter",
15        "default_value": "en","required": true},
16       {"name": "models","type": "parameter",
17        "default_value": "model_1;model_2","
            required": true},
18       ...],
19     "body": {
20       "content": "documentContentNIF"
21     },
22     "headers": [
23       {"name": "Accept","type": "header",
24        "default_value": "text/turtle","
            required": true},
25       {"name": "Content-Type","type": "header"
           ,
26        "default_value": "text/turtle","
            required": true}
27     ]
28   }
29 }
```

Listing 1: Example of a Controller definition that connects to an external REST API service.

```
1  {
2    "taskName": "NER Task",
3    "taskId": "NERTask",
4    "controllerId": "NER",
5    "component_type": "rabbitmqrestapi"
6  }
```

Listing 2: Example of a Task definition.

The third element, *template*, specifies which micro-services are included in the workflow. Basic identification information is specified in `workflowTemplateId`. The different micro-services included in the template are contained in `tasks`. Inside this element, the following information is specified:

1. `ParallelTask` executes multiple tasks in parallel.

2. `SequentialTask` executes tasks sequentially.

3. `split` splits the input information to every output.

4. `waitcombiner` waits until all connected inputs have finished to combine their results and proceed.

Listing 3 shows an example of the `template` element.

```
 1  {
 2    "workflowTemplateName": "GLK",
 3    "workflowTemplateId": "ML_GLK",
 4    "workflowTemplateDescription": "...",
 5    "tasks": [
 6    {
 7      "order": 1,
 8      "taskId": "ParallelTask",
 9      "features":{
10      "input": {"component_type": "split"},
11      "output": {"component_type": "
             waitcombiner"},
12      "tasks":[
13        {"order": 1, "taskId": "NERTask"},
14        {"order": 2, "taskId": "GEOTask"},
15        ...]
16      }
17    },
18    ...]
19  }
```

Listing 3: Example of a workflow definition.

We plan to improve this basic scheme and will make it compliant with BPMN V2.0 in its next iteration.

5. Curation Workflow Manager Architecture

In Section 4, the description of the JSON-based workflow definition language outlines how to instruct the workflow manager to perform complex tasks. In this section, we outline how these task definitions are translated into processes and procedures, by explaining the workflow manager architecture. Our previous work includes a generic workflow manager for curation technologies (Bourgonje et al., 2016; Rehm et al., 2020b), and two indicative descriptions of an initial prototype of a workflow manager that we conceptualised based on use cases in the legal domain (Moreno-Schneider and Rehm, 2018a; Moreno-Schneider and Rehm, 2018b). Figure 1 illustrates this architecture, its individual components are described in the following subsections.

5.1. Workflow Execution Engine

The core component of the workflow manager is the Workflow Execution Engine. This component manages workflows, from their definition to the management of its execution to the final results that are produced. In the CWM a workflow is composed of the three components described in Section 4, and a workflow execution. More specifically:

- A *controller* is a component whose main purpose is to communicate with a service (see Section 5.2).

- A *task* can be anything that has to do with taking input in a certain format, and producing output. This can be enriching text though NLP components, converting data to a required format for specific other tasks, combining information from different upstream tasks, or deciding which task to perform next, depending on parameters that are either set in the configuration, or that are the outcome of upstream processing.

- A *template* is an abstract definition of a workflow composed of a combination of tasks. It is, in the literal sense of the word, a preset for a collection of tasks that together form a logical processing pipeline. In the object-oriented programming paradigm, it would be the equivalent of a class, i.e., the definition of an object (and the objects would be *tasks*).

- A *workflow execution* is an instance of a workflow template, i.e., a complete workflow created with specific *task* objects. The *workflow execution* would be equivalent to an instantiated object in the object-oriented analogy.

5.2. Controllers

Every service is required to be accessible through a REST API and must allow both sending and receiving of task-specific messages. Because the services are independently developed, and their behaviour may change with new versions, the way to communicate with them may change as well. We, therefore, introduce the concept of a proxy element between the messaging control system (for which we use RabbitMQ, see Section 5.3) and the service. This proxy element is the *controller*. We attempt to maximise flexibility by updating the *controller* whenever the service changes, so that the rest of the communication chain can remain untouched.

In the current implementation, the controller connects to RabbitMQ and waits for receiving messages. Whenever a message is received, the controller processes its contents and generates a HTTP request for the corresponding service. Depending on whether or not the service in question executes in a synchronous or asynchronous way, the controller waits for the response, or checks back in to collect it later, and subsequently communicates the result.

5.3. Communication Module

The communication module, based on the message control system RabbitMQ, allows the exchange of information between the different workflow components, or with components external to the workflow. As mentioned above,

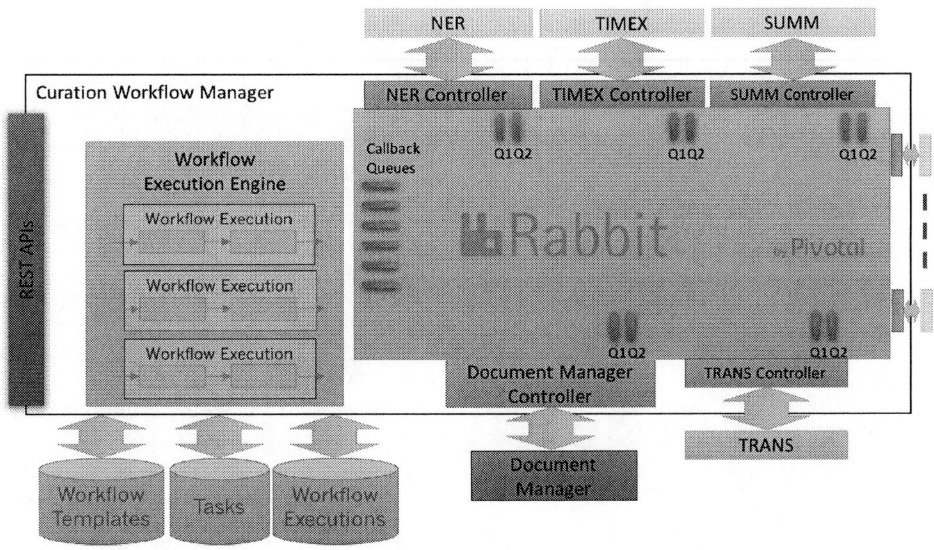

Figure 1: Architecture of the Curation Workflow Manager (CWM)

our system requires individual services to be accessible via REST API, and supports both synchronous and asynchronous execution of services.

This communication entails both information relating to tasks to be performed, as well as the result or output of the tasks themselves. We use RabbitMQ, because it allows larger message contents than some of its competitors (Apache Kafka, for example). RabbitMQ handles the communication between the workflow execution engine and the services (through *controllers*). Both the workflow execution engine and the *controllers* send messages to and receive messages from RabbitMQ during the execution of a workflow. The workflow execution engine sends a message to every service (through its proxy element, the *controller*), to execute a processing step. After finishing the processing, the service sends a new message with the result (again, through the *controller*) to the workflow execution engine.

The CWM is designed to cover complex curation tasks, which can potentially include large files. Since we want to avoid such larger files to use and thereby block resources for other processes, we implemented a priority feature in RabbitMQ queues. We reserve high priority processes for smaller documents and/or processes that take place in (semi-)real-time, while larger documents or more complex tasks can use normal/low priority for offline processing.

5.4. Information Exchange Format

Since interoperability is a key feature of the CWM, we must settle on a shared annotation format which all (or at least most[21]) micro-services can work with and further augment in case of pipeline processing. Instead of defining our own format for this, we use the NLP Interchange Format (NIF) (Hellmann et al., 2013). NIF includes an ontology that defines the way in which documents are annotated,

with strong roots in the Linked Data paradigm. This allows for easy referencing of external knowledge bases (such as Wikidata) in the annotations on a document. NIF can be serialised in XML-like (RDF-XML), JSON-like (JSON-LD) or N3/turtle (RDF triple) formats. This serialised format is what is communicated as input or output for specific services. An example NIF (turtle) document with annotated named entities is shown in Listing 4 in the Appendix.

5.5. Access Control

Access control for the various API endpoints is defined by the corresponding module, which specifies which operations are allowed for the endpoints of the different components, i. e., how a workflow is modified.

This module defines 12 methods that allow a user to (i) initialize and stop the CWM, (ii) view, create, modify and delete elements necessary to define workflows (i. e., *tasks*, *controllers*, *templates* and *workflow executions*, (iii) execute a specific workflow, and (iv) obtain the result of a workflow. An overview is provided in Figure 2.

In addition to the above mentioned functionalities, this module also handles security by allowing only users included in a pre-defined list to access the functionalities listed in Figure 2. We are currently working on more detailed user management by implementing user profiles, allowing certain users to access certain procedures only. This improvement will be included in a future version of the workflow manager.

6. Conclusions and Future Work

We present an approach of connecting services and tools developed on different platforms and environments, in order to make them work together by means of a Curation Workflow Manager. The tool is built around the key principles of *generality*, *flexibility*, *scalability* and *efficiency*. It allows the combination of different tools, i. e., containerised micro-services, in the wider area of NLP, Information

---

[21]This is, first and foremost, relevant if tasks are relying on output of upstream tasks, or their output is input to downstream tasks.

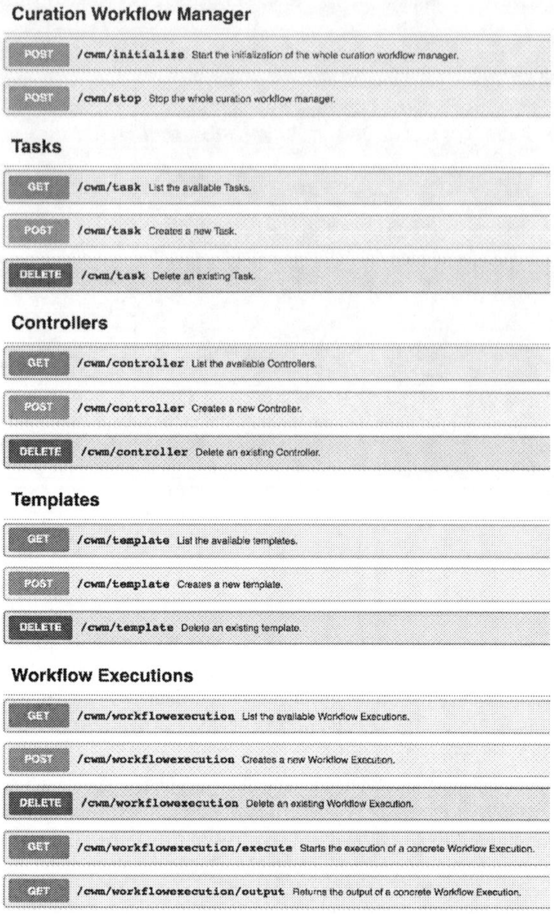

Figure 2: REST APIs

Retrieval, Question Answering, and Knowledge Management (triple stores) and uses a shared annotation format (NIF) throughout, addressing, respectively, the *generality* and *flexibility* principles. Our main motivation for developing the workflow manager, which comes with its own JSON-based definition language, was to address – under the umbrella of a larger Curation Technology platform – interoperability challenges and hardware-based resource-sharing and -handling issues in one go, addressing, respectively, the *scalability* and *efficiency* principles.

The CWM is meant to process large documents, but is, as of now, restricted to text documents. As part of future work, we will also include the processing of multimedia files (images, audio, video). The curation workflow manager's design will be revised and extended accordingly. Furthermore, we plan to evaluate the workflow manager in a real-world use case provided by one of the partners in the QURATOR project. Additionally, we plan to integrate the CWM in the ELG platform in the medium to long term (Rehm et al., 2020a; Labropoulou et al., 2020; Rehm et al., 2020c). We currently work on extensions to the workflow definition language; its next iteration will be compliant with the standardised Business Process Model and Notation, in-

creasing the sustainability and adaptability of our approach. Finally, we are currently considering the development of a visual editor (i. e., a GUI) to define and modify workflows, inspired by the GUI offered by Camunda[22].

The source code of the Curation Workflow Manager is available on Gitlab.[23]

Acknowledgements

The work presented in this paper has received funding from the German Federal Ministry of Education and Research (BMBF) through the project QURATOR (Wachstumskern no. 03WKDA1A) as well as from the European Union's Horizon 2020 research and innovation programme under grant agreements no. 825627 (European Language Grid) and no. 780602 (Lynx).

7. Bibliographical References

Bourgonje, P., Moreno-Schneider, J., Nehring, J., Rehm, G., Sasaki, F., and Srivastava, A. (2016). Towards a Platform for Curation Technologies: Enriching Text Collections with a Semantic-Web Layer. In Harald Sack, et al., editors, *The Semantic Web*, number 9989 in Lecture Notes in Computer Science, pages 65–68. Springer, June. ESWC 2016 Satellite Events. Heraklion, Crete, Greece, May 29 – June 2, 2016 Revised Selected Papers.

Cunningham, H., Maynard, D., Bontcheva, K., Tablan, V., Aswani, N., Roberts, I., Gorrell, G., Funk, A., Roberts, A., Damljanovic, D., Heitz, T., Greenwood, M. A., Saggion, H., Petrak, J., Li, Y., and Peters, W. (2011). *Text Processing with GATE (Version 6)*.

Ferrucci, D. and Lally, A. (2004). UIMA: An Architectural Approach to Unstructured Information Processing in the Corporate Research Environment. *Natural Language Engineering*, 10(3-4):327–348, sep.

Hellmann, S., Lehmann, J., Auer, S., and Brümmer, M. (2013). Integrating NLP using Linked Data. In *12th International Semantic Web Conference*. 21-25 October.

Hinrichs, E. and Krauwer, S. (2014). The CLARIN Research Infrastructure: Resources and Tools for eHumanities Scholars. In *Proceedings of the Ninth International Conference on Language Resources and Evaluation (LREC'14)*, pages 1525–1531, Reykjavik, Iceland, May. European Language Resources Association (ELRA).

Labropoulou, P., Gkirtzou, K., Gavriilidou, M., Deligiannis, M., Galanis, D., Piperidis, S., Rehm, G., Berger, M., Mapelli, V., Rigault, M., Arranz, V., Choukri, K., Backfried, G., Pérez, J. M. G., and Garcia-Silva, A. (2020). Making Metadata Fit for Next Generation Language Technology Platforms: The Metadata Schema of the European Language Grid. In Nicoletta Calzolari, et al., editors, *Proceedings of the 12th Language Resources and Evaluation Conference (LREC 2020)*, Marseille, France, May. European Language Resources Association (ELRA). Accepted for publication.

---

[22]https://camunda.com/products/modeler/

[23]https://gitlab.com/qurator-platform/dfki/
curationworkflowmanager

Moreno-Schneider, J. and Rehm, G. (2018a). Curation Technologies for the Construction and Utilisation of Legal Knowledge Graphs. In Georg Rehm, et al., editors, *Proceedings of the LREC 2018 Workshop on Language Resources and Technologies for the Legal Knowledge Graph*, pages 23–29, Miyazaki, Japan, May. 12 May 2018.

Moreno-Schneider, J. and Rehm, G. (2018b). Towards a Workflow Manager for Curation Technologies in the Legal Domain. In Georg Rehm, et al., editors, *Proceedings of the LREC 2018 Workshop on Language Resources and Technologies for the Legal Knowledge Graph*, pages 30–35, Miyazaki, Japan, May. 12 May 2018.

OMG. (2011). Business Process Model and Notation (BPMN), Version 2.0, January.

Rehm, G., Berger, M., Elsholz, E., Hegele, S., Kintzel, F., Marheinecke, K., Piperidis, S., Deligiannis, M., Galanis, D., Gkirtzou, K., Labropoulou, P., Bontcheva, K., Jones, D., Roberts, I., Hajic, J., Hamrlová, J., Kacena, L., Choukri, K., Arranz, V., Vasiljevs, A., Anvari, O., Lagzdins, A., Melnika, J., Backfried, G., Dikici, E., Janosik, M., Prinz, K., Prinz, C., Stampler, S., Thomas-Aniola, D., Pérez, J. M. G., Silva, A. G., Berrío, C., Germann, U., Renals, S., and Klejch, O. (2020a). European Language Grid: An Overview. In Nicoletta Calzolari, et al., editors, *Proceedings of the 12th Language Resources and Evaluation Conference (LREC 2020)*. European Language Resources Association (ELRA), May. Accepted for publication.

Rehm, G., Bourgonje, P., Hegele, S., Kintzel, F., Schneider, J. M., Ostendorff, M., Zaczynska, K., Berger, A., Grill, S., Räuchle, S., Rauenbusch, J., Rutenburg, L., Schmidt, A., Wild, M., Hoffmann, H., Fink, J., Schulz, S., Seva, J., Quantz, J., Böttger, J., Matthey, J., Fricke, R., Thomsen, J., Paschke, A., Qundus, J. A., Hoppe, T., Karam, N., Weichhardt, F., Fillies, C., Neudecker, C., Gerber, M., Labusch, K., Rezanezhad, V., Schaefer, R., Zellhöfer, D., Siewert, D., Bunk, P., Pintscher, L., Aleynikova, E., and Heine, F. (2020b). QURATOR: Innovative Technologies for Content and Data Curation. In Adrian Paschke, et al., editors, *Proceedings of QURATOR 2020 – The conference for intelligent content solutions*, Berin, Germany, February. CEUR Workshop Proceedings, Volume 2535. 20/21 January 2020.

Rehm, G., Galanis, D., Labropoulou, P., Piperidis, S., Welß, M., Usbeck, R., Köhler, J., Deligiannis, M., Gkirtzou, K., Fischer, J., Chiarcos, C., Feldhus, N., Moreno-Schneider, J., Kintzel, F., Montiel, E., Doncel, V. R., McCrae, J. P., Laqua, D., Theile, I. P., Dittmar, C., Bontcheva, K., Roberts, I., Vasiljevs, A., and Lagzdins, A. (2020c). Towards an Interoperable Ecosystem of AI and LT Platforms: A Roadmap for the Implementation of Different Levels of Interoperability. In Georg Rehm, et al., editors, *Proceedings of the 1st International Workshop on Language Technology Platforms (IWLTP 2020, co-located with LREC 2020)*, Marseille, France, 5. 16 May 2020. Accepted for publication.

Richardson, L., Amundsen, M., and Ruby, S. (2013). *RESTful Web APIs*. O'Reilly Media, Inc.

Appendix

```
<http://dkt.dfki.de/documents/#char=0,25>
 a                          nif:RFC5147String, nif:String, nif:Context ;
 nif:beginIndex             "0"^^xsd:nonNegativeInteger ;
 nif:endIndex               "25"^^xsd:nonNegativeInteger ;
 nif:isString               "Monteux was born in Paris"^^xsd:string .

<http://dkt.dfki.de/documents/#char=20,25>
 a                          nif:RFC5147String, nif:String ;
 nif:anchorOf               "Paris"^^xsd:string ;
 nif:beginIndex             "20"^^xsd:nonNegativeInteger ;
 nif:endIndex               "25"^^xsd:nonNegativeInteger ;
 nif:entity                 <http://dkt.dfki.de/ontologies/nif#LOC> ;
 nif:referenceContext       <http://dkt.dfki.de/documents/#char=0,25> ;
 itsrdf:taIdentRef          <http://www.geonames.org/2988507> .

<http://dkt.dfki.de/documents/#char=0,7>
 a                          nif:RFC5147String, nif:String ;
 nif:anchorOf               "Monteux"^^xsd:string ;
 nif:beginIndex             "0"^^xsd:nonNegativeInteger ;
 nif:endIndex               "7"^^xsd:nonNegativeInteger ;
 nif:entity                 <http://dkt.dfki.de/ontologies/nif#PER> ;
 nif:referenceContext       <http://dkt.dfki.de/documents/#char=0,25> ;
 itsrdf:taIdentRef          <http://d-nb.info/gnd/122700198> .
```

Listing 4: An example NIF document.

Proceedings of the 1st International Workshop on Language Technology Platforms (IWLTP 2020), pages 81–88
Language Resources and Evaluation Conference (LREC 2020), Marseille, 11–16 May 2020

A Processing Platform Relating Data and Tools for Romanian Language

Vasile Păiş, Radu Ion, Dan Tufiş
Research Institute for Artificial Intelligence "Mihai Drăgănescu", Romanian Academy
CASA ACADEMIEI, 13 "Calea 13 Septembrie", Bucharest 050711, ROMANIA
{vasile, radu, tufis}@racai.ro

Abstract

This paper presents RELATE (http://relate.racai.ro), a high-performance natural language platform designed for Romanian language. It is meant both for demonstration of available services, from text-span annotations to syntactic dependency trees as well as playing or automatically synthesizing Romanian words, and for the development of new, annotated corpora. It also incorporates the search engines for the large CoRoLa reference corpus of contemporary Romanian and the Romanian wordnet. It integrates multiple text and speech processing modules and exposes their functionality through a web interface designed for the linguist researcher. It makes use of a scheduler-runner architecture, allowing processing to be distributed across multiple computing nodes. A series of input/output converters allows large corpora to be loaded, processed and exported according to user preferences.

Keywords: natural language processing, web platform, Romanian language processing

1. Introduction

Today's natural language processing challenges require the use of very complex pipelines applied on huge datasets. In this context, existing pipelines must be integrated and adapted for usage inside high performance environments such as clusters, grids or even in the cloud. The entire flow needs to be supervised and resume mechanisms must be in place in order to recover processing in case of unforeseen hardware or software errors.

Even though existing Romanian language resources are an order of magnitude less than those existing for English language, several new large data sets become available each year. For each new project that we are involved in, we are faced with processing hundreds of thousands of text files, in the several gigabytes range. Due to large sizes involved, combined with the pipeline's complexity, this usually implies many days of processing time. Thus, the ability to distribute processing across multiple computing nodes becomes a necessity in order to reduce the required processing time. Furthermore, in order to allow scientists to focus on their research and not on technical issues, a user-friendly interface was needed, allowing easy interaction with the system.

RELATE is a Romanian language technology platform developed at the Institute for Artificial Intelligence of the Romanian Academy, integrating different state-of-the art tools and algorithms for processing Romanian language, developed either in-house or by our partners in different research projects. It evolved from our previous TEPROLIN platform (Ion, 2018) from a demonstrative, single file multi-level processing pipeline, to a more complex platform allowing for user-friendly interaction with Romanian language technologies as well as storage, processing, visualizing and downloading of large sets of annotated data. It was constructed using a task-based approach, where the user can load a corpus (usually as an archive) then start a number of annotation tasks and finally export the resulting data. The platform hides the complexities of distributing the load across the available processing nodes, waiting for data to be processed, error recovery and final gathering of results. Instead, the user is presented with an easy to use web interface where she/he can interact with the already annotated files and see the status of the entire annotation process. RELATE was constructed with the goal of making it accessible to at least two types of researchers: 1) theoretical linguists, Romanian language teachers and anyone interested in studying Romanian language by providing a nice visualization of the automatic analysis for any Romanian sentence and 2) NLP researchers wishing to either have access to off-the-shelf Romanian annotators or evaluating Romanian language technologies.

2. Related work

Speaking of language resource *inventories and search engines*, META-SHARE[1] (Federmann et al., 2012) together with CLARIN[2] are the biggest, publicly available European websites for research and development in the field. ELRC-SHARE[3] (European Language Resource Coordination Share) is another website dedicated to European language resources, specifically for machine translation. Both ELRC-Share and META-SHARE offer search boxes through which one can easily find various language resources (language tool, annotated, text or audio corpora, etc.) for any (European) language. Beside language resources for Romanian, our language of interest, there are *complex processing pipelines* such as NLP-Cube (Boroş et al., 2018) or TTL (Ion, 2007) that are able to do tokenization, POS tagging, lemmatization, chunking and dependency parsing. To use them, one has to be tech savvy, know Python 3 or Perl programming and be comfortable installing required open-source libraries (actually, this is the story of any open-source language technology tool, thus limiting its use to those that possess the knowledge to take the required steps).

To make the composition of the language processing chains more user-friendly, GATE (Cunningham, 2002) and TextFlows (Perovšek et al., 2016) allow for dragging and dropping text processing widgets into a graphical processing workflow to create the processing pipelines that the likes of NLP-Cube and TTL require computer programming to achieve. While graphically composing language processing chains is a big step towards the usability of the respective language technologies, their output is not enhanced with specialized visualization tools that allow access into the computational resources used for annotation.

---

[1] http://www.meta-share.org

[2] https://www.clarin.eu

[3] https://elrc-share.eu/

RELATE aims specifically at doing automatic text processing, with annotations at multiple levels, along with annotation visualization and expansion into the corresponding linguistic computational resources. Compared to other platforms, such as (Wanxiang et al., 2010), our platform does not focus on exposing APIs, even though such text processing APIs do exist, either directly from the different components or as an indirect result of integrating several components. Instead, RELATE is designed to be an integrated environment accessible via the web interface. In some ways it is similar to (Morton and LaCivita, 2003) work, with the addition of the web interface and parallel processing capabilities. Currently, the RELATE platform does not contain yet any functionality for automatic training of new models, such as more recent platforms like (Gardner et al., 2018). Furthermore, compared to the WebLicht (Hinrichs et al, 2010) platform, developed within the CLARIN project, RELATE is focused on Romanian language tools. Even more, besides integrating tagging capabilities, the platform also integrates other tools, such as WordNet, translation, speech recognition and synthesis.

The processing workflow is guided via addition of tasks which, by design, can work with the internal format produced by any other tasks. Thus, no workflow editor, such as the one used in (Perovšek et al., 2016), was needed at the moment. Tasks can be chained together, one after another, without the need for complex "wiring".

3. Platform Architecture

RELATE has two main areas (see Figure 1): a public area and a private area. The public area allows running most of the annotation tasks as well as exploring other platform features without any data storage facilities. Therefore, this is intended either for familiarizing a user with the platform or for small scale annotations (like single sentences or small files which do not require long term storage in the platform). The private part requires a user name and password[4] to be provided for user authentication and allows access to all platform features, including annotation of large corpora and storage of both raw and annotated data.

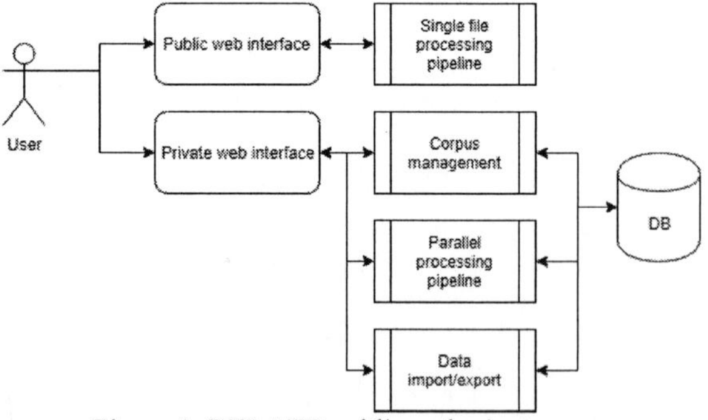

Figure 1: RELATE public and private areas

---

[4] The credentials are provided free of charge by request sent to one of the authors.

3.1 Platform components

The RELATE platform was constructed using an approach based on multiple interconnected layers. From the user's perspective, the first layer is the web front-end. It is in charge of displaying data to the user and employs visualizations such as: text views (for displaying raw text files as well as annotated files if the user opts for a text like visualization), data grids (for visualizing table information, such as annotation results in different formats), tree-views (useful for displaying dependency parsing information), integration of Brat rapid annotation tool (Stenetorp et al., 2012) for named entity visualization. Furthermore, the visualization layer interconnects with visualizations made available from other projects, such as the interrogation tools from the Reference Corpus for Contemporary Romanian Language (CoRoLa) (Mititelu et al., 2018).

The second layer of the platform is the back-end layer. This is in charge of orchestrating user requests between the various integrated modules. In turn, this happens either via an ephemerous flow, with results communicated directly to the web front-end, or via the task system with final storage in the platform's file system. The multi-layer architecture is presented in Figure 2.

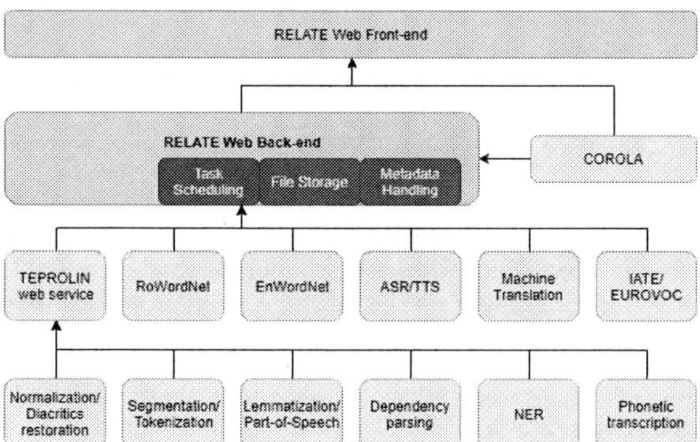

Figure 2: RELATE multiple layers architecture

Components integrated in the RELATE platform are written in different programming languages, such as: C/C++, Java, Python, scripts (bash, php). Furthermore, most of them were not exposing any web API and the few who had such an API available used completely different invocation flows. This created serious integration challenges, as described in more detail in (Păiş et al., 2019). Basically, we had to either create a web API wrapper for the tools or execute them as separate processes and collect the produced temporary files. In order to guarantee a uniform interrogation for multiple, related, modules, we used the TEPROLIN web service which integrates modules written in Python and other programming languages and exposes them in the same web API. This is in turn consumed by the back-end layer modules. Different modules are integrated either for textual annotation, as detailed below in the "Available annotations" sub-section, or only for enhancing the user visualization experience and allowing the researcher to make additional enquiries. Such is the case for integrating the Romanian WordNet aligned with the English WordNet which allows the user to research cross-lingually various senses of annotated words.

3.2 Available annotations

TEPROLIN and its web service[5] interface is a text preprocessing platform for Romanian (Ion, 2018) that currently offers 15 types of text transformation/annotations, from text-span annotations to syntactic dependency trees. Below is a brief account of these modules and corresponding annotations:

1. **Text normalization**: removal of multiple consecutive spaces and Romanian diacritical codes normalization;
2. **Diacritics restoration**: automatic detection of texts lacking Romanian diacritics and automatic diacritic insertion;
3. **Word hyphenation** (Stan et al., 2011);
4. **Word stressed syllable identification** (Stan et al., 2011);
5. **Word phonetic transcription** (Stan et al., 2011) using the SAMPA phonemes for Romanian[6];
6. **Numeral rewriting** (Stan et al., 2011): automatic transformation of number to their written form, useful in text-to-speech synthesis (e.g. 93 → "ninety-three");
7. **Abbreviation rewriting** (Stan et al., 2011): automatic expansion of abbreviations or acronyms to their full form, also useful for text-to-speech synthesis (e.g. art. → "article" or AI → "Artificial Intelligence");
8. **Sentence splitting** (Ion, 2007; Boroş et al., 2018);
9. **Tokenization** (Ion, 2007; Boroş et al., 2018);
10. **POS tagging** (Ion, 2007; Boroş et al., 2018) using the Morpho-Syntactic Descriptors (MSD) for Romanian tag set[7];
11. **Lemmatization** (Ion, 2007; Boroş et al., 2018);
12. **Named entity recognition (NER)** with four labels: person-PER, location-LOC, organization-ORG and time-TIME (Păiş 2019);
13. **Biomedical NER** (Boroş et al., 2018) with four labels: disorder (DISO), anatomical part (ANAT), medical procedure (PROC) and chemical (CHEM). The sequence labeler was trained on the MoNERo corpus (Mitrofan et al., 2018), (Carp (Mitrofan), 2019);
14. **Chunking** (Ion, 2007) with four types of non-recursive syntactic phrases: noun (Np), verb (Vp), adjectival/adverbial (Ap) and prepositional (Pp);
15. **Dependency parsing** (Boroş et al., 2018) with the Romanian Universal Dependencies label set[8].

Each module was adapted and made available for integration as part of the ReTeRom project[9]. Development of individual modules was realized by the ReTeRom partners, as indicated in the references and on the project's website.

TEPROLIN is a Python 3 module that integrates various NLP applications by requiring them to implement the TEPROLIN application programming interface:

- Resource loading, which usually takes from tens of seconds to minutes when the NLP application starts, is

only allowed inside a specialized method which is called once when the implementing object is instantiated;

- If the NLP application is not written in Python 3, TEPROLIN expects that the application runs on the same machine as the platform; the communication with the resident process is done via an established inter-process communication mechanism (e.g. sockets or named pipes).

When adding a new NLP application, the software engineer has to insert its name and operations in the TEPROLIN operation graph. Using this graph, TEPROLIN is able to automatically resolve the requirements of the new operation (e.g. before doing POS tagging, the text has to be tokenized first).

Pushing the "DEMO" button in the TEPROLIN Web Service/Complete Flow menu entry will run the full (all 15 operations) processing chain on two sample Romanian sentences. These two sentences were chosen such that every annotation that TEPROLIN is able to give is present and can be visualized. The output of this run can be visualized in computer readable formats: JSON, CoNLL-U[10], CoNLL-X, XML, and as well as graphically: in "Tree" mode (the most informative) and in "Entities" mode where NER annotations can be visualized graphically.

3.3 Task-based processing

In order to achieve better performance by harnessing the CPU resources available on different servers, the RELATE platform uses a task-based scheduler engine which in turn distributes the load across the available computing nodes. Since we targeted a mixed environment, with computing nodes of different sizes and performances, as well as a mixture of operating systems, we decided to develop our own task-engine for the purposes of the platform. It has two components: the scheduler, which is the first to receive a new task and decides where it should be executed, and the task runners which take care of actually running the task and storing final files on the file system.

Each task runner process keeps track of the files already processed so that it can resume processing in case of a system failure. Furthermore, the process is activated via a cron job which ensures automatic restart in case the task runner itself encounters a fatal error. Even more, logging is performed at operating system level ensuring all relevant messages are recorded and available for investigation. However, this is not displayed to the end user, being considered a very technical information, useful for platform developers. Entire processing pipelines are kept in-memory and accessed by task runners via URL endpoints. This ensures the possibility to distribute the tasks on any computing nodes, regardless of their location: same local area network (similar to a cluster environment), multiple networks (a grid environment) or across the Internet (cloud environment). Of course, the location of the computing resources can influence the overall processing time due to the differences in transfer speeds. Nevertheless, in case of large corpora, we

---

[5] http://relate.racai.ro:5000

[6] https://www.phon.ucl.ac.uk/home/sampa/rom-uni.htm

[7] http://nl.ijs.si/ME/V4/msd/html/msd-ro.html

[8] http://universaldependencies.org/ro/index.html

[9] http://www.racai.ro/p/reterom/index_en.html

[10] https://universaldependencies.org/format.html

consider the parallelization outweighs transfer times, thus reducing the total time required to process the files.

In order to avoid costly synchronization issues that usually occur in distributed systems, the RELATE platform does not make use of any shared resources. The scheduler process allocates disjunct slices of the corpus to each of the task runners. This allows for parallel computation throughout the pipelines without the need to synchronize with other processes.

Finally, the last runner who finishes work related to any particular task will also be in charge of composing the final result if needed. Even though, most of the tasks do not require final assembly of data since each annotation happens on a separate file. The scheduler and runners architecture is presented in Figure 3.

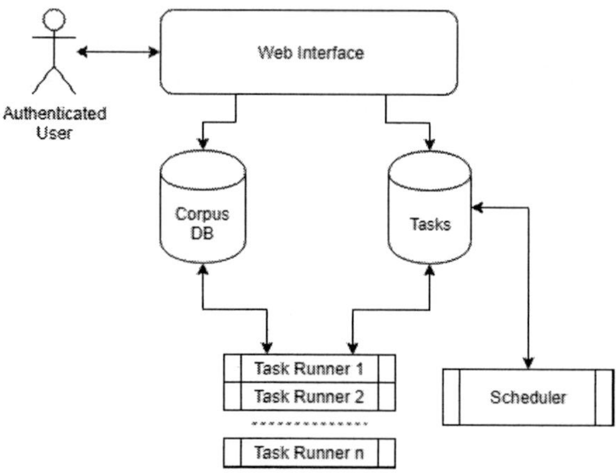

Figure 3: Task execution inside the RELATE platform

3.4 File formats

The platform was designed to allow corpora to be uploaded in the user's format, then processed and annotated to an internal platform format and finally exported to another user specified format. For this purpose, the platform has an import/export interface which can be extended with new functionality to export different user specified formats. Currently, the input format is either raw text files or comma separated files (CSV). In the second case, the user can specify in the interface the column or columns containing text data.

The internal format used throughout the platform is CoNLL-U Plus[11] format. This is a tab separated set of columns, usually considered to be an extension of the CoNLL-U format. In order to allow for a greater compatibility with CoNLL-U aware applications (and users), we have decided to keep the first 10 columns in the order of CoNLL-U specification and extend this with additional information available in the platform, such as named entities, IATE and EUROVOC annotations (Coman et al., 2019).

For output, the platform allows for a number of formats to be used, including: JSON, CoNLL-U (with limited annotations), CoNLL-U Plus variations, XML. In the case of CoNLL-U Plus, one possibility is to export the internal format, containing all the produced annotations, or a subset of those as required for different projects. The actual annotations available in the output file depend on the annotations tasks that were executed.

Since different modules in the pipeline require additional internal formats, other converters are available internally inside the platform, but are not exposed as input/output options.

3.5 Available visualizations

Apart from the annotation options described in section 3.2 above, RELATE integrates several visualization components, allowing the researcher user to better interact with the data. These components can be accessed either directly, via the proper links present in the platform's main menu, or via action buttons made available when interacting with the annotated data.

The "Tree" visualization mode is the most comprehensive of all, displaying generated annotations as well as *on the fly query results of other Romanian computational resources for the selected word*. In other words, the user can *relate* (hence the name of the portal) the output of the automatic language processing chain with information stored in the associated Romanian computational resources, thus seeing if the resource contains (or not) the relevant information and whether this information is useful when studying Romanian or how could it inform other automated Romanian processing algorithms. The "Tree" visualization mode has the dependency tree of a sentence in the center of the frame (one can see individual sentences using the arrows on the left/right of the current sentence). Dependency label names can be seen on the relations. If the user clicks a node in the tree, a panel of information about that word is opened to the right of the dependency tree: search in the CoRoLa corpus, search in the Romanian WordNet, listen to the native pronunciation of the word (if it is stored in the corpus) or synthesizing it (if not existing in the speech corpus), using the SSLA Text-to-Speech module[12] (Boroş et al., 2018b).

Besides linking other Romanian computational language resources and language tools, token annotations can also be inspected in the "Tree" view (e.g. POS tag, lemma, chunk membership, etc.) "Similar Words" will display up to 10 most similar words to the clicked word, computed using word embeddings extracted from the CoRoLa corpus (Păiş and Tufiş, 2018). A lemma with POS version of the similar words list is also available.

Romanian wordnet, RoWordNet, as described in (Tufiş and Mititelu, 2014), is made available for interrogation in the platform, either by itself or aligned with the English wordnet (Miller, 1995). The second option involves searching for a Romanian lemma in the wordnet, seeing the identified synsets and, based on the synset id, the corresponding English information is also displayed.

CoRoLa (Mititelu et al., 2018) which was constructed as a priority project of the Romanian Academy, between 2014 and 2017, contains both written texts and oral recordings. For each of these components, dedicated query interfaces were made available. These were also integrated in the RELATE platform, allowing words to be researched for occurrences in CoRoLa. In the case of written data, interrogation is performed by integration of the KorAP corpus management platform, developed at the Institute for German Language (Leibniz-Institut für Deutsche

---

[11] https://universaldependencies.org/ext-format.html

[12] http://slp.racai.ro/index.php/ssla/

Sprache) in Mannheim (Bański et al. 2014; Diewald et al. 2016). Similarly, for interrogation of audio transcriptions aligned with voice recordings, the Oral Corpus Query platform (OCQP) (Boroş et al., 2018b) developed for CoRoLa was integrated allowing the user to listen for the pronunciation of different words.

Since only a fraction of Romanian words are available in the audio component of the CoRoLa corpus, two speech synthesis components were integrated in the platform, allowing to user to listen for pronunciation of other words as well. One such system is the Speech Synthesis for Lightweight Applications (SSLA), described in (Boroş and Dumitrescu, 2015). Another, more recent development, is a system derived from our ROBIN project. Furthermore, from the ROBIN project resulted also an automatic speech recognition component which was also integrated in the RELATE platform.

In the case of text automatically recognized from speech, this can be automatically processed through the RELATE platform text annotation components, even though at this moment we lack the integration of an automatic capitalization and punctuation restoration component. Therefore, this particular integration currently has its use only in the case of small sentences.

A machine translation component is also available for interrogation within the RELATE platform. This is derived from the project "CEF Automated Translation toolkit for the Rotating Presidency of the Council of the EU", TENtec no. 28144308, led by TILDE, a linguistic technology company specializing in neural automatic translation. As part of this project, the translation system (Ro-En and En-Ro)[13] was developed in partnership with the Institute of Research for Artificial Intelligence "Mihai Draganescu" and is available for short translations within the RELATE platform.

Apart from the dedicated components, the platform makes use of advanced data grids whenever such a display option makes sense. For this purpose, we integrated the PqGrid[14] component which allows for features like: maximized view of data grid, column reordering, sorting, searching and integration with JSON based APIs. Furthermore, dependency parsed sentences are displayed in a tree-like visualization which is enhanced with action buttons allowing exploration of words within the other visualization components as detailed above.

3.6 Statistics

For each corpus, a dedicated task can be started for computing corpus statistics. These are computed at various levels: entire corpus, word form, lemma. After being computed, they can be visualized in the RELATE interface or downloaded as CSV files. Similar to other tasks, the statistics task makes use of the parallel runners in order to reduce the overall time required.

Corpus level statistics include: number of raw documents, number of annotated documents, number of sentences, number of tokens, number of "words" (strings separated by space characters), number of lines, number of characters. For each named entity type, the identified number of entities of that type is computed. Similarly, for each universal part of speech tag the corresponding number of occurrences is computed.

Word form (token) statistics include number of tokens, number of unique tokens and for each unique word form the total number of occurrences as well as the total number of files containing the particular word form are computed. Furthermore, the statistics task computes the number of words occurring only once in the entire corpus (also known as "hapax legomena"), the words occurring only two times and the words occurring only three times. Lemma statistics include number of unique lemmas as well as the number of occurrences for each lemma.

4. Case Study: Annotation of Romanian Legal Corpus

Within the "Multilingual Resources for CEF.AT in the legal domain" (MARCELL)[15] project, the seven participating teams cooperated in order to produce a comparable corpus aligned at the top-level domains identified by EUROVOC descriptors[16]. For Romanian language, the legal database created includes more than 140K legislative documents issued starting with 1881. These were gathered from the Romanian legislative portal[17] and converted from HTML to raw text format. This resulted in 2.7GB of raw text. During the conversion process certain metadata was also retrieved from within the HTML pages, but only information required for the project's use cases was stored (such as the publication year of the document).

For upload in the RELATE platform, the raw text was compressed into a zip archive, which had the size of 550Mb. After uploading to the platform, it was automatically decompressed by a task runner and its content was made available through the interface. Following a quick visual inspection to ensure the files were properly imported, an annotation task was launched.

Given the large size of the corpus, the annotation process took about one month on the two physical servers which were made available for project's purposes. Allocation of text files to pipeline components was orchestrated by the RELATE platform using the scheduler-runners approach described in 2.3 above. During this time, one server restart occurred due to a power outage which demonstrated the platform's ability to recover in case of unexpected errors and resume annotation. Furthermore, during task running, annotated files started to become available in the interface as they were finished. This allowed the researchers involved in the project to look at the produced annotations and identify potential issues.

Once the basic annotation task ended, a separate, dedicated task was started for IATE[18] and EUROVOC annotations, using the method described in (Coman et al., 2019). This was again orchestrated by the RELATE platform and split across 10 processes which managed to process the entire corpus in less than half hour. Similar to the previous step, annotations were made available in the RELATE web interface and were consulted by the project's team. Figure 5 shows a data grid visualization of one of the annotated files. This is performed using the CoNLL-U Plus format.

The large difference in the required time for the two annotation tasks is due to the number of processes

---

[13] https://ro.presidencymt.eu/#/text
[14] https://paramquery.com/

[15] https://marcell-project.eu/
[16] https://eur-lex.europa.eu/browse/eurovoc.html
[17] http://legislatie.just.ro/
[18] https://iate.europa.eu/home

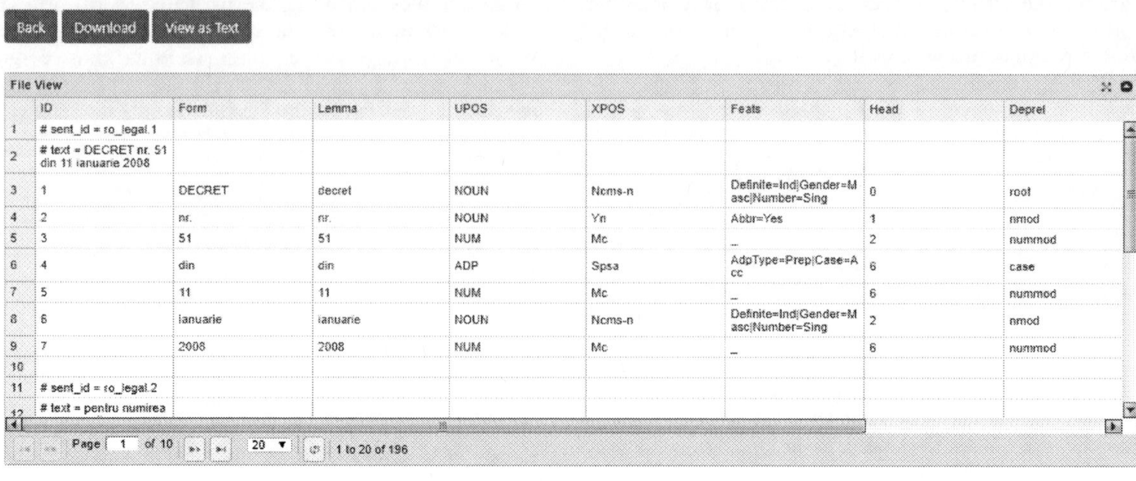

	ID	Form	Lemma	UPOS	XPOS	Feats	Head	Deprel
1	# sent_id = ro_legal.1							
2	# text = DECRET nr. 51 din 11 ianuarie 2008							
3	1	DECRET	decret	NOUN	Ncms-n	Definite=Ind|Gender=Masc|Number=Sing	0	root
4	2	nr.	nr.	NOUN	Yn	Abbr=Yes	1	nmod
5	3	51	51	NUM	Mc	_	2	nummod
6	4	din	din	ADP	Spsa	AdpType=Prep|Case=Acc	6	case
7	5	11	11	NUM	Mc	_	6	nummod
8	6	ianuarie	ianuarie	NOUN	Ncms-n	Definite=Ind|Gender=Masc|Number=Sing	2	nmod
9	7	2008	2008	NUM	Mc	_	6	nummod
10								
11	# sent_id = ro_legal.2							
12	# text = pentru numirea							

Figure 5: Datagrid visualization of an annotated file from the Romanian legal corpus

involved and their respective complexity. The IATE/EUROVOC annotator used the already tokenized and annotated documents from the previous step. More important, the Aho-Corasick algorithm (Aho and Corasick, 1975) used for detecting the corpus occurrences of the terms stored in the trie dictionary made of IATE Romanian terms runs in linear-time (see details in (Coman et al., 2019)).

Following the two annotation stages, a statistics task was executed, in order to compute the overall statistics on the corpus, useful for reporting purposes. This was executed using 13 processes orchestrated by the platform and took about one hour and half to compute the statistical indicators described in section 2.6 above. Table 1 presents some of the computed statistics.

Number of documents	144,131
Number of tokens	456,079,723
Unique tokens	1,528,228
Unique lemmas	1,195,484
Tokens occurring only once	772,141

Table 1: Statistics from the Romanian legal corpus obtained using the RELATE platform

Finally, a MARCELL specific preparation task was executed, ensuring the output format agreed within the project. This is also a CoNLL-U Plus based format. Each document begins with a line describing the columns followed by a "newdoc" marker holding the file id (# newdoc id = ro.legal). Each sentence in a document is labelled by a unique ID (example: "# sent id = ro legal.4"), followed by the text of the respective sentence (# text = ...). Following is a tab separated list of 14 columns, according to the first descriptor line in the file. It contains the word id, word form, lemma, universal part of speech tag, language specific part of speech tag, list of morphological features, head of the current word, universal dependency relation, underscore in columns nine and ten (since we don't use any enhanced dependency graph features or miscellaneous features),

named entities in BIO format, NP chunk information, IATE and EUROVOC annotations.

The entire annotated corpus has a size of 29GB and was archived using an archiving task, resulting a zip archive of 4.3GB, downloadable through the platform and was later stored in the MARCELL repository.

5. Conclusion

This paper presented an integrated, high performance platform for Romanian language, called RELATE. It allows researchers to upload a large corpus and perform annotations as well as complex analysis on the data. To achieve parallelization of time-consuming annotation operations, the platform uses a scheduler-runners mechanism. This allows CPU-intensive operations to be distributed across multiple processing nodes across a network or even across the Internet.

By integrating current state of the art modules for processing Romanian language, developed by different research partners, the RELATE platform strives to become a national reference portal.

Multiple input and output file formats are supported, while the internal format used by the platform is the CoNLL-U Plus format. Large archives can be uploaded, processed and finally downloaded in a standard annotated format.

The platform is loosely coupled with the processing pipelines, by means of URLs accessed by the task runner processes, thus complying with a micro-services architecture. Therefore, one of the key future developments for the platform is envisaged to be its containerization in the form of multiple docker containers: one for the interface and one for the processing pipeline. This would allow for quick deployment on new processing nodes as well as increased durability when faced with operating system updates or changes in external libraries.

RELATE will be further enhanced with new Romanian language technologies/computational resources as they become available. While we do not aim at standardizing language technologies interoperation or annotation visualization, thus admitting supplementary programming effort for each new addition, our *focus* is to keep thinking on how to best visualize and link automatically generated annotations with their supporting computational resources in such a way that the widest interested audience is best served doing their work.

In the spirit of European Language Grid, as National Center of Competence for Romania, we will try to persuade all the developers of technologies and resources for Romanian to adhere and contribute to the RELATE portal with new tools and data-sets.

6.   Acknowledgements

Part of this work was conducted in the context of the ReTeRom project. Part of this work was conducted in the context of the Marcell project. Speech recognition and synthesis components referenced in this work were developed within the ROBIN project. Machine translation components referenced in this work were developed within the "CEF Automated Translation toolkit for the EU Council Presidency", TENtec no. 28144308.

7.   Bibliographical References

Aho, A. and Corasick, M. (1975). Efficient string matching: An aid to bibliographic search. *Commun. ACM.* 18:6, 333-340.

Bański, P., Diewald, N., Hanl, M., Kupietz, M. and Witt, A. (2014). Access Control by Query Rewriting. The Case of KorAP. In *Proceedings of the Ninth Conference on International Language Resources and Evaluation (LREC'14)*. Reykjavik, European Language Resources Association (ELRA).

Boroș, T., Dumitrescu, D.Ș. and Burtică, R. (2018). NLP-Cube: End-to-End Raw Text Processing With Neural Networks. In *Proceedings of the CoNLL 2018 Shared Task: Multilingual Parsing from Raw Text to Universal Dependencies.* Association for Computational Linguistics, pages 171-179.

Boroș, T., Dumitrescu, D.Ș. and Păiș, V. (2018b). "Tools and resources for Romanian text-to-speech and speech-to-text applications", in *Proceedings of the International Conference on Human-Computer Interaction – RoCHI 2018*, pp 46-53.

Boroș, T. and Dumitrescu, D.Ș. (2015). Robust deep learning models for text-to-speech synthesis support on embedded devices. In *Proceedings of the 7th International Conference on Management of computational and collective IntElligence in Digital EcoSystems (MEDES'15)*, Caraguatatuba, Brasil.

Carp (Mitrofan) M. (2019). Extragere de cunoștințe din texte în limba română și date structurate cu aplicații în domeniu medical. PhD Thesis, Romanian Academy, 144 pages.

Che, W., Li, Z. and Liu, T. (2010). LTP: a Chinese Language Technology Platform. In *Proceedings of the 23rd International Conference on Computational Linguistics: Demonstrations (COLING '10)*. Association for Computational Linguistics, Stroudsburg, PA, USA, 13-16.

Coman, A., Mitrofan, M. and Tufis, D. (2019). Automatic identification and classification of legal terms in Romanian law texts, In *Proceedings of ConsILR 2019*, Cluj, România, pp 39-49.

Cunningham, H. (2002). GATE, a General Architecture for Text Engineering. *Computers and the Humanities*, 36(2):223—254.

Diewald, N., Hanl, M., Margaretha, E., Bingel, J., Kupietz, M., Bański, P. and Witt, A. (2016). KorAP Architecture – Diving in the Deep Sea of Corpus Data. In: Calzolari, Nicoletta et al. (eds.): *Proceedings of the Tenth International Conference on Language Resources and Evaluation (LREC'16)*, Portoroz, European Language Resources Association (ELRA).

Federmann, C., Giannopoulou, I., Girardi, C., Hamon, O., Mavroeidis, D., Minutoli, S. and Schröder, M. (2012). META-SHARE v2: An Open Network of Repositories for Language Resources including Data and Tools. In *Proceedings of the Eighth International Conference on Language Resources and Evaluation (LREC 2012)*, Turkey, pages 3300-3303.

Gardner, M., Grus, J., Neumann, M., Tafjord, O., Dasigi, P., Liu, N., Peters, M., Schmitz, M., and Zettlemoyer, L. (2018). AllenNLP: A Deep Semantic Natural Language Processing Platform. arXiv:1803.07640.

Hinrichs, M., Zastrow, T., and Hinrichs, E. W. (2010). WebLicht: Web-based LRT Services in a Distributed eScience Infrastructure. In *Proceedings of the International Conference on Language Resources and Evaluation, LREC 2010*, pp 489-493.

Ion, R. (2007). Word Sense Disambiguation Methods Applied to English and Romanian. PhD Thesis, Romanian Academy, 148 pages (in Romanian).

Ion, R. (2018). TEPROLIN: An Extensible, Online Text Preprocessing Platform for Romanian. In *Proceedings of the International Conference on Linguistic Resources and Tools for Processing Romanian Language (ConsILR 2018)*, November 22-23, 2018, Iași, Romania.

Miller, G.A. (1995). WordNet: A Lexical Database for English, *Communications of the ACM*, Vol. 38, No. 11:39-41.

Mititelu, B.V., Tufiș, D. and Irimia, E. (2018). The Reference Corpus of Contemporary Romanian Language (CoRoLa). In *Proceedings of the 11th Language Resources and Evaluation Conference – LREC'18*, Miyazaki, Japan, European Language Resources Association (ELRA).

Morton, T. and LaCivita, J. (2003). WordFreak: an open tool for linguistic annotation. In *Proceedings of the 2003 Conference of the North American Chapter of the Association for Computational Linguistics on Human Language Technology: Demonstrations - Volume 4 (NAACL-Demonstrations '03)*, Vol. 4. Association for Computational Linguistics, Stroudsburg, PA, USA, 17-18. DOI: https://doi.org/10.3115/1073427.1073436.

Păiș, V. (2019). Contributions to semantic processing of texts; Identification of entities and relations between textual units; Case study on Romanian language. PhD Thesis, Romanian Academy, 114 pages.

Păiș, V., Tufiș, D. and Ion, R. (2019). Integration of Romanian NLP tools into the RELATE platform. In *Proceedings of the International Conference on Linguistic Resources and Tools for Processing Romanian Language – CONSILR 2019*, pages 181-192.

Perovšek, M., Kranjc, J., Erjavec, T., Cestnik, B. and Lavrač, N. (2016). TextFlows: A visual programming platform for text mining and natural language processing, *Science of Computer Programming*, Volume 121, Pages 128-152.

Stan, A., Yamagishi, J., King, S. and Aylett, M. (2011). The Romanian Speech Synthesis (RSS) corpus: building a high quality HMM-based speech synthesis system using a high sampling rate. *Speech Communication* 53(3):442—450.

Stenetorp, P., Pyysalo, S., Topić, G., Ohta, T., Ananiadou, S. and Tsujii, J. (2012). brat: a Web-based Tool for NLP-Assisted Text Annotation. In *Proceedings of the Demonstrations Session at EACL 2012*

Tufiş, D. and Mititelu, B.V. (2014). The Lexical Ontology for Romanian. In Nuria Gala, Reinhard Rapp, Gemma Bel-Enguix (eds) Recent Advances in Language Production, Cognition and the Lexicon, pages 491–504, Springer, 2014

Proceedings of the 1st International Workshop on Language Technology Platforms (IWLTP 2020), pages 89–95
Language Resources and Evaluation Conference (LREC 2020), Marseille, 11–16 May 2020
© European Language Resources Association (ELRA), licensed under CC-BY-NC

LinTO Platform: A Smart Open Voice Assistant for Business Environments

Ilyes Rebai, Kate Thompson, Sami Benhamiche, Zied Sellami, Damien Laine, Jean-Pierre Lorre
Linagora R&D Labs
75 Route de Revel, 31400 Toulouse, France
{irebai, cthompson, sbenhamiche, zsellami, dlaine, jplorre}@linagora.com

Abstract

In this paper, we present LinTO, an intelligent voice platform and smart room assistant for improving efficiency and productivity in business. Our objective is to build a Spoken Language Understanding system that maintains high performance in both Automatic Speech Recognition (ASR) and Natural Language Processing while being portable and scalable. In this paper we describe the LinTO architecture and our approach to ASR engine training which takes advantage of recent advances in deep learning while guaranteeing high-performance real-time processing. Unlike the existing solutions, the LinTO platform is open source for commercial and non-commercial use.

Keywords: Smart room assistant, Spoken Language Understanding, Speech recognition, Accuracy and real-time performance

1. Introduction

Speech processing is an active research topic in the signal processing community. There has been a growing interest, both commercial and academic, in creating intelligent machines that interact with humans by voice, suggesting the capability of not only recognizing what is said, but also of extracting the meaning from the spoken language (TURING, 1950).

Advances in machine learning, Automatic Speech Recognition (ASR), and Natural Language Processing (NLP) have lead to dramatic advances in Spoken Language Understanding (SLU) during the last two decades, evolving from relatively simple tasks such as spoken keyword extraction to much more complicated ones involving language understanding in more extended natural language interactions (Serdyuk et al., 2018; Coucke et al., 2018). These achievements have unlocked many practical voice applications, e.g. voice assistants, which are now used in many contexts, including autonomous vehicles (Pfleging et al., 2012), and smart homes[1] (Coucke et al., 2018). Popular commercial solutions for voice assistance include Cortana-Microsoft[2], DialogFlow-Google[3], Watson-IBM[4] or Alexa-Amazon.

SLU is an active research and development field at the intersection of ASR and NLP that focuses on the task of extracting meaning from spoken utterances. Unlike speech recognition, SLU is not a single technology but a combination of technologies: it is a system that requires each of its interdependent components to perform well with respect to speech, speech recognition errors, various characteristics of uttered sentences, and speaker intent detection. This is significantly more difficult to achieve than written language understanding (Tur and De Mori, 2011).

Our objective in this paper is to introduce the LinTO Voice Platform designed for business environments, a competitive solution for voice assistance. Unlike the previous solutions, all the components of our platform are open source[5] for commercial and non-commercial use. All models and components are made available for download for use on our platform.

We outline the design of a SLU system that achieves high performance in terms of response time and accuracy with cloud computing based solutions. This is done by optimizing the trade-off between accuracy and computational efficiency of the two main ASR components: the acoustic model and the language model. While the acoustic model component must be trained on a large corpus using sophisticated deep learning techniques requiring a lot of computational resources in order to achieve high performance, the language model component can be trained on the linguistic domain of the application assistant rather than the domain of the entire spoken language. The total computational cost of the ASR is thus reduced by reducing the cost of the language model while even improving its in-domain accuracy.

2. LinTO Platform

LinTO is an open-source client-server system that enables the conception, deployment and maintenance of software and hardware clients with a voice-activated user interface. The system boosts the ease of use and productivity in both administrative management and customer application contexts, offering hands-free vocal control processes, multiple-speaker speech recognition, and voice access for customer applications.

The LinTO platform features a friendly user console, the LinTO admin, used to design, build and manage specific voice assistants. Each assistant is composed of the models and resources necessary to execute its desired functions, and may include any number of *skills*, or intention-action pairs defined for a particular process, e.g. delivering a verbal weather report if asked about the weather (see section 4.). These are represented in the LinTO admin as an easily manipulable workflow (see Figure 1).

The workflow defines and runs the models of the corresponding SLU pipeline (Figure 2) which is composed of

---

[1]https://demo.home-assistant.io/
[2]https://www.microsoft.com/en-us/cortana
[3]https://cloud.google.com/dialogflow
[4]https://www.ibm.com/watson

[5]https://doc.linto.ai/#/repos

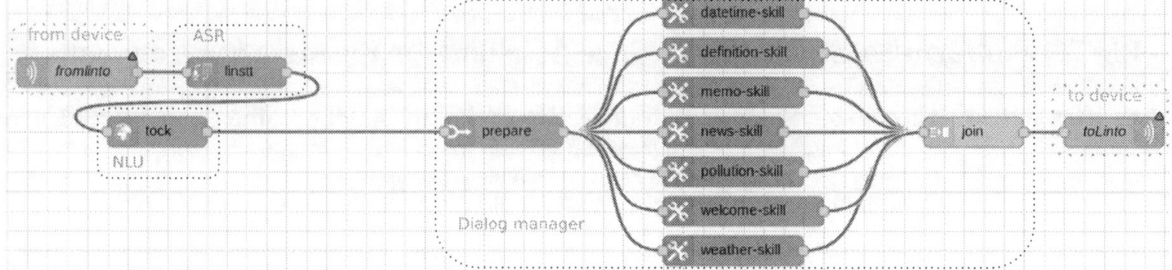

Figure 1: A LinTO Admin workflow describing a voice assistant that incorporates several skills

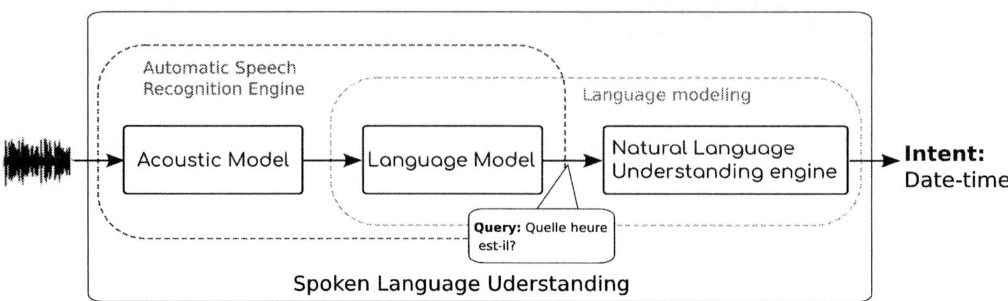

Figure 2: The LinTO SLU architecture

the ASR and NLU engines. The ASR engine recognizes spoken language and transcribes it into text by first mapping the audio stream into a sequence of probabilities over acoustic units (or phones) using an acoustic model (AM), and then converting the outputs of the AM to text using a language model (LM). The NLU engine interprets the language. Specifically, it goes beyond speech recognition to determine a user's intent from her decoded spoken language input (e.g. a query about the weather forecast). Once the user query is interpreted, the final step is to compute a response using a dialogue manager. The response can take multiple forms depending on the request, e.g., an audio response if asked about the weather or an action on a connected device if asked to play a song.

In accordance with our performance, portablity and scalability objectives, we developed an SLU system using cloud-based technologies and offering a service that meets three basic requirements:

1. Can be deployed in any system

2. Can handle a high number of queries

3. Responds in real time with high accuracy

To address the first requirement, we take advantage of Docker technology in order to create "containerized" services that can be used in any OS environment. For the scalability requirement, we implement Docker Swarm, a container orchestration tool that helps manage multiple containers deployed across multiple host machines, such that the service can be scaled up or down depending on the number of queries (see Figure 3). Finally, in order to provide an accurate, real-time response, we design the SLU

components to optimize the trade-off between accuracy and computational efficiency. For instance, since the size of the AM architecture has an impact on the computational cost and the accuracy, we determine the final model size by taking into account target resources and the desired accuracy. Similarly for the LM and the NLU components, the models are trained to reduce size and increase in-domain accuracy by restricting the vocabulary as well as the variety of the queries they should model.

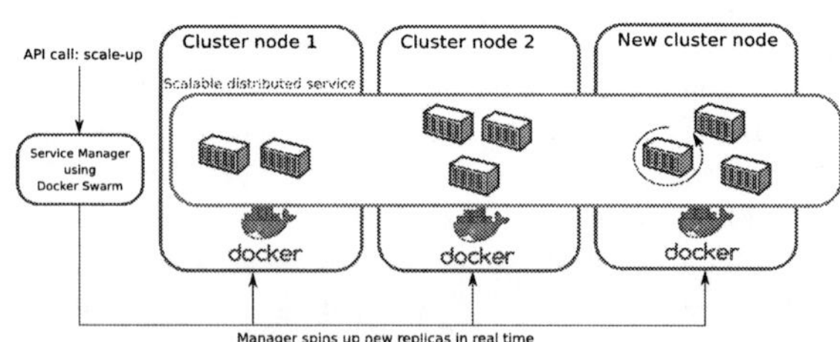

Figure 3: Service manager using Docker Swarm for container orchestration

The LinTO platform and all its services and components are released publicly[6], at no cost for commercial and non-commercial use. The language currently supported by our platform is French.

3. The Acoustic Model

The AM is the first component of ASR engine and first step of the SLU pipeline, and is therefore crucial to the functioning of the entire system. It is responsible for converting raw audio data to a sequence of acoustic units, or phones. It is

---

[6]https://doc.linto.ai/

usually trained on large speech corpus using deep networks in order to model context variations, speaker variations, and environmental variations. Given that these variations are the main factors impacting the accuracy of a speech recognition system, robust modeling of them is imperative to successful speech-to-text transcription.

There are two major research directions in acoustic modeling. The first one focuses on collecting a large, in-domain speech corpus adapted to the context of application of the assistant in order to build a robust model. The second one focuses on improving machine learning techniques to better model the long temporal speech contexts. In the next subsections, we will address both directions, first detailing our methods for collecting, processing and validating training data, and then describing the acoustic model architecture.

3.1. Data preparation

A large amount of transcribed data is needed in order to train the deep networks used for speech recognition models, including AMs. A robust AM requires several thousand hours of audio training data with corresponding transcripts. This data must be formatted to include a set of audio extracts and matching transcripts which are cut into segments of lengths suitable for acoustic training (optimally a few tenths a of second).

In recent years there has been a rapid increase in the amount of open source multimedia content on the internet, making collecting a large speech corpus more feasible. We have created a French corpus using various publicly available sources, including those made available by the LibriVox project[7], a community of volunteers from all over the world who record public domain texts. We reformat this data by segmenting and realigning the transcripts, and we also remove any transcription errors. Our corpus preparation process is presented in Figure 4 and detailed in the following subsections.

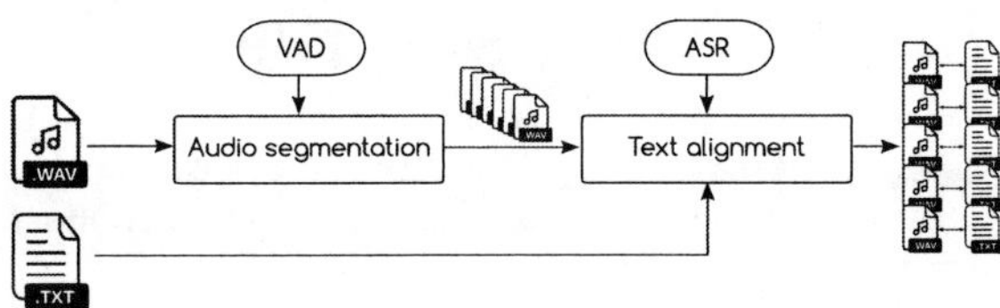

Figure 4: Audio alignment procedure used in the creation of the corpus

3.1.1. Audio segmentation

We segment the audio recordings using Vocal Activity Detection (VAD) technique, which detects the presence or absence of human speech. We use the detected non-speech intervals to split the audio at intervals of 0.5 seconds or less. After segmentation, we must re-align the audio snippets with their transcriptions.

3.1.2. Text alignment

To match the audio segments with the original text, we use a pre-trained acoustic model with a language model biased to the specific vocabulary in order to transcribe each audio segment. The proposed procedure consists of two stages. During the first stage, we normalize the original text in order to adapt it for language model generation. Additionally, the obtained text is extended by a set of extra-words including numbers, ordinal numbers, most common abbreviations, and punctuation signs in order to anticipate annotation errors. Next, both the normalized original text and the audio segments are split into n parts. The text in each part is then converted into a decoding graph. This is done to avoid automatic transcription errors by increasing the likelihood that the audio will be matched to some portion of the text. Finally, we transcribe each audio segment using the pre-trained acoustic model along with the decoding graph that matches the audio.

In order to analyze the quality of the transcription, we develop an alignment algorithm to get the best match between the transcriptions and the normalized original text. We are inspired by Levenshtein alignment algorithm (Levenshtein, 1966). Once the alignment is obtained, the word error rate (WER), a common metric used to compare the accuracy of the transcripts produced by speech recognition, is computed between the reference and the hypothesis. Possible sources of text-audio mismatch include inaccuracies in ASR prediction, as well as in the original text (e.g., normalization errors, annotation errors). At this stage, it is possible to retain the segments that are below a low WER threshold and discard the others.

We then move to the second stage, where we further improve the audio transcription using a custom-generated decoding graph for each audio segment. This is done as follows. First, the decoding graph is formed from a combination of three original text segments. Our aim is to have a decoding graph with a high bias in order to overcome the ASR errors, and to increase the accuracy of the transcription with respect to the first stage. Then, we always use the pre-trained acoustic model with the new decoding graphs to decode the audio segments. Figure 5 shows different examples of errors and the results generated during alignment stage 1 and 2. At the end of this stage, we retain only the segments with a WER of 0.

3.1.3. AM training data

We have collected about 500 hours of read French speech from various freely available sources, including: Commonvoice[8], M-AILabs[9] and librivox. The alignment process produces a set of aligned audio of size approximately 200 hours performed mainly on librivox data. For the first and second decoding pass, we use a pre-trained triphone deep neural network-based AM.

3.2. Acoustic model architecture

Hybrid acoustic models are widely adopted in the current state-of-the-art systems combining a Hidden Markov Model (HMM) with a Deep Neural Network (DNN). The HMM describes temporal variability while the DNN computes emission probabilities from HMM states in order to

---

[7]https://librivox.org/

[8]https://voice.mozilla.org/
[9]https://www.caito.de/2019/01/the-m-ailabs-speech-dataset/

a-

Reference: aux artistes ou aux savants dont l' appui aide à percer dans la branche où ils priment

Hypothesis (Stage 1): aux artistes ou aux savants dont l' appui aide à **entre guillemets** percer dans la branche où ils priment

Hypothesis (Stage 2): aux artistes ou aux savants dont l' appui aide à **entre guillemets** percer dans la branche où ils priment

b-

Reference: pour lesquels ils n' admettent pas la critique qu' ils acceptent aisément **s' il s' agit** de leurs chefs d' oeuvre

Hypothesis (Stage 1): pour lesquels ils n' admettent pas la critique qu' ils acceptent aisément **s' agit** de leurs chefs d' oeuvre

Hypothesis (Stage 2): pour lesquels ils n' admettent pas la critique qu' ils acceptent aisément **s' il s' agit** de leurs chefs d' oeuvre

c-

Reference: lui préféreront même des adversaires comme **mm** ribot et deschanel

Hypothesis (Stage 1): lui préféreront même des adversaires comme **messieurs** ribot et deschanel

Hypothesis (Stage 2): lui préféreront même des adversaires comme **messieurs** ribot et deschanel

Figure 5: Examples of the audio transcription obtained in the first and second stage. a- Errors in text normalization overcome in the first and second stage. b- Words deleted in the first stage but correctly recognized in the second one. c- 'messieurs' expanded abbreviation in the original text perfectly transcribed by ASR.

model and map acoustic features to phones (Hinton et al., 2012).

Over the last few years, various deep learning techniques have been proposed to improve the emission probabilities estimation (Graves et al., 2013). In fact, modeling long term temporal dependencies is critical in acoustic modeling: by modeling the temporal dynamics in speech, the acoustic model can effectively capture the dependencies between acoustic events and thus improve speech recognition performance (Peddinti et al., 2015). One of the most popular techniques is the Time-Delay Neural Network (TDNN) (Waibel et al., 1989) which has been shown to be effective in modeling long range temporal dependencies (Peddinti et al., 2015).

Our AM is designed to guarantee high transcription accuracy while requiring fewer computational resources. We use a neural network that maps sequences of speech frames to sequences of triphone HMM state probabilities. The speech frames are obtained by computing the mel-frequency cepstral coefficients (MFCC) from the audio signal. The neural network combines a time-delay layers and an attention mechanism that selects the temporal locations over the input frame sequence where the most relevant information is concentrated (Bahdanau et al., 2016). The selection of elements from the input sequence is a weighted sum:

$$c_t = \sum_l \alpha_{tl} \mathbf{h}_l \qquad (1)$$

where α_{tl} are the attention weights. This mechanism helps to improve the acoustic modeling of the network and to subsequently improve speech recognition performance (Bahdanau et al., 2016; Lu, 2019).

In the literature, the acoustic model achieving human parity (Xiong et al., 2016) is a complex neural network, composed of several hundred of million parameters. The size of these models along with the language model, increase the computational resources necessary not only to perform real time decoding, but also to scale them. Models with a variable number of parameters, i.e. different number of layers and neurons, can be trained and evaluated in terms of accuracy and computational cost. This can help to select the most appropriate model that optimizes a trade-off between accuracy and computation time.

We train deep neural AMs using the Kaldi toolkit [10]. Our typical architectures have 7 time-delay layers and an attention layer. The input vector to the model consists of 40 MFCC features, and 100 speaker and channel features computed using an i-vector speaker-adaptive model (Garimella et al., 2015). It is trained with the lattice-free MMI criterion (Povey et al., 2016), using gradient descent with start and final learning rates of 0.001 and 0.0001 respectively.

4. The Language Model

The language model is the second component of the ASR engine and of the SLU pipeline. Like the acoustic model, it is designed to optimize a trade-off between transcription, precision and computational cost.

The LM converts the sequence of probabilities over acoustic units predicted by the AM into a probable word sequence, while taking into account the probability of word co-occurrence (Chelba et al., 2012b). Once the text is obtained, the NLU module extracts the intent of the user from the decoded query. The LM and NLU have to be mutually consistent in order to optimize the accuracy of the SLU engine, and together they make up the language modeling component.

A large vocabulary LM consisting of several million n-grams (Chelba et al., 2012a) can adequately capture the linguistic knowledge of a target language (e.g. syntax and semantics) in order to more accurately transcribe a sequence of acoustic units. But this results in a large search space that greatly increases decoding time for the LM, and effects ASR performance as a whole. To avoid such limitations to

---

[10]https://github.com/kaldi-asr/kaldi

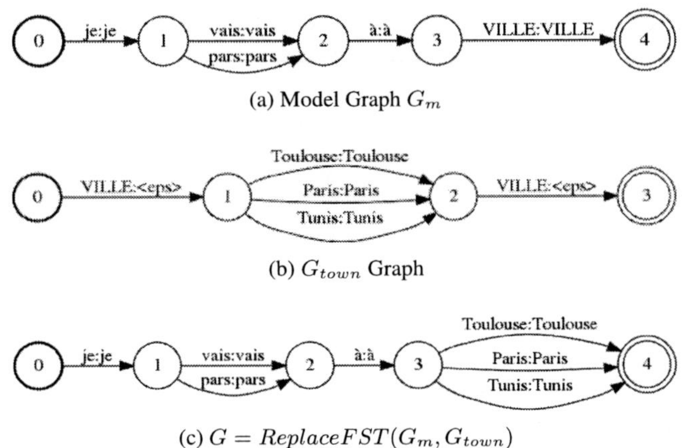

(a) Model Graph G_m

(b) G_{town} Graph

(c) $G = ReplaceFST(G_m, G_{town})$

Figure 6: Graph G creation process with a simple query of the form "je vais à #VILLE" (in English "I am going to #TOWN"

the performance of our SLU, we restrict the vocabulary of the LM to a particular use case domain.

This domain is defined by the set of skills the assistant is designed to handle (e.g. SmartRoomEquipment, MeetingReport, MeetingControl for a smart business assistant, or SmartLights, SmartMusic skills for smart home assistant). Each skill contains one or multiple intents (i.e. user-intentions[11]), that furnish a concentrated vocabulary which is sufficient to correctly model the sentences encountered by the assistant. While the AM is trained once per language, this specialized LM can be trained quickly on the reduced vocabulary, which is sufficient to with improvements to the overall performance of the SLU.

4.1. LM training data

The data used to train the specialized LM (as well as the NLU) consists of sentences expressing the desired intents. These are the queries listed manually by the user to which one or more entities can be bound. For example, the skill MeetingReport contains the intent ShowMeetingReport, to which the entities *date* and *report-type* are bound, giving "show the meeting *summary* of the date *21 April 2019*" to the dialogue manager which then executes the correct action.

Entities are predefined and provided by the platform – e.g. numbers, colors, date and times, etc, and can be bound to different intents. Using the same example, the values associated with the date and report-type entities in the query can be specified as follows: "show the meeting (summary)[report-type] of the date (21 April 2019)[date]". The entity report-type is a custom list of values (e.g. full transcription, summary, notes).

4.2. Model generation

The map from the output of the acoustic model to the most likely sequence of words is carried out using a Viterbi search in a decoding graph which is a weighted finite state transducer (wFST) (Mohri et al., 2002). This graph is the composition of four wFST graphs: H contains the HMM

definitions, C represents the context-dependency, L is the lexicon, and G is a bigram or a trigram language model. For more details refer to (Mohri et al., 2002) and references therein. In this paper, we focus on the construction of the L graph and G graph since they are the most important parts of the decoding graph that must be adapted to the domain-specific data.

The lexicon (i.e. dictionary) consists of a set of words with their phonetic pronunciations. This pair (word/phonemes) allows us to associate a sequence of words with the predicted phonetic sequence provided by the acoustic model. In this work we use an open-source lexicon (French Prosodylab dictionary[12]), composed of more than 100,000 words with their SAMPA phonetization (McAuliffe et al., 2017). Since this lexicon may not include all possible words, the new words in the data used to train the G graph are first automatically phoneticized and then added to the lexicon in order to allow the decoding graph to correctly predict these words. The word's phonetization is performed using a Grapheme-to-Phoneme (G2P) model trained using phonetisaurus toolkit[13]. The obtained lexicon is then converted into L graph using a Kaldi function.

After preparing the L graph, the first step in building G is the preparation of the set of queries that the user may make to the assistant. Given the data described in section 4.1., the values of each entities in the queries are replaced by an identifier of the entity. For example, the query "show the meeting (summary)[report-type] of the date (21 April 2019)[date]" is mapped to "show the meeting *#report-type* of the date *#date*". Next, an n-gram model is trained on the resulting queries and then converted to a wFST, which we called the main graph G_m.

In order to bind the entities to the main graph, each entity e is converted into an acceptor graph G_e that encodes the list of values of that entity. Next, these graphs G_e are merged with the main graph G_m to obtain the final graph G. This process is illustrated by a sample query in Figure 6.

---

[11]Overall, a user intent spots what a user is looking for when conducting a search query

[12]https://montreal-forced-aligner.readthedocs.io/en/latest/pre-trained_models.html

[13]https://github.com/AdolfVonKleist/Phonetisaurus

5. Performance Evaluation

The aim of this work is to develop an SLU system that achieves high performance in terms of response time and accuracy. This system must correctly predict the intent and the entities of a spoken utterance in order to execute the correct action. In this paper, our focus is to improve the performance of the ASR engine which has a strong impact on the SLU performance.

In this section, we present the different experiments carried out under different conditions. The objective is to evaluate the ASR engine and in particular the LM of a smart business assistant. While the response time is used to analyse the speed of the decoder, the accuracy of the transcription is usually measured using the word error rate (WER). The experiments are conducted on French language. Thirteen queries related to the context of the meeting are chosen for evaluation. Examples are:

- "Baisse la lumière de (10)[number] pourcent" (Turn down the light 10 percent)

- "Active le chronomètre pour (4 heures)[time] de réunion" (Activate the chronometer for 4 hours)

- "Affiche le compte-rendu de la réunion du (12 septembre 2018)[date] concernant le (résumé automatique)[subject]" (Post the meeting minutes from the September 12 meeting about automatic summarization.

- "Invite (Sonia)[person] à la visioconférence de (demain)[date]" (Invite Sonia to the video-conference tomorrow)

These queries are recorded in order to build an evaluation corpus. For this purpose, we record the queries with 16 speakers (14 native and 2 non-native, including 10 men and 6 women between 21 and 30 years old). The recording are carried out with the YETI – Blue Microphone in a meeting room, with a sampling frequency of 16 Khz and a speaker/microphone distance of 80 cm.

We varied the number of the queries (intents) on which the LM is trained to evaluate the quality of recognition based on the number of skills. Four models are built, defined as follows:

- First Model: using only the thirteen evaluation queries

- Second Model: using 76 queries which represents the following 7 skills:

    - control-equipment: manage the meeting room equipment (contains 8 queries);

    - time: gives the time (contains 8 queries);

    - meeting_time: gives the meeting time (contains 11 queries);

    - chrono: adjust the stopwatch of the meeting (9 queries);

    - meeting-report: which gives the meeting report (5 queries);

    - meeting-participant: manage the meeting participants (5 queries);

    - videoconf: manage the video conference (17 queries).

- Third Model: We use 171 queries in this model which represent 14 skills: weather, news, mail, note, meeting-control (recording, meeting mode), traffic, control-Linto, control-equipment, time, meeting-time, chrono, meeting-report, meeting-participant, videoconf.

- Fourth Model: In this model, we use 237 queries which represents 22 skills.

In order to evaluate the impact of the adapted language model over the large vocabulary model on the response time, we use a large vocabulary model trained on the text of the speech corpus.

Results

The results of the evaluations in terms of WER, SER (Sentence/Command Error Rate) as well as the response time are presented in the following table.

Table 1: Performance evaluation in terms of WER for the different language models.

	WER[%]	SER[%]	Time[s]
Large vocabulary model	25.75	70.67	237
Adapted language model (1)	4.28	20.67	195
Adapted language model (2)	4.62	22.12	199
Adapted language model (3)	5.23	25.00	204
Adapted language model (4)	5.37	25.48	216

The first evaluation consists of comparing the results obtained using a conversational recognition mode (using the large vocabulary model) on the one hand, and an adapted language model on the other. The objective of this evaluation is to highlight the performance and response time of the control systems.

As shown in Table 1, the WER results of the control systems are better than those obtained by the large vocabulary system with a gain of 20%. It can be concluded that the models adapted to the assistant are more advantageous. Additionally, the response time of these models is shorter than that of the conversational system thanks to the relatively small size of the language models in terms of vocabulary (words).

The second series of evaluations allows us to analyze the consequence of the complexity of the language model in terms of the number of commands trained on the recognition performance.

Table 1 shows a slight loss in WER (1%) obtained by switching from a 13-queries model (Model 1) to a 237-queries model (Model 4). On the other hand, in terms of response time, we see a loss of 21s / 208 evaluated queries from the M4 model compared to the M1 model.

6. Conclusion

In this paper, we presented LinTO, an open-source voice platform for business environments. It is a spoken language understanding system that achieves high performance in terms of accuracy and response time, is portable and scalable, and can be tailored to meet the needs of specific business contexts in the form of skills. We described the techniques and adaptations applied to the system's acoustic model and language model: for the acoustic model, we took advantage of recent advances in machine learning while optimizing computational cost; for the language model we trained the adapted automatic speech recognition component to correctly model only the sentences that are found in the domain supported by the SLU, which is implemented in a particular context. Overall, these techniques optimize a trade-off between the accuracy and computational cost by biasing and thus reducing the size of the language model.

7. Acknowledgements

This work was carried out as part of the research project assessed by Bpifrance (Public Investment Bank): LinTO - Open-source voice assistant that respects personal data for the company. The latter is financed by the French government as part of the "Programme des Investissements d'Avenir - Grands Défis du Numérique".

8. Bibliographical References

Bahdanau, D., Chorowski, J., Serdyuk, D., Brakel, P., and Bengio, Y. (2016). End-to-end attention-based large vocabulary speech recognition. In *2016 IEEE international conference on acoustics, speech and signal processing (ICASSP)*, pages 4945–4949. IEEE.

Chelba, C., Bikel, D., Shugrina, M., Nguyen, P., and Kumar, S. (2012a). Large scale language modeling in automatic speech recognition. *arXiv preprint arXiv:1210.8440*.

Chelba, C., Schalkwyk, J., Harb, B., Parada, C., Allauzen, C., Johnson, L., Riley, M., Xu, P., Jyothi, P., Brants, T., Ha, V., and Neveitt, W. (2012b). Language modeling for automatic speech recognition meets the web: Google search by voice.

Coucke, A., Saade, A., Ball, A., Bluche, T., Caulier, A., Leroy, D., Doumouro, C., Gisselbrecht, T., Caltagirone, F., Lavril, T., et al. (2018). Snips voice platform: an embedded spoken language understanding system for private-by-design voice interfaces. *arXiv preprint arXiv:1805.10190*.

Garimella, S., Mandal, A., Strom, N., Hoffmeister, B., Matsoukas, S., and Parthasarathi, S. H. K. (2015). Robust i-vector based adaptation of dnn acoustic model for speech recognition. In *Sixteenth Annual Conference of the International Speech Communication Association*.

Graves, A., Mohamed, A.-r., and Hinton, G. (2013). Speech recognition with deep recurrent neural networks. In *2013 IEEE international conference on acoustics, speech and signal processing*, pages 6645–6649. IEEE.

Hinton, G., Deng, L., Yu, D., Dahl, G. E., Mohamed, A.-r., Jaitly, N., Senior, A., Vanhoucke, V., Nguyen, P., Sainath, T. N., et al. (2012). Deep neural networks for acoustic modeling in speech recognition: The shared views of four research groups. *IEEE Signal processing magazine*, 29(6):82–97.

Levenshtein, V. I. (1966). Binary codes capable of correcting deletions, insertions, and reversals. In *Soviet physics doklady*, volume 10, pages 707–710.

Lu, L. (2019). A transformer with interleaved self-attention and convolution for hybrid acoustic models. *arXiv preprint arXiv:1910.10352*.

McAuliffe, M., Socolof, M., Mihuc, S., Wagner, M., and Sonderegger, M. (2017). Montreal forced aligner: Trainable text-speech alignment using kaldi. In *Interspeech*, pages 498–502.

Mohri, M., Pereira, F., and Riley, M. (2002). Weighted finite-state transducers in speech recognition. *Computer Speech & Language*, 16(1):69–88.

Peddinti, V., Povey, D., and Khudanpur, S. (2015). A time delay neural network architecture for efficient modeling of long temporal contexts. In *Sixteenth Annual Conference of the International Speech Communication Association*.

Pfleging, B., Schneegass, S., and Schmidt, A. (2012). Multimodal interaction in the car: combining speech and gestures on the steering wheel. In *Proceedings of the 4th International Conference on Automotive User Interfaces and Interactive Vehicular Applications*, pages 155–162.

Povey, D., Peddinti, V., Galvez, D., Ghahremani, P., Manohar, V., Na, X., Wang, Y., and Khudanpur, S. (2016). Purely sequence-trained neural networks for asr based on lattice-free mmi. In *Interspeech*, pages 2751–2755.

Serdyuk, D., Wang, Y., Fuegen, C., Kumar, A., Liu, B., and Bengio, Y. (2018). Towards end-to-end spoken language understanding. *CoRR*, abs/1802.08395.

Tur, G. and De Mori, R. (2011). *Spoken language understanding: Systems for extracting semantic information from speech*. John Wiley & Sons.

TURING, I. B. A. (1950). Computing machinery and intelligence-am turing. *Mind*, 59(236):433.

Waibel, A., Hanazawa, T., Hinton, G., Shikano, K., and Lang, K. J. (1989). Phoneme recognition using time-delay neural networks. *IEEE transactions on acoustics, speech, and signal processing*, 37(3):328–339.

Xiong, W., Droppo, J., Huang, X., Seide, F., Seltzer, M., Stolcke, A., Yu, D., and Zweig, G. (2016). Achieving human parity in conversational speech recognition. *arXiv preprint arXiv:1610.05256*.

Proceedings of the 1st International Workshop on Language Technology Platforms (IWLTP 2020), pages 96–107
Language Resources and Evaluation Conference (LREC 2020), Marseille, 11–16 May 2020
© European Language Resources Association (ELRA), licensed under CC-BY-NC

Towards an Interoperable Ecosystem of AI and LT Platforms:
A Roadmap for the Implementation of Different Levels of Interoperability

Georg Rehm[1], Dimitrios Galanis[2], Penny Labropoulou[2], Stelios Piperidis[2], Martin Welß[3], Ricardo Usbeck[3],
Joachim Köhler[3], Miltos Deligiannis[2], Katerina Gkirtzou[2], Johannes Fischer[4], Christian Chiarcos[5], Nils Feldhus[1],
Julián Moreno-Schneider[1], Florian Kintzel[1], Elena Montiel[6], Víctor Rodríguez Doncel[6], John P. McCrae[7], David Laqua[3],
Irina Patricia Theile[3], Christian Dittmar[4], Kalina Bontcheva[8], Ian Roberts[8], Andrejs Vasiljevs[9], Andis Lagzdiņš[9]

[1] DFKI GmbH, Germany • [2] ILSP/Athena RC, Greece • [3] Fraunhofer IAIS, Germany • [4] Fraunhofer IIS, Germany •
[5] Goethe University Frankfurt, Germany • [6] Universidad Politécnica de Madrid, Spain •
[7] National University of Ireland Galway, Ireland • [8] University of Sheffield, UK • [9] Tilde, Latvia

Corresponding author: Georg Rehm – georg.rehm@dfki.de

Abstract

With regard to the wider area of AI/LT platform interoperability, we concentrate on two core aspects: (1) cross-platform search and
discovery of resources and services; (2) composition of cross-platform service workflows. We devise five different levels (of increasing
complexity) of platform interoperability that we suggest to implement in a wider federation of AI/LT platforms. We illustrate the
approach using the five emerging AI/LT platforms AI4EU, ELG, Lynx, QURATOR and SPEAKER.

Keywords: LR Infrastructures and Architectures, LR National/International Projects, Tools, Systems, Applications, Web Services

1. Introduction

Due to recent breakthroughs in deep neural networks, artificial intelligence has been increasingly ubiquitous in the society and media. AI is now widely considered a continuous game-changer in every technology sector. While critical aspects need to be carefully considered, AI is perceived to be a big opportunity for many societal and economical challenges. As a prerequisite, a large number of AI platforms are currently under development, both on the national level, supported through local funding programmes, and on the international level, supported by the European Union. In addition to publicly-supported endeavours, many companies have been developing their own clouds to offer their respective services or products in their targeted sectors (including legal, finance, health etc.). Positioned orthogonally to these verticals, Language Technology (LT) platforms typically offer domain-independent, sometimes domain-specific, services for the analysis or production of written or spoken language. LT platforms can be conceptualised as language-centric AI platforms: they use AI methods to implement their functionalities. Various European LT platforms exist, both commercial and non-commercial, including large-scale research infrastructures.

The enormous fragmentation of the European AI and LT landscape is a challenge and bottleneck when it comes to the identification of synergies, market capitalisation as well as boosting technology adoption and uptake (Rehm et al., 2020c). The fragmentation also relates to the number and heterogeneity of AI/LT platforms. If we do not make sure that all these platforms are able to exchange information, data and services, their increasing proliferation will further contribute to the fragmentation rather than solve it. This can be achieved by agreeing upon and implementing standardised ways of exchanging repository entries and other types of metadata or functional services, or enabling multi-platform and multi-vendor service workflows, benefitting

from their respective unique offerings. Only by discussing and agreeing upon standards as well as technical and operational concepts for AI/LT platform interoperability, can we benefit from the highly fragmented landscape and its specialised platforms. This paper takes a few initial steps, which we demonstrate primarily using the two platforms AI4EU and ELG (European Language Grid) but also including QURATOR, Lynx and SPEAKER. These platforms are introduced in Section 2, where we also compare their architectures. Section 3 introduces requirements and prerequisites for platform interoperability, including shared semantics as well as legal and operational interoperability, followed by a description of five levels of platform interoperability that exhibit an increasing level of conceptual complexity. Section 4 summarises the paper and presents next steps. We contribute to the challenge of platform interoperability by identifying this topic as a crucial common development target and by suggesting a roadmap for the implementation of different levels of interoperability.

2. The Platforms

In the following, we describe the platforms AI4EU (Section 2.1), ELG (Section 2.2), QURATOR (Section 2.3), Lynx (Section 2.4) and SPEAKER (Section 2.5).

2.1. AI4EU

In January 2019, the AI4EU consortium with more than 80 partners started its work to build the first European AI on-demand platform. The main goals are: the creation and support of a large European ecosystem to facilitate collaboration between all European AI actors (scientists, entrepreneurs, SMEs, industries, funding agencies, citizens etc.); the design of a European AI on-demand platform to share AI resources produced in European projects, including high-level services, expertise in research and innovation, components and data sets, high-powered computing resources and access to seed funding for innovative

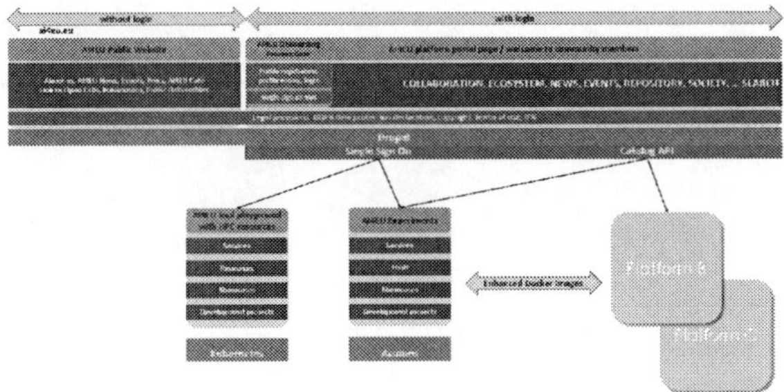

Figure 1: AI4EU logical structure

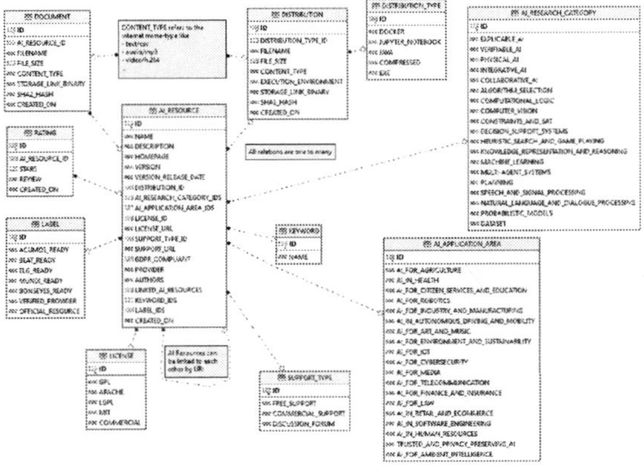

Figure 2: AI4EU metadata model

projects; the implementation of industry-led pilots, which demonstrate the platform's capabilities to enable real applications and foster innovation; research in five key areas (explainable AI, physical AI, verifiable AI, collaborative AI, integrative AI); the creation of a European ethical observatory to ensure that European AI projects adhere to high ethical, legal, and socio-economical standards; the preparation of a Strategic Research Innovation Agenda for Europe.

The AI4EU platform consists of several subsystems. In this paper, we focus on the AI4EU Repository and AI4EU Experiments, which are at the core of all interoperability topics. The repository exposes the Catalog API, which is based on the AI4EU metadata model, in the center of which is the AI resource: this can be any relevant entity like trained models, data sets, tools for symbolic AI, tools to build AI pipelines etc. AI resources can be linked to each other, e. g., a trained model could be linked to the data set used for training. The license information is mandatory demonstrating the emphasis on lawful reuse of resources. Documents, pictures and binary artefacts can be associated with a resource. However, AI resources cannot be combined or worked with in the repository itself. That leads us to the AI4EU Experiments subsystem, which enables the quick and visual composition of AI solutions using tools with published, well-known interfaces. These solutions can be training or production pipelines or pipelines to check or verify models. The subsystem enables easily to connect tools to data sets via databrokers or datastreams. It includes tools and models for symbolic AI, ethical AI and verifiable AI, and allows

for collaboration and feedback (discussion, ratings, workgroups). It also supports mixed teams, e. g., with business users and external AI experts to bootstrap AI adoption in SMEs. To combine tools to runnable pipelines, the expected format of an AI resource is an enhanced Docker container, which (1) contains a license file for the resource; (2) includes a self-contained protobuf[1] specification of the service, defining all input and output data structures; (3) exposes the above service using gRPC.[2] Protobuf and gRPC are both open source and programming language-neutral and, thus, a solid foundation for interoperability, especially when combined with Docker.

Interoperability is addressed at the following levels: (1) AI4EU supports the bidirectional exchange of metadata of AI resources, i. e., to send and receive catalog entries. Since AI4EU is prepared to connect with other platforms, it takes the approach of focussing the metadata on the least common denominator. This docking point is the Catalog API. (2) To contribute to a distributed search across several platforms, AI4EU provides a search API. It accepts remote queries, executes them on the catalog and returns a list of matches from the AI4EU repository. (3) The Docker container format used in AI4EU Experiments.

2.2. European Language Grid (ELG)

Multilingualism and cross-lingual communication in Europe can only be enabled through Language Technologies (LTs) (Rehm et al., 2016). The European LT landscape is fragmented (Vasiljevs et al., 2019), holding back its impact. Another crucial issue is that many languages are under-resourced and, thus, in danger of digital extinction (Rehm and Uszkoreit, 2012; Kornai, 2013; Rehm et al., 2014). There is an enormous need for an European LT platform as a unifying umbrella (Rehm and Uszkoreit, 2013; Rehm et al., 2016; STOA, 2017; Rehm, 2017; Rehm and Hegele, 2018; European Parliament, 2018; Rehm et al., 2020c).

The project European Language Grid (2019-2021) attempts to establish the primary platform and marketplace for the European LT community, both industry and research (Rehm et al., 2020a). This scalable cloud platform will provide access to hundreds of LTs for all European languages, including running services as well as data sets. ELG will enable the European LT community to upload their technologies and data sets, to deploy them, and to connect with other resources. ELG caters for *commercial* and *non-commercial LTs* (i. e., LTs with a high Technology Readiness Level, TRL), both *functional* (processing and generation, written and spoken) and *non-functional* (data sets etc.). The platform has a user interface, backend components and APIs. Functional services are made available through containerisation and by wrapping them with the ELG LT Service API.[3] These services, provided initially by members of the ELG consortium and ultimately by many external partners, can be used through APIs or the web UI (Figure 3).

The *base infrastructure* is operated on a Kubernetes[4] cluster in the data centre of a Berlin-based cloud provider. All

---

[1] https://developers.google.com/protocol-buffers
[2] https://grpc.io
[3] https://gitlab.com/european-language-grid/platform/
[4] https://kubernetes.io

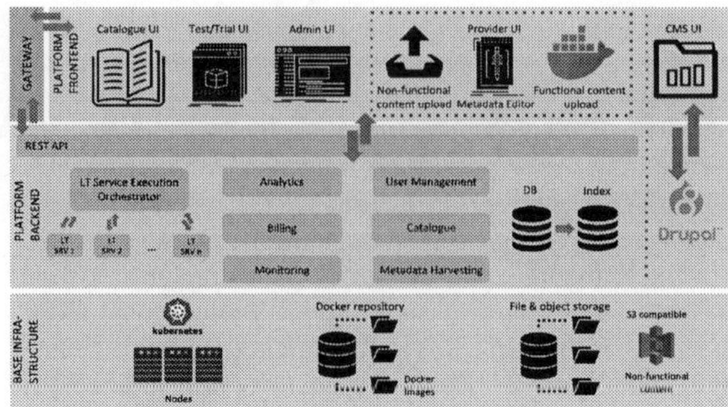

Figure 3: Technical architecture of the ELG

infrastructural components of the three layers run in this cluster as Docker containers. They are built with robust, scalable, reliable and widely used technologies and frameworks, e. g., Django, Drupal, ReactJS, AngularJS.

The *backend* contains the catalogue, i. e., the list of metadata records of services, resources, organisations (e. g., companies, universities, research centres), service types, languages etc. Stakeholders will be able to register themselves, ensuring increased reach and visibility. Users can filter and search for organisations, services, data sets and more, by language, service type, domain, and country. Functionalities are offered via REST services. Metadata records are stored in PostgreSQL and ElasticSearch. The LT Service Execution Server offers a common REST API.

The *frontend* consists of UIs for different user types, e. g., LT providers, buyers and system administrators. These include catalogue UIs, test UIs for functional services, provider UIs for uploading/registering services etc.

ELG uses Docker containers to encapsulate all components, settings and libraries of an individual LT service in one self-contained unit. Docker images can be built locally by their developers and ingested into the ELG, where they can be started, terminated and scaled out on demand. Containers can be also replaced easily.

Kubernetes is used for container orchestration. It decides autonomously how many replicas of an LT service are needed at any given point in time.[5] The integration of a service into the ELG currently consists of six steps: (1) adapt the service to the ELG API; (2) create a Docker image; (3) push the Docker image into a registry (e. g., ELG Gitlab); (4) request, from the ELG administrators, a Kubernetes namespace, in case of a proprietary service with restricted access; (5) deploy the service by creating a Kubernetes config file; (6) add the service to the ELG catalogue by providing the metadata. For some of the approx. 175 services currently in the ELG, this process took a few days, for others, only a few hours. Our goal is to bring this effort down to a minimum, at least for the most common cases.

The ELG metadata schema (Labropoulou et al., 2020) supports discovery and operation for humans and machines. It describes Language Resources and Technologies (LRTs) and related entities (organizations, persons, projects, etc.; Figure 4). The schema is organised around three concepts:

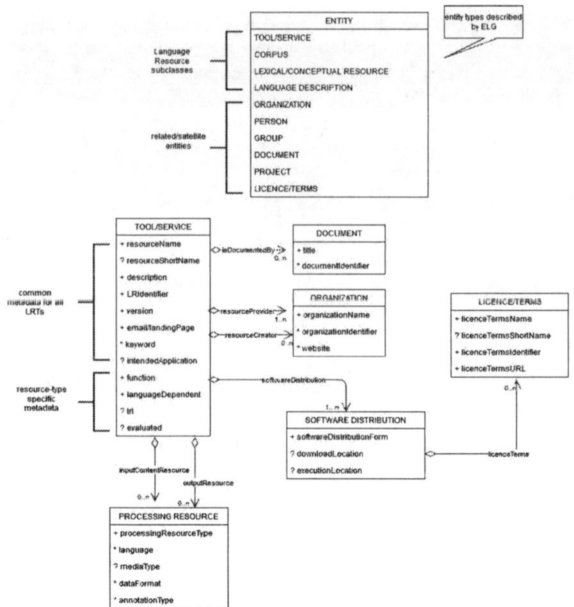

Figure 4: Excerpt of the ELG metadata schema

resource type (tool or service, corpus, lexical or conceptual resource, language description), *media type* (text, audio, video, image) and *distribution*, i. e., the physical form of the resource (e. g., software distributed as web services, source or binary code). Administrative and descriptive metadata (e. g., identification, contact, licensing information, etc.) are common to all LRTs, while technical metadata differ across resource/media type and distributions.

Interoperability is addressed at the following levels: (1) exchange of metadata records from and to other, external catalogues: the schema exploits an RDF/OWL ontology (McCrae et al., 2015) with links to widespread vocabularies and ontologies and the possibility to be further enriched with those of collaborating initiatives; (2) interoperability across resource types, supporting the automatic match of (a) candidate resources that can be combined together to form a workflow (e. g., matching input and output formats of tools to create pipelines, models of a specific type with tools that can utilize them), and (b) data resources with functional services that can be used for their processing (e. g., an English NER tool with English data sets etc.).

2.3. QURATOR: Curation Technologies

Online content has recently gained immense importance in many areas of society. Some of the challenges include better support and smarter technologies for content curators who are exposed to an ever increasing stream of heterogeneous information they need to process, e. g., knowledge workers in libraries digitize archives, add metadata and publish them online, journalists need to continuously stay up to date on their current topic of investigation. Many work environments would benefit immensely from technologies that support content curators (Rehm and Sasaki, 2015).

The QURATOR consortium consists of ten partners from industry and research (Rehm et al., 2020b). The project de-

---

[5]For autoscaling and scale-to-zero functionalities, ELG uses Knative (https://cloud.google.com/knative).

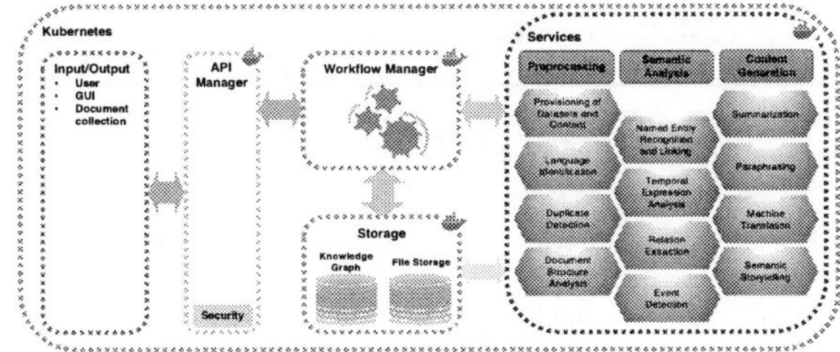

Figure 5: Technical architecture of the QURATOR platform

velops a curation technology platform, which is also being populated with services, simplifying and accelerating the curation of content (Bourgonje et al., 2016a; Rehm et al., 2019a; Schneider and Rehm, 2018a; Schneider and Rehm, 2018b). The project develops, evaluates and integrates services for preprocessing, analyzing and generating content, spanning use cases from the sectors of culture, media, health and industry. To process and transform incoming data, text or multimedia streams into device-adapted, publishable content, various groups of components, services and technologies are applied. These include adapters to data, content and knowledge sources, as well as infrastructural tools and AI methods for the acquisition, analysis and generation of content. All these different technologies are combined into pilots and prototypes for selected use case.

The QURATOR platform (Figure 5) is designed together with all partners who also contribute services, which can be divided into three broad groups: (1) *Preprocessing* encompasses services for obtaining and processing information from different content sources so that they can be used in the platform and integrated into other services (Schneider et al., 2018), e. g., provisioning content, language and duplicate detection as well as document structure recognition. (2) *Semantic analysis services* process a document and add information in the form of annotations, e. g., NER, temporal expression analysis, relation extraction, event detection, fake news as well as discourse analysis (Bourgonje et al., 2016b; Srivastava et al., 2016; Rehm et al., 2017b; Ostendorff et al., 2019). (3) *Content generation services* enable the creation of a new piece of content, e. g., summarization, paraphrasing, and semantic storytelling (Rehm et al., 2019c; Rehm et al., 2018; Moreno-Schneider et al., 2017; Rehm et al., 2017a; Schneider et al., 2017; Schneider et al., 2016).

Interoperability is addressed at the following levels: Since the QURATOR platform is a closed ecosystem, the platform can be thought of as an experimental toolbox with services customised by the partners for their own use cases. As the platform is used only by the QURATOR partners, it does not contain a catalogue or any kind or structured metadata. However, two of the ten QURATOR projects have a focus on service composition and workflows with prototypical implementations under development (Moreno-Schneider et al., 2020a), using NIF as a joint annotation format (Hellmann et al., 2013).

2.4. Lynx: Legal Knowledge Graph Platform

The project Lynx produces a multilingual Legal Knowledge Graph (LKG), in which data sources from different jurisdic-

tions, languages and orders are aggregated and interlinked by a collection of analysis and curation services. Lynx aims to facilitate compliance of SMEs and other companies in internationalisation processes, leveraging European legal and regulatory open data duly interlinked and offered through cross-sectorial, cross-lingual services. The platform is tested in three pilots that develop solutions for legal compliance, regulatory regimes and compliance, where legal provisions, case law, administrative resolutions, and expert literature are interlinked, analysed, and compared to inform strategies for legal practice.

The platform (Figure 6) focuses upon three main components: (1) semantic services for the extraction of information from large and heterogeneous sets of documents; (2) the LKG (Montiel-Ponsoda and Rodríguez-Doncel, 2018; Schneider and Rehm, 2018a; Martín-Chozas et al., 2019) stores linguistic and legal information from documents; (3) the workflow manager realises complex use cases.

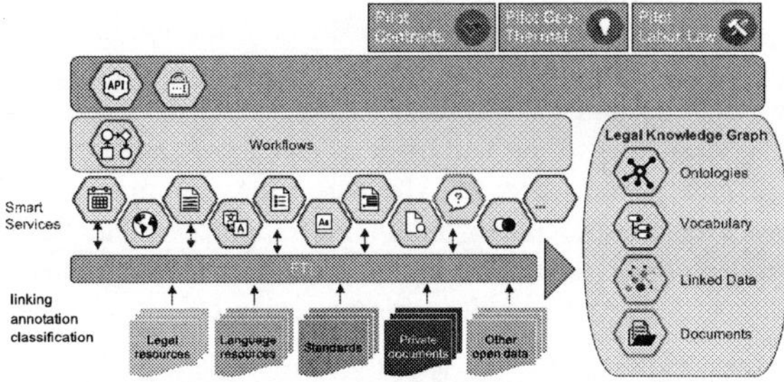

Figure 6: The Lynx technology platform

The platform's microservice architecture is a variant of the service-oriented architecture (SOA), in which an application is structured as a collection of loosely coupled services. It uses Docker containers hosted and managed through OpenShift, a containerisation software built on top of Kubernetes.[6] Services communicate through REST APIs. The platform includes a heterogeneous set of services (Rehm et al., 2019b).[7] Some of the services make use of others, some extract or annotate information, while others operate on full documents, yet others provide a user interface. The Document Manager provides the storage and annotation of documents with an emphasis on keeping them synchronized, providing read and write access, as well as updates of documents and annotations. It can be queried in terms of annotations and documents, through REST APIs. The interface includes a set of create, read, update, and delete APIs to manage collections, documents and annotations. The orchestration and execution of services involved in more complex tasks is addressed by a Workflow Manager. It defines combinations of services as workflows (Moreno-Schneider et al., 2020b; Bourgonje et al., 2016a; Schneider and Rehm, 2018a; Schneider and Rehm, 2018b). Workflows are described using BPMN and executed using Camunda.[8]

Interoperability is addressed at the following levels: Like all previously described platforms, the Lynx platform

---

[6]https://www.openshift.com
[7]http://lynx-project.eu/doc/api/
[8]https://camunda.com

is based on microservices orchestrated as containers. Like the QURATOR platform, the Lynx platform does not contain a structured catalogue with metadata entries other than Open API descriptions, because some services have restricted access and, so far, are only used by the project partners. While the QURATOR platform is populated with a large variety of services, the development of the domain-specific Lynx services is primarily driven by three focused use cases. The Lynx platform includes a workflow manager. Lynx defines an RDF-based data model, which reuses NIF (Hellmann et al., 2013), ELI (European Legislation Identifier) metadata elements and other standard specifications. A SHACL-based validator grants conformance and favours interoperability.

2.5. SPEAKER

The SPEAKER project develops a B2B conversational agent platform "Made in Germany". A secondary aim is the creation of a vivid ecosystem. Numerous partners, such as large industrial companies, SMEs, start-ups and research partners ensure the project's practical relevance, as well as academic excellence. Industry expressed a strong demand for a speech assistant platform that can accommodate specific application scenarios. These use cases comprise, e. g., an automated speech recognition (ASR) component that can be adapted to recognize technical terms or the unification of company-internal knowledge graphs using NLP.

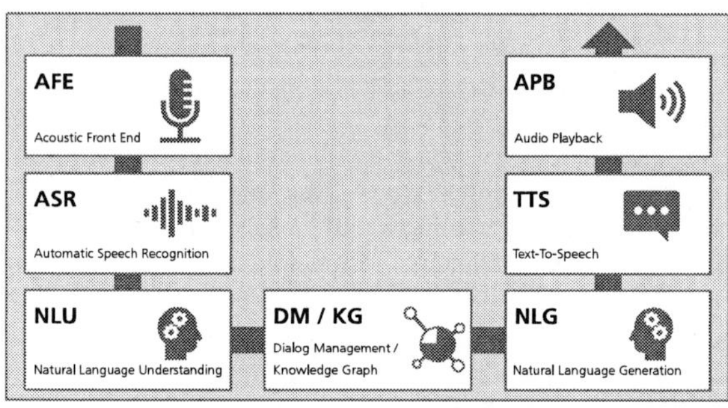

Figure 7: Flexible workflow components in SPEAKER

The speech solutions developed by the large technology providers based on other continents do not offer the required customizability nor do they comply with GDPR. Thus, they do not meet the data protection standards required by many of the SPEAKER industry partners. In many use cases, data that needs to be handled by a conversational agent is either sensitive (e. g., medical records) or company secrets, the confidentiality of which must not be jeopardized.

The platform will comprise core modules such as AFE, ASR, NLU, DM/KG, NLG, TTS and APB. These can be combined to implement complete B2B voice assistant applications (Figure 7). Each module can also be deployed individually, customized to the targeted use case. Platform interoperability will be investigated during the lifetime of the project. The SPEAKER partners have the necessary know-how and expertise (Usbeck, 2014; Both et al., 2014; Singh et al., 2018; Shet et al., 2019; Govalkar et al., 2019; Fischer et al., 2016; Chakrabarty and Habets, 2019), enabling them to develop this flexible and scalable platform.

Interoperability is addressed at the following levels: SPEAKER will provide a modular, customizable platform based on mature, existing components. It is intended to implement the industry partners' use cases in a close to production ready fashion. Thus, high quality and reliable services with the additional privacy features are required. SPEAKER will investigate interfaces to other platforms in order to facilitate interoperability. SPEAKER is less open to ensure a high level of trust and data privacy. In contrast to QURATOR and Lynx, it will have a structured service catalog for self-servicing. SPEAKER will offer an orchestration component to enable the flexible composition of voice assistants. Services will be containerised using Docker and hence be pluggable into on-premise computing landscapes.

2.6. Common Aspects and Functionalities

The five platforms share several common aspects but also differ substantially with regard to other dimensions and requirements. Table 1 provides a comparison. While AI4EU caters for AI at large, ELG concentrates on LT, i. e., language-centric AI. Lynx, QURATOR and SPEAKER focus upon specific domains and application areas within LT. AI4EU and ELG are community-driven, open platforms through which third parties can make available services or resources, while the other three are closed, i. e., populated by their respective project consortia with the goal of commercial exploitation. All platforms make use of microservices and orchestrate their containers through base infrastructures that provide mechanisms for scaling. Structured repositories of services and resources are maintained in AI4EU, ELG and SPEAKER; all platforms with a repository also have a graphical user interface enabling search and discovery of resources. Workflows are at least partially addressed in all platforms except ELG; however, it is planned to evaluate if the QURATOR approach can be integrated into the ELG platform (Moreno-Schneider et al., 2020a). Table 1 also includes ranges with regard to the targeted Technology Readiness Level (TRL) of the platforms and their services.[9] The individual TRLs indicate the range between a rather experimental and a more production-ready stage of the platform initiatives and their services.

Technically and conceptually, interoperability between these or other AI/LT platforms can be addressed with regard to the repository layer, the API layer, the functional service layer (workflows) or the computation layer.

3. Platform Interoperability

Platform interoperability can be achieved with regard to various different aspects. We concentrate on two that are inspired by the heterogeneous European landscape: (1) cross-platform search and discovery of resources and (2) composition of cross-platform workflows. The broad and robust implementation of these two feature sets makes it possible to use the search functionality of platform A with specific criteria and to receive matches, if any, from all platforms attached to platform A. The cross-platform composition of service workflows enables putting together distributed processing pipelines that make use of REST services hosted

---

[9]https://en.wikipedia.org/wiki/Technology_readiness_level

	Scope	Domain-specific	Open vs. Closed	Infrastructure	Structured Catalogue	Functional Microservices	Workflows possible	Targeted TRL of …	
								platform	services
AI4EU → https://www.ai4eu.eu – Runtime: 01/2019–12/2021	Europe	no (AI at large)	Open	Kubernetes, Acumos, Drupal	yes	yes	yes	7-9	6-9
ELG → https://www.european-language-grid.eu – Runtime: 01/2019–12/2021	Europe	no (LT at large)	Open	Kubernetes, Drupal	yes	yes	no	7-9	5-9
Lynx → http://lynx-project.eu – Runtime: 12/2017–11/2020	Europe	Legal domain	Closed	OpenShift	no	yes	yes	7-8	6-8
QURATOR → https://qurator.ai – Runtime: 11/2018–10/2021	Germany	Curation services	Closed	Kubernetes	no	yes	partially	4-6	3-8
SPEAKER → https://www.speaker.fraunhofer.de – Runtime: 04/2020–03/2023	Germany	Voice Assistants	Closed	Kubernetes	yes	yes	yes	8-9	8-9

Table 1: Central characteristics of selected emerging European AI/LT platforms

on different platforms. We can even think of more complex service development scenarios in which we, e. g., take a data set, hosted on ELG, ingest it into the AI4EU Experiments instance, train a new model and move the resulting Kubernetes artefact back into ELG, describing it with metadata, making it available to all platforms.

Before we provide more details on the five levels of platform interoperability (Sections 3.2 to 3.6), we discuss the benefits of using a shared semantic space for achieving interoperability; we also describe a solution for creating it in the form of a reference model acting as a bridge between the metadata schemas of the different platforms and that may also provide interoperability on the level of exchange formats or annotations (Section 3.1). Finally, Section 3.7 discusses the aspect of legal and operational interoperability.

3.1. Shared Semantic Space

For the more advanced levels of platform interoperability (Level 2 and upwards), a shared semantic space is needed as a joint, ontologically grounded and machine-readable vocabulary, into which all platform-specific concepts and terminologies can be mapped so that abstract conceptualisations originating in a platform, e. g., names of service categories or specific annotation labels, can be interpreted. Such a shared semantic space explicitly represents knowledge about various different aspects, including, among others: (1) categories of resources including different types of data resources (data set, corpus, lexicon, terminology, language model, etc.) and different types of tools and functional services (NER, parser, image classifier, facial expression detector, etc.); (2) abstract descriptions of the I/O requirements of tools and services (data formats, languages, modalities etc.); (3) attributes and values used in specific annotation formats and tagsets including metadata about annotation formats themselves.

As a first step, interoperability can be achieved by mapping two schemas onto each other and creating converters. However, such an approach does not scale because we would need to create new converters for each new platform "attached" to this federation of platforms. In contrast, the proposed shared semantic space can function as a reference model that is able to represent all crucial information typically contained in the respective platform-specific metadata scheme. Alternatively, all platforms should adhere to a joint RDF/OWL ontology for their semantic metadata. On top

of the domain-independent semantic categories, there is the challenge of representing domain-specific terms and concepts. Even for general categories, communities tend to use different terms for similar concepts, which makes the adoption of a single joint ontology an almost impossible task (Labropoulou et al., 2018).

This is not the first attempt at such a shared semantic space. Previous experience does, however, show, that centralized repositories for data categories may face long-term sustainability issues (Langendoen, 2019; Warburton and Wright, 2019). As an alternative, one may consider to follow a Linked Data approach, where concepts and definitions of different providers are defined in a self-contained formal model, e. g., an ontology, and subsequently refer to vocabularies or reference concepts developed in a distributed fashion by the broader community.

This approach can be exemplified by the Ontologies of Linguistic Annotation (Chiarcos, 2008; Chiarcos and Sukhareva, 2015), a central hub for linguistic annotation terminology in the web of data. OLiA was designed for mediating between various terminology repositories on the one hand and annotated resources (i. e., their annotation schemes), on the other. Four different types of ontologies are distinguished (Fig. 8): (1) The OLiA Reference Model is an OWL ontology that specifies the common terminology that different annotation schemes can refer to. (2) Multiple OLiA Annotation Models formalize annotation schemes and tagsets. Fig. 8 illustrates this with an annotation model developed as part of the Korean NLP2RDF stack (Hahm et al., 2012). (3) For every annotation model, a linking model defines subclass-relationships between concepts in the annotation model and the reference model. Linking models are interpretations of annotation model concepts and properties in terms of the reference model. (4) Similarly, other community-maintained vocabularies are linked with OLiA, e. g., the CLARIN Concept Registry (Chiarcos et al., 2020). OLiA was developed as part of an infrastructure for the sustainable maintenance of linguistic resources (Wörner et al., 2006; Schmidt et al., 2006; Rehm et al., 2008b; Witt et al., 2009; Rehm et al., 2009). Its field of application included the formalization of annotation schemes and concept-based querying over heterogeneously annotated corpora (Rehm et al., 2008a). As several institutions and resources from various disciplines were involved, no holistic annotation standard could be enforced onto the contributors.

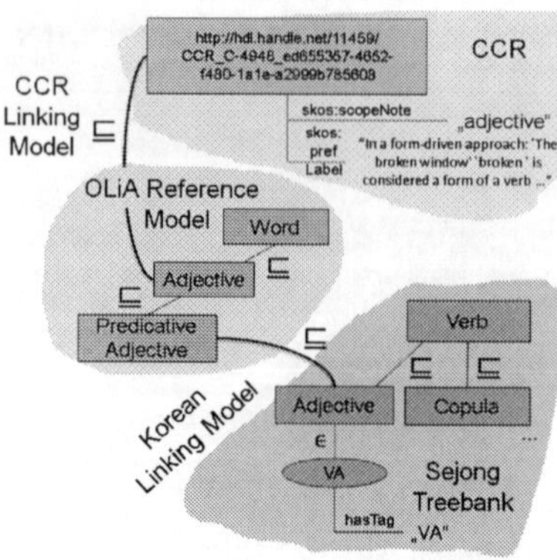

Figure 8: Modular OLiA ontologies

3.2. Level 1: Simple Cross-Platform Search through Public APIs

The first level of platform interoperability relates to simple cross-platform search through publicly available search and discovery APIs for resources offered by the platforms, i. e., data sets, functional services, tools, workflows, lists of organisations etc. Making the search API of a platform available to third parties enables other platform providers to integrate it in their own search facilities and, thus, to include the resources of this platform into their search space. This way, a query would return matches from all platforms. Search results need to show only minimal metadata and redirect the user to the original platform. Realising this level of interoperability requires only a limited amount of discussion and agreement between the platform operators with regard to metadata schemes, their semantics or the data format returned by the search API.

3.3. Level 2: Complex Cross-Platform Search through the Exchange of Metadata Records

One disadvantage of Level 1 interoperability relates to the fact that the user experience will be rather lacking because the search results retrieved from external platforms are difficult to integrate and aggregate into the search results of the local platform due to the lack of a shared semantic space; ranking search results is equally difficult. Level 2 foresees either aligning all platforms involved in such a federation of platforms along a shared semantic space that explicitly provides semantics for the metadata fields and their values, or agreeing upon the same metadata scheme or at least upon a certain (obligatory) subset (Labropoulou et al., 2020; McCrae et al., 2015). Such a more detailed, semantics-driven approach enables more efficient and more user-friendly search results from multiple platforms that can be visually aggregated and also easily ranked. The actual search can be performed through publicly available APIs but returned objects would be semantically richer. Alternatively, the metadata records of external repositories can be harvested using standard protocols such as OAI-PMH, which allow the construction of a master index out of decentralised inventories (Piperidis, 2012). A known issue that needs to be addressed using such an approach involves the detection of duplicate resources.

3.4. Level 3: Manual Service Composition into Cross-Platform Workflows

While the two previous levels refer to search and discovery, the other three levels relate to cross-platform service workflows. The idea is to make use of the respective platforms' specific services to benefit from the best possible workflows as bespoke processing pipelines. The easiest way to realise cross-platform workflows is to develop them manually; this requires knowledge of the APIs and technologies used for each service/tool involved in the workflow and the development of the required wrappers for making them compatible with the workflow execution system.

Figure 9 demonstrates a working example for automated translation from German to Latvian (through English), followed by running the Latvian translation through a dependency parser. If a workflow is developed manually, incompatibilities with regard to data formats are not relevant. Furthermore, regardless of their implementation as server- or client-side code, such workflows could be described as first-class citizens of the respective repository using its metadata scheme (i. e., the workflow gets a name, ID, description etc.) and stored in the repository so that other users can discover, retrieve, potentially modify and apply them.

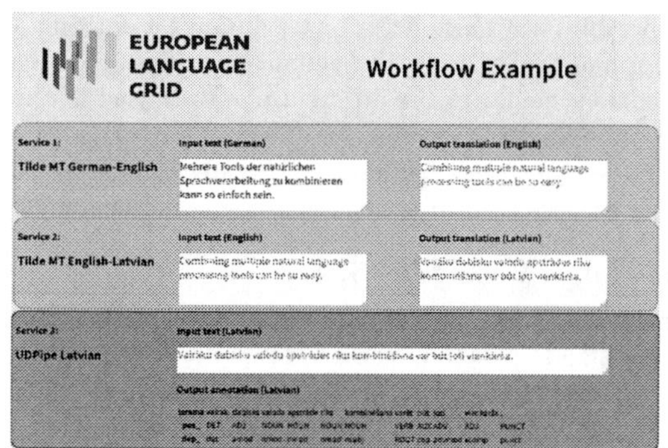

Figure 9: A cross-platform workflow example

A similar approach was implemented in the project Open-MinTeD (OMTD) (Labropoulou et al., 2018) using the Galaxy workflow management system.[10] Three types of LT components are supported: (1) components packaged in Docker images that follow the OMTD specifications; (2) components wrapped with UIMA or GATE, available in a Maven repository; (3) Text and Data Mining web services that run outside the OMTD platform and that follow the OMTD specifications. Each component is registered in the OMTD repository by providing a metadata record. These are curated by the platform administrators and published in the catalogue when the components have been checked for conformity to the OMTD specifications. For each component, a Galaxy wrapper was automatically created from the metadata record and ingested to the Galaxy server. A Galaxy wrapper is an XML file[11] that allows (1) adding the component to the toolbox of the workflow editor and (2) invoking the component. The LT providers or other OMTD

---

[10]https://galaxyproject.org

[11]https://docs.galaxyproject.org/en/latest/dev/schema.html

Level	Description	Complexity	What is required from each participating platform?
1	Simple cross-platform search	*	Publicly available repository index or repository search API
2	Complex cross-platform search	**	Exchange of repository metadata records with shared semantics
3	Manuel composition of cross-platform workflows	***	Publicly available service APIs; legal and organisational interoperability
4	Automated service composition into cross-platform workflows	****	Publicly available service APIs with complete semantic descriptions
5	Sophisticated cross-platform development workflows	*****	Protocols for the automated training and exchange of resources (models etc.)

Table 2: Five levels of AI/LT platform interoperability (focusing upon service discovery as well as workflow composition)

users can use Galaxy to chain LT components into workflows, set parameters and publish the workflow. Each processing step is executed as a command line tool within a Docker container in a Mesos cluster.

3.5. Level 4: Automated Service Composition into Cross-Platform Workflows

In addition to Level 3, we can foresee a more sophisticated way of composing cross-platform workflows grounded in deep semantic descriptions of the corresponding APIs and data formats. If the workflow manager has access to semantic metadata that describe the services' requirements regarding APIs and data formats, workflows can be partially automated through GUIs that enable their composition. The difference to Level 3 is that the workflow manager, or the different platforms, have access to explicitly represented knowledge that describes which services are interoperable, i. e., the manual mapping of data formats and their attributes or values is not necessary. For this to work, services and workflows need to be first class citizens of the metadata scheme (including persistence, discovery, retrieval, billing etc.); all data formats need to be agreed upon or made interoperable through a shared semantic space.

3.6. Level 5: Sophisticated Cross-Platform AI/LT Development Workflows

The last level of platform interoperability relates to fully realised and automated AI/LT development workflows. This scenario enables the automated development of new AI/LT tools by providing fully interoperable data and tool exchange pipelines. For example, an annotated data set available in ELG could be made available to AI4EU by ingesting it into AI4EU's Experiments instance, training a new model and then moving the resulting Kubernetes artefact back into ELG with an automatically pre-filled partial metadata record. As the metadata records are available cross-platform, the resulting new resource is also automatically discoverable through AI4EU's search (Levels 1 and 2).

3.7. Legal and Operational Interoperability

In addition to the technical and organisational aspects, which are the main focus of this article, there are the dimensions of legal and operational interoperability, which are equally complex and which also need to be successfully addressed to arrive at full platform interoperability. Here, we can only scratch the surface.

An important aspect relates to authentication and authorisation. Do platforms only expose services and resources that can be freely shared? Can a registered user of platform X, who searches for service A on platform X and finds it in platform Y, use service A in platform Y, in which the user is *not* registered? Technically, this can be solved easily but in order to arrive at a solution that works for all parties and platforms involved, legal interoperability must be reached, i. e., collaboration agreements and policies need to be drawn up and endorsed by all. Legal interoperability also relates to the standard licenses that platforms need to agree upon for sharing different types of digital objects, from data sets to language models to containerised processing services. Especially with regard to commercial services and cross-platform workflows that include such services, policies and mechanisms for billing and brokering need to be agreed upon. For the formal representation of licensing terms and policies, the W3C standard Open Digital Rights Language (ODRL) offers a good solution (Iannella et al., 2018; Iannella and Villata, 2018).

4. Conclusions and Next Steps

The interoperability of the AI and LT platforms our community develops is of crucial importance collaboratively to develop something that is, jointly, more useful and more innovative than the sum of its parts. However, achieving platform interoperability requires commitment and effort by all parties involved, i. e., the platform developers need to be cooperative and actually *want* to participate in a wider group of interoperable platforms. To achieve Level 1 interoperability, a participating platform needs to offer a documented and public search API for (parts of) its repository and, for more advanced levels, also access to documented and public APIs for its processing services to enable the manual or automated composition of service workflows (Table 2).

Platform interoperability can be realised on various levels, from simple to highly complex. As an initial roadmap, the authors would like to suggest to the AI/LT community to start implementing platform interoperability at Level 1 and then attempt to realise the various stages up to Level 5. There is a multitude of aspects that can and must be addressed in addition to cross-platform search and cross-platform service workflows, among others, user authentication, shared data storage, shared compute infrastructure as well as shared organisational and legal approaches. An instrument to arrive at joint understanding of shared technical concepts is standardisation, which could include processing APIs and the shared semantic space (vocabulary, location, functionalities etc.). A joint European approach towards platform interoperability could provide a competitive advantage when compared to the very-large-industry-driven developments followed on other continents.

Acknowledgments

The work presented in this paper has received funding from the European Union's Horizon 2020 research and innovation programme under grant agreements no. 825627 (European Language Grid), no. 825619 (AI4EU), no. 825182 (Prêt-à-LLOD) and no. 780602 (Lynx) as well as from the German Federal Ministry of Education and Research (BMBF) through the project QURATOR (Wachstumskern no. 03WKDA1A) and from the German Federal Ministry for Economic Affairs and Energy (BMWi) through the project SPEAKER (no. 01MK19011). Finally, the authors would like to thank all project teams involved in the different projects for their respective contributions.

5. Bibliographical References

Both, A., Ngonga, A.-C. N., Usbeck, R., Lukovnikov, D., Lemke, C., and Speicher, M. (2014). A service-oriented search framework for full text, geospatial and semantic search. In *SEMANTiCS 2014*.

Bourgonje, P., Moreno-Schneider, J., Nehring, J., Rehm, G., Sasaki, F., and Srivastava, A. (2016a). Towards a Platform for Curation Technologies: Enriching Text Collections with a Semantic-Web Layer. In Harald Sack, et al., editors, *The Semantic Web*, number 9989 in Lecture Notes in Computer Science, pages 65–68. Springer, June. ESWC 2016 Satellite Events. Heraklion, Crete, Greece, May 29 – June 2, 2016 Revised Selected Papers.

Bourgonje, P., Schneider, J. M., Rehm, G., and Sasaki, F. (2016b). Processing Document Collections to Automatically Extract Linked Data: Semantic Storytelling Technologies for Smart Curation Workflows. In Aldo Gangemi et al., editors, *Proceedings of the 2nd International Workshop on Natural Language Generation and the Semantic Web (WebNLG 2016)*, pages 13–16, Edinburgh, UK, September. The Association for Computational Linguistics.

Chakrabarty, S. and Habets, E. A. (2019). Time–frequency masking based online multi-channel speech enhancement with convolutional recurrent neural networks. *IEEE Journal of Selected Topics in Signal Processing*, 13(4):787–799.

Chiarcos, C. and Sukhareva, M. (2015). OLiA – Ontologies of Linguistic Annotation. *Semantic Web Journal*, 518:379–386.

Chiarcos, C., Fäth, C., and Abromeit, F. (2020). Annotation interoperability in the post-ISOCat era, May. Accepted for publication.

Chiarcos, C. (2008). An ontology of linguistic annotations. *LDV Forum*, 23(1):1–16.

European Parliament. (2018). Report on language equality in the digital age. http://www.europarl.europa.eu/doceo/document/A-8-2018-0228_EN.html, September. (2018/2028(INI)). Committee on Culture and Education (CULT), Committee on Industry, Research and Energy (ITRE); Rapporteur: Jill Evans.

Fischer, J., Bhardwaj, K., Breiling, M., Leyh, M., and Bäckström, T. (2016). Ultra-low power acoustic front-ends for natural language user interfaces. In *VDE Kongress Internet der Dinge*.

Govalkar, P., Fischer, J., Zalkow, F., and Dittmar, C. (2019). A comparison of recent neural vocoders for speech signal reconstruction. In *Proc. 10th ISCA Speech Synthesis Workshop*, pages 7–12.

Hahm, Y., Lim, K., Park, J., Yoon, Y., and Choi, K.-S. (2012). Korean nlp2rdf resources. In *Proceedings of the 10th Workshop on Asian Language Resources*, pages 1–10.

Hellmann, S., Lehmann, J., Auer, S., and Brümmer, M. (2013). Integrating nlp using linked data. In *The Semantic Web – ISWC 2013. 12th International Semantic Web Conference, 21-25 October 2013, Sydney, Australia*, number 8219 in Lecture Notes in Computer Science, pages 98–113.

Iannella, R. and Villata, S. (2018). ODRL Information Model 2.2. https://www.w3.org/TR/odrl-model/, February. W3C Recommendation 15 February 2018.

Iannella, R., Steidl, M., Myles, S., and Rodríguez-Doncel, V. (2018). ODRL Vocabulary and Expression 2.2. https://www.w3.org/TR/odrl-vocab/, February. W3C Recommendation 15 February 2018.

Kornai, A. (2013). Digital Language Death. *PLoS ONE*, 8(10). https://doi.org/10.1371/journal.pone.0077056.

Labropoulou, P., Galanis, D., Lempesis, A., Greenwood, M., Knoth, P., Eckart de Castilho, R., Sachtouris, S., Georgantopoulos, B., Martziou, S., Anastasiou, L., Gkirtzou, K., Manola, N., and Piperidis, S. (2018). OpenMinTeD: A Platform Facilitating Text Mining of Scholarly Content. In *WOSP 2018 Workshop Proceedings, Eleventh International Conference on Language Resources and Evaluation (LREC 2018)*, pages 7–12, Miyazaki, Japan. European Language Resources Association (ELRA).

Labropoulou, P., Gkirtzou, K., Gavriilidou, M., Deligiannis, M., Galanis, D., Piperidis, S., Rehm, G., Berger, M., Mapelli, V., Rigault, M., Arranz, V., Choukri, K., Backfried, G., Pérez, J. M. G., and Garcia-Silva, A. (2020). Making Metadata Fit for Next Generation Language Technology Platforms: The Metadata Schema of the European Language Grid. In Nicoletta Calzolari, et al., editors, *Proceedings of the 12th Language Resources and Evaluation Conference (LREC 2020)*, Marseille, France, May. European Language Resources Association (ELRA). Accepted for publication.

Langendoen, D. (2019). Whither GOLD? In Antonio Pareja-Lora, et al., editors, *Development of Linguistic Linked Open Data Resources for Collaborative Data-Intensive Research in the Language Sciences*. MIT Press, Cambridge, Massachusetts.

Martín-Chozas, P., Montiel-Ponsoda, E., and Rodríguez-Doncel, V. (2019). Language resources as linked data for the legal domain. *Knowledge of the Law in the Big Data Age*, 317:170.

McCrae, J. P., Labropoulou, P., Gracia, J., Villegas, M., Rodríguez-Doncel, V., and Cimiano, P. (2015). One Ontology to Bind Them All: The META-SHARE OWL Ontology for the Interoperability of Linguistic Datasets on the Web. In Fabien Gandon, et al., editors, *The Semantic Web: ESWC 2015 Satellite Events*, Lecture Notes in Computer Science, pages 271–282. Springer International Publishing.

Montiel-Ponsoda, E. and Rodríguez-Doncel, V. (2018). Lynx: Building the Legal Knowledge Graph for Smart Compliance Services. In Georg Rehm, et al., editors, *Proc. of the LREC 2018 Workshop on Language Resources and Technologies for the Legal Knowledge Graph*, pages 23–29, Miyazaki, Japan, May.

Moreno-Schneider, J., Srivastava, A., Bourgonje, P., Wabnitz, D., and Rehm, G. (2017). Semantic Storytelling, Cross-lingual Event Detection and other Semantic Services for a Newsroom Content Curation Dashboard. In Octavian Popescu et al., editors, *Proc. of the Second Workshop on Natural Language Processing meets Journalism – EMNLP 2017 Workshop (NLPMJ 2017)*, pages 68–73, Copenhagen, Denmark.

Moreno-Schneider, J., Bourgonje, P., Kintzel, F., and Rehm, G. (2020a). A Workflow Manager for Complex NLP and Content Curation Workflows. In Georg Rehm, et al., editors, *Proceedings of the 1st International Workshop on Language Technology Platforms (IWLTP 2020, co-located with LREC 2020)*, Marseille, France, May. 16 May 2020. Accepted for publication.

Moreno-Schneider, J., Rehm, G., Montiel-Ponsoda, E., Rodriguez-Doncel, V., Revenko, A., Karampatakis, S., Khvalchik, M., Sageder, C., Gracia, J., and Maganza, F. (2020b). Orchestrating NLP Services for the Legal Domain. In Nicoletta Calzolari, et al., editors, *Proceedings of the 12th Language Resources and Evaluation Conference (LREC 2020)*, Marseille, France, May. European Language Resources Association (ELRA). Accepted for publication. Submitted version available as preprint.

Ostendorff, M., Bourgonje, P., Berger, M., Moreno-Schneider, J., and Rehm, G. (2019). Enriching BERT with Knowledge Graph Embeddings for Document Classification. In Steffen Remus, et al., editors, *Proceedings of the GermEval Workshop 2019 – Shared Task on the Hierarchical Classification of Blurbs*, Erlangen, Germany, 10. 8 October 2019.

Piperidis, S. (2012). The META-SHARE Language Resources Sharing Infrastructure: Principles, Challenges, Solutions. In Nicoletta Calzolari (Conference Chair), et al., editors, *Proceedings of the Eight International Conference on Language Resources and Evaluation (LREC'12)*, Istanbul, Turkey, May. European Language Resources Association (ELRA).

Rehm, G. and Hegele, S. (2018). Language Technology for Multilingual Europe: An Analysis of a Large-Scale Survey regarding Challenges, Demands, Gaps and Needs. In Nicoletta Calzolari, et al., editors, *Proceedings of the 11th Language Resources and Evaluation Conference (LREC 2018)*, pages 3282–3289, Miyazaki, Japan, 5. European Language Resources Association (ELRA).

Rehm, G. and Sasaki, F. (2015). Digitale Kuratierungstechnologien – Verfahren für die Effiziente Verarbeitung, Erstellung und Verteilung Qualitativ Hochwertiger Medieninhalte. In *Proceedings der Frühjahrstagung der Gesellschaft für Sprachtechnologie und Computerlinguistik (GSCL 2015)*, pages 138–139, Duisburg, 9. 30. September–2. Oktober.

Georg Rehm et al., editors. (2012). *META-NET White Paper Series "Europe's Languages in the Digital Age"*. Springer, Heidelberg, New York, Dordrecht, London. 31 volumes on 30 European languages. http://www.meta-net.eu/whitepapers.

Georg Rehm et al., editors. (2013). *The META-NET Strategic Research Agenda for Multilingual Europe 2020*. Springer, Heidelberg, New York, Dordrecht, London.

Rehm, G., Eckart, R., Chiarcos, C., and Dellert, J. (2008a). Ontology-Based XQuery'ing of XML-Encoded Language Resources on Multiple Annotation Layers. In Nicoletta Calzolari (Conference Chair), et al., editors, *Proceedings of the 6th Language Resources and Evaluation Conference (LREC 2008)*, pages 525–532, Marrakesh, Morocco, May.

Rehm, G., Schonefeld, O., Witt, A., Chiarcos, C., and Lehmberg, T. (2008b). SPLICR: A Sustainability Platform for Linguistic Corpora and Resources. In Angelika Storrer, et al., editors, *KONVENS 2008 (Konferenz zur Verarbeitung natürlicher Sprache) – Textressourcen und lexikalisches Wissen*, pages 86–95, Berlin, 9.

Rehm, G., Schonefeld, O., Witt, A., Hinrichs, E., and Reis, M. (2009). Sustainability of Annotated Resources in Linguistics: A Web-Platform for Exploring, Querying and Distributing Linguistic Corpora and Other Resources. *Literary and Linguistic Computing*, 24(2):193–210. Selected papers from Digital Humanities 2008.

Rehm, G., Uszkoreit, H., Dagan, I., Goetcherian, V., Dogan, M. U., Mermer, C., Váradi, T., Kirchmeier-Andersen, S., Stickel, G., Jones, M. P., Oeter, S., and Gramstad, S. (2014). An Update and Extension of the META-NET Study "Europe's Languages in the Digital Age". In Laurette Pretorius, et al., editors, *Proceedings of the Workshop on Collaboration and Computing for Under-Resourced Languages in the Linked Open Data Era (CCURL 2014)*, pages 30–37, Reykjavik, Iceland, 5.

Rehm, G., Uszkoreit, H., Ananiadou, S., Bel, N., Bieleviciené, A., Borin, L., Branco, A., Budin, G., Calzolari, N., Daelemans, W., Garabík, R., Grobelnik, M., García-Mateo, C., van Genabith, J., Hajic, J., Hernáez, I., Judge, J., Koeva, S., Krek, S., Krstev, C., Lindén, K., Magnini, B., Mariani, J., McNaught, J., Melero, M., Monachini, M., Moreno, A., Odijk, J., Ogrodniczuk, M., Pezik, P., Piperidis, S., Przepiórkowski, A., Rögnvaldsson, E., Rosner, M., Pedersen, B. S., Skadina, I., Smedt, K. D., Tadic, M., Thompson, P., Tufiş, D., Váradi, T., Vasiljevs, A., Vider, K., and Zabarskaite, J. (2016). The strategic impact of META-NET on the regional, national and international level. *Lang. Resour. Evaluation*, 50(2):351–374.

Rehm, G., He, J., Schneider, J. M., Nehring, J., and Quantz, J. (2017a). Designing User Interfaces for Curation Technologies. In Sakae Yamamoto, editor, *Human Interface and the Management of Information: Information, Knowledge and Interaction Design, 19th International Conference, HCI International 2017 (Vancouver, Canada)*, number 10273 in Lecture Notes in Computer Science (LNCS), pages 388–406, Cham, Switzerland, July. Springer. Part I.

Rehm, G., Schneider, J. M., Bourgonje, P., Srivastava,

A., Nehring, J., Berger, A., König, L., Räuchle, S., and Gerth, J. (2017b). Event Detection and Semantic Storytelling: Generating a Travelogue from a large Collection of Personal Letters. In Tommaso Caselli, et al., editors, *Proc. of the Events and Stories in the News Workshop*, pages 42–51, Vancouver, Canada, August. Association for Computational Linguistics.

Rehm, G., Schneider, J. M., Bourgonje, P., Srivastava, A., Fricke, R., Thomsen, J., He, J., Quantz, J., Berger, A., König, L., Räuchle, S., Gerth, J., and Wabnitz, D. (2018). Different Types of Automated and Semi-Automated Semantic Storytelling: Curation Technologies for Different Sectors. In Georg Rehm et al., editors, *Language Technologies for the Challenges of the Digital Age: 27th International Conference, GSCL 2017, Berlin, Germany, September 13-14, 2017, Proceedings*, number 10713 in Lecture Notes in Artificial Intelligence (LNAI), pages 232–247, Cham, Switzerland, January. Gesellschaft für Sprachtechnologie und Computerlinguistik e.V., Springer. 13/14 September 2017.

Rehm, G., Lee, M., Schneider, J. M., and Bourgonje, P. (2019a). Curation Technologies for a Cultural Heritage Archive: Analysing and Transforming a Heterogeneous Data Set into an Interactive Curation Workbench. In Apostolos Antonacopoulos et al., editors, *Proceedings of DATeCH 2019: Digital Access to Textual Cultural Heritage*, Brussels, Belgium, May. 8-10 May 2019. In print.

Rehm, G., Moreno-Schneider, J., Gracia, J., Revenko, A., Mireles, V., Khvalchik, M., Kernerman, I., Lagzdins, A., Pinnis, M., Vasilevskis, A., Leitner, E., Milde, J., and Weißenhorn, P. (2019b). Developing and Orchestrating a Portfolio of Natural Legal Language Processing and Document Curation Services. In Nikolaos Aletras, et al., editors, *Proceedings of Workshop on Natural Legal Language Processing (NLLP 2019)*, pages 55–66, Minneapolis, USA, 6. Co-located with NAACL 2019. 7 June 2019.

Rehm, G., Zaczynska, K., and Schneider, J. M. (2019c). Semantic Storytelling: Towards Identifying Storylines in Large Amounts of Text Content. In Alipio Jorge, et al., editors, *Proc. of Text2Story – Second Workshop on Narrative Extraction From Texts co-located with 41th European Conf. on Information Retrieval (ECIR 2019)*, pages 63–70, Cologne, Germany, April. 14 April 2019.

Rehm, G., Berger, M., Elsholz, E., Hegele, S., Kintzel, F., Marheinecke, K., Piperidis, S., Deligiannis, M., Galanis, D., Gkirtzou, K., Labropoulou, P., Bontcheva, K., Jones, D., Roberts, I., Hajic, J., Hamrlová, J., Kačena, L., Choukri, K., Arranz, V., Vasiļjevs, A., Anvari, O., Lagzdiņš, A., Meļņika, J., Backfried, G., Dikici, E., Janosik, M., Prinz, K., Prinz, C., Stampler, S., Thomas-Aniola, D., Pérez, J. M. G., Silva, A. G., Berrío, C., Germann, U., Renals, S., and Klejch, O. (2020a). European Language Grid: An Overview. In Nicoletta Calzolari, et al., editors, *Proceedings of the 12th Language Resources and Evaluation Conference (LREC 2020)*, Marseille, France, May. European Language Resources Association (ELRA). Accepted for publication.

Rehm, G., Bourgonje, P., Hegele, S., Kintzel, F., Schneider, J. M., Ostendorff, M., Zaczynska, K., Berger, A., Grill, S., Räuchle, S., Rauenbusch, J., Rutenburg, L., Schmidt, A., Wild, M., Hoffmann, H., Fink, J., Schulz, S., Seva, J., Quantz, J., Böttger, J., Matthey, J., Fricke, R., Thomsen, J., Paschke, A., Qundus, J. A., Hoppe, T., Karam, N., Weichhardt, F., Fillies, C., Neudecker, C., Gerber, M., Labusch, K., Rezanezhad, V., Schaefer, R., Zellhöfer, D., Siewert, D., Bunk, P., Pintscher, L., Aleynikova, E., and Heine, F. (2020b). QURATOR: Innovative Technologies for Content and Data Curation. In Adrian Paschke, et al., editors, *Proceedings of QURATOR 2020 – The conference for intelligent content solutions*, Berlin, Germany, 02. CEUR Workshop Proceedings, Volume 2535. 20/21 January 2020.

Rehm, G., Marheinecke, K., Hegele, S., Piperidis, S., Bontcheva, K., Hajic, J., Choukri, K., Vasiļjevs, A., Backfried, G., Prinz, C., Pérez, J. M. G., Meertens, L., Lukowicz, P., van Genabith, J., Lösch, A., Slusallek, P., Irgens, M., Gatellier, P., Köhler, J., Bars, L. L., Auksoriūtė, A., Bel, N., Branco, A., Budin, G., Daelemans, W., Smedt, K. D., Garabík, R., Gavriilidou, M., Gromann, D., Koeva, S., Krek, S., Krstev, C., Lindén, K., Magnini, B., Odijk, J., Ogrodniczuk, M., Ras, E., Rögnvaldsson, E., Rosner, M., Pedersen, B., Skadina, I., Tadić, M., Tufiş, D., Váradi, T., Vider, K., Way, A., and Yvon, F. (2020c). The European Language Technology Landscape in 2020: Language-Centric and Human-Centric AI for Cross-Cultural Communication in Multilingual Europe, May. Accepted for publication.

Georg Rehm, editor. (2017). *Language Technologies for Multilingual Europe: Towards a Human Language Project. Strategic Research and Innovation Agenda.* CRACKER and Cracking the Language Barrier federation, 12. Version 1.0. Unveiled at META-FORUM 2017 in Brussels, Belgium, on November 13/14, 2017. Prepared by the Cracking the Language Barrier federation, supported by the EU-funded project CRACKER.

Schmidt, T., Chiarcos, C., Lehmberg, T., Rehm, G., Witt, A., and Hinrichs, E. (2006). Avoiding Data Graveyards: From Heterogeneous Data Collected in Multiple Research Projects to Sustainable Linguistic Resources. In *Proceedings of the E-MELD 2006 Workshop on Digital Language Documentation: Tools and Standards – The State of the Art*, East Lansing, Michigan, 6.

Schneider, J. M. and Rehm, G. (2018a). Curation Technologies for the Construction and Utilisation of Legal Knowledge Graphs. In Georg Rehm, et al., editors, *Proc. of the LREC 2018 Workshop on Language Resources and Technologies for the Legal Knowledge Graph*, pages 23–29, Miyazaki, Japan, May.

Schneider, J. M. and Rehm, G. (2018b). Towards a Workflow Manager for Curation Technologies in the Legal Domain. In Georg Rehm, et al., editors, *Proc. of the LREC 2018 Workshop on Language Resources and Technologies for the Legal Knowledge Graph*, pages 30–35, Miyazaki, Japan, May.

Schneider, J. M., Bourgonje, P., Nehring, J., Rehm, G., Sasaki, F., and Srivastava, A. (2016). Towards Semantic Story Telling with Digital Curation Technologies. In Larry Birnbaum, et al., editors, *Proceedings of Natural Language Processing Meets Journalism – IJCAI-16*

Workshop (NLPMJ 2016), New York, July.

Schneider, J. M., Bourgonje, P., and Rehm, G. (2017). Towards User Interfaces for Semantic Storytelling. In Sakae Yamamoto, editor, *Human Interface and the Management of Information: Information, Knowledge and Interaction Design, 19th Int. Conf., HCI International 2017 (Vancouver, Canada)*, number 10274 in Lecture Notes in Computer Science (LNCS), pages 403–421, Cham, Switzerland, July. Springer. Part II.

Schneider, J. M., Roller, R., Bourgonje, P., Hegele, S., and Rehm, G. (2018). Towards the Automatic Classification of Offensive Language and Related Phenomena in German Tweets. In Josef Ruppenhofer, et al., editors, *Proceedings of the GermEval Workshop 2018 – Shared Task on the Identification of Offensive Language*, pages 95–103, Vienna, Austria, September. 21 September 2018.

Shet, R., Davcheva, E., and Uhle, C. (2019). Segmenting multi-intent queries for spoken language understanding. *Studientexte zur Sprachkommunikation: Elektronische Sprachsignalverarbeitung 2019*, pages 141–147.

Singh, K., Radhakrishna, A. S., Both, A., Shekarpour, S., Lytra, I., Usbeck, R., Vyas, A., Khikmatullaev, A., Punjani, D., Lange, C., Vidal, M., Lehmann, J., and Auer, S. (2018). Why reinvent the wheel: Let's build question answering systems together. In *Proceedings of the 2018 World Wide Web Conference on World Wide Web, WWW 2018, Lyon, France, April 23-27, 2018*, pages 1247–1256.

Srivastava, A., Sasaki, F., Bourgonje, P., Moreno-Schneider, J., Nehring, J., and Rehm, G. (2016). How to Configure Statistical Machine Translation with Linked Open Data Resources. In Joaǐfo Esteves-Ferreira, et al., editors, *Proceedings of Translating and the Computer 38 (TC38)*, pages 138–148, London, UK, November. Editions Tradulex.

STOA. (2017). Language equality in the digital age – Towards a Human Language Project. STOA study (PE 598.621), IP/G/STOA/FWC/2013-001/Lot4/C2, March 2017. Carried out by Iclaves SL (Spain) at the request of the Science and Technology Options Assessment (STOA) Panel, managed by the Scientific Foresight Unit (STOA), within the Directorate-General for Parliamentary Research Services (DG EPRS) of the European Parliament, March. http://www.europarl.europa.eu/stoa/.

Usbeck, R. (2014). Combining linked data and statistical information retrieval. In *11th Extended Semantic Web Conference, PhD Symposium*. Springer.

Vasiljevs, A., Choukri, K., Meertens, L., and Aguzzi, S. (2019). Final study report on CEF Automated Translation value proposition in the context of the European LT market/ecosystem. DOI 10.2759/142151. A study prepared for the European Commission, DG Communications Networks, Content & Technology by Crosslang, Tilde, ELDA, IDC.

Warburton, K. and Wright, S. (2019). A data category repository for language resources. In Antonio Pareja-Lora, et al., editors, *Development of Linguistic Linked Open Data Resources for Collaborative Data-Intensive Research in the Language Sciences*. MIT Press, Cambridge, Massachusetts.

Witt, A., Rehm, G., Hinrichs, E., Lehmberg, T., and Stegmann, J. (2009). SusTEInability of Linguistic Resources through Feature Structures. *Literary and Linguistic Computing*, 24(3):363–372.

Wörner, K., Witt, A., Rehm, G., and Dipper, S. (2006). Modelling Linguistic Data Structures. In B. Tommie Usdin, editor, *Proceedings of Extreme Markup Languages 2006*, Montréal, Canada, 8.

Proceedings of the 1st International Workshop on Language Technology Platforms (IWLTP 2020), pages 108–111
Language Resources and Evaluation Conference (LREC 2020), Marseille, 11–16 May 2020
© European Language Resources Association (ELRA), licensed under CC-BY-NC

The COMPRISE Cloud Platform

Raivis Skadiņš, Askars Salimbajevs
Tilde, Vienibas gatve 75a, Riga, Latvia, LV-1004
University of Latvia, Raina bulvaris 19, Riga, Latvia, LV-1586
{raivis.skadins, askars.salimbajevs}@tilde.lv

Abstract
This paper presents the COMPRISE cloud platform that is developed in the H2020 project. We present an overview of the COMPRISE project, its main goals, components, and how the cloud platform fits in the context of the overall project. The COMPRISE cloud platform is presented in more detail – main users, use scenarios, functions, implementation details, and how it will be used by both COMPRISE's targeted audience and the broader language-technology community.

Keywords: cloud platform, voice dialog systems

1. Introduction

The COMPRISE project[1] (Cost-effective, Multilingual, Privacy-driven voice-enabled Services) is a Research and Innovation Action funded by the European Union's Horizon 2020 programme. It aims to develop the next generation of voice interaction technology that will be more affordable, inclusive and, above all, secure.

Voice-operated technologies and tools have multiplied in recent years, voice is rapidly replacing touch or text as the main means of interaction with modern devices. COMPRISE aims to support, this expansion by providing the tools and methodology to make voice interaction more secure, more cost-effective, and more inclusive for a variety of languages.

Due to the cost of voice data collection and labelling, current voice interaction technologies have a strong bias in favour of languages with a wider user base (such as English), thus potentially excluding some users. In addition, they often rely on cloud-based algorithms to analyse voice signals, but there are few guarantees (if any) regarding how data stored in the cloud is used and will be used in the future by cloud service providers. COMPRISE is employing deep learning methodologies to improve speech-to-text and machine understanding of different languages and domains. In addition, it aims to create a methodology that protects the users' data, in order to ensure their privacy.

2. Approach

COMPRISE implements a fully private-by-design methodology and tools to reduce the cost and increase the inclusiveness of voice interaction technologies. To do so, we focus on the following key technologies:

• privacy-driven transformations to delete private information from the users' speech and the corresponding text data obtained by speech-to-text (Srivastava et al., 2020; Quian et al., 2018; Sundermann and Ney, 2003; Chou et al., 2019),

• joint centralized (H2020 COMPRISE project, 2019) and local learning to train large-scale systems from these transformed data while personalizing them for every user in a privacy-preserving way,

• weakly supervised learning to leverage both multiple automatic labelers for all utterances and manual labeling for a few utterances thereby drastically reducing the human labeling cost (Tam et al., 2014; Byambakhishig et al., 2014; Oualil et al., 2015; Kang et al. 2014; Zhou et al., 2019),

• robust integration of machine translation (MT) with speech and dialog processing tools to translate on-the-fly from one language to another and to generate additional training data by translating data available in other languages.

Building on scientific advances, we are implementing a cross-platform software development kit (SDK) and a sustainable cloud-based platform (Figure 1).

The SDK and the platform will ease the design of multilingual voice-enabled applications and their advancement.

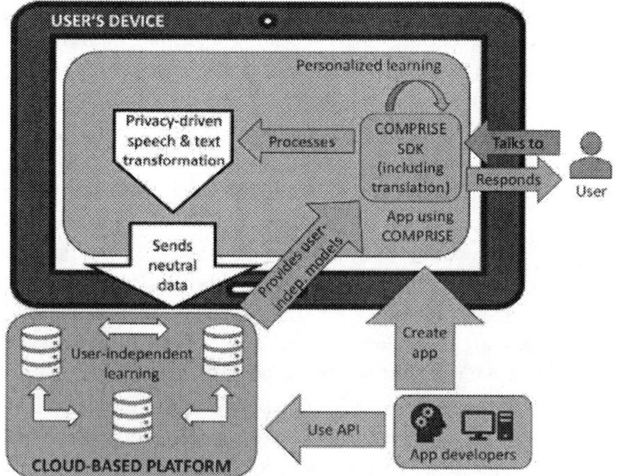

Figure 1. COMPRISE framework.

The COMPRISE framework leverages new web technologies largely supported by mobile browsers to make its solution also available for mobile devices, which are our primary targeted environment. The COMPRISE framework will not only provide a speech-to-text framework but rather a complete interactive conversational multilingual framework. The COMPRISE framework will embed the technologies in charge of analyzing, understanding and interpreting the voice of the user

---

[1] https://www.compriseh2020.eu

considering the spoken language, the accent, the mic encoding quality, etc.

the cost for both industrial providers and industrial users of voice interaction technologies.

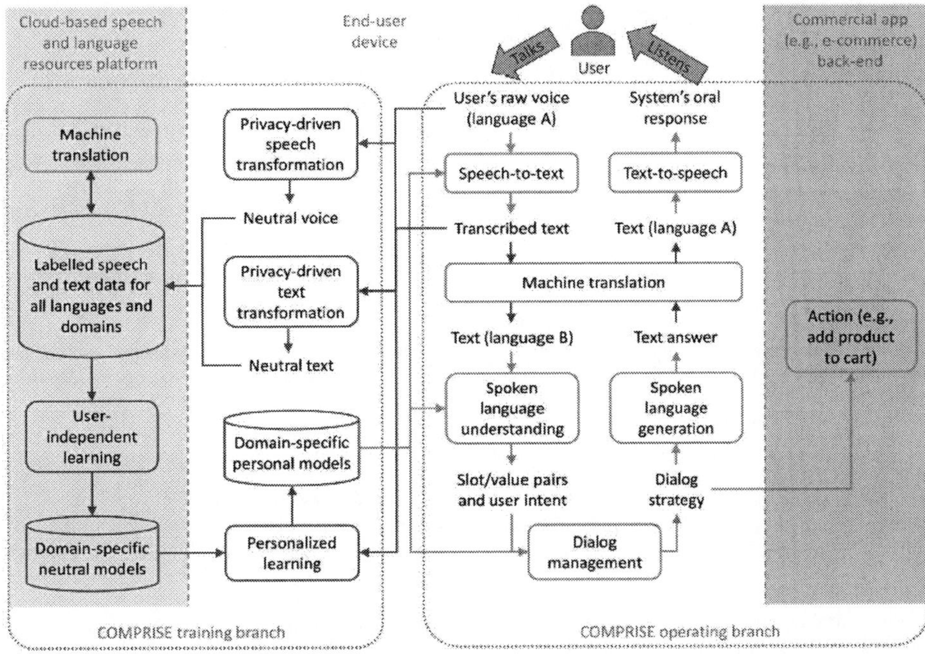

Figure 2. Detailed data flow of the COMPRISE voice interaction system.

The COMPRISE voice interaction system involves two branches running in parallel: the operating branch and the training branch (Figure 2).

The COMPRISE operating branch shown in the right half of the figure involves the usual chain of speech and language processing tools: speech-to-text, spoken language understanding, dialog management, spoken language generation, and text-to-speech. This branch conducts voice based interaction with the user in order to understand his/her request and fulfil it. This branch is similar to today's voice interaction systems, except that it runs locally on the user's device, it uses personalized models of speech and dialog, and it leverages machine translation to interface tools in different languages. The Operating branch is implemented as a cross-platform COMPRISE SDK that provides an easy to-use interface for multilingual voice-enabled application developers. By providing access to all tools developed within COMPRISE and by abstracting language- and platform-specific issues, the SDK significantly reduces the development time compared to existing SDKs from third-party vendors, thereby resulting in quicker time-to-market and major cost savings for industrial users of language technologies.

The COMPRISE training branch shown in the left half of the figure aims to collect large-scale in domain speech and language data for many languages and application domains and learn domain-specific personalized models from these data for speech-to-text, spoken language understanding, and dialog management in a privacy-preserving way. This branch is completely new and relies on research advances made in the project. This guaranties privacy and reduces

The COMPRISE Cloud platform is accessed by the SDK via REST API to exchange data and models. The platform will be used to store the neutral data and the models in a secure way, curate and label them, and update the models whenever sufficient additional data has been received. This platform fills a gap in the current ecosystem: existing resource repositories are good for speech resource description, dissemination, sharing, and distribution, but according to our knowledge there is no platform that would facilitate speech data creation, labelling, and curation. The COMPRISE platform is designed and developed for this purpose. It is a backbone on which all other components of the COMPRISE training branch are relying.

3. Cloud Platform

The neutral data and the corresponding (manual or automatic) labels are stored in the COMPRISE Cloud platform. The platform allows users to upload, store and manage data and labels and train or access large-scale user-independent models trained on these data. The platform functionality includes secure cloud-based data and model storage, scalable and dynamic cloud-based high-performance computing, APIs for continuous data upload and occasional model download, and general platform features (user interface, authentication, usage analytics, etc.) and procedures for data labeling and curation.

Two types of data will be handled by the platform: (1) speech and (2) text. The platform will allow training acoustic and language models for speech-to-text (STT), and intent detection models for spoken language understanding (SLU) on collected data. In the future support for other types of data and models might be added.

The main user of the cloud-based COMPRISE platform is a developer who uses COMPRISE SDK which will exchange data and models via REST API. Communications between the platform and the users' devices will be secured via state-of-the-art encryption and full compliance with the GDPR (e.g., regarding data retention) will be ensured.

3.1 User profiles

To specify user requirements for the COMPRISE Cloud platform first it's necessary to understand who platform users will be and how they will use the platform. We have identified four main user profiles – (1) COMPRISE Client apps, (2) developers, (3) data annotators and (4) administrators.

COMPRISE Client apps are machine users - applications that use COMPRISE SDK client components for STT and/or SLU and for communication with the COMPRISE Cloud platform. To achieve the best possible user experience, COMPRISE Client App wants to use the best neutral STT and/or SLU models for a particular usage domain. This is achieved by periodically (at runtime): (1) uploading new neutral speech and/or text data to the COMPRISE Cloud platform, and (2) downloading the latest models from the platform (e.g. on application start).

Developers use COMPRISE SDK to create voice-enabled privacy-preserving applications (e.g. personal assistant). To achieve the best possible user experience, the developer wants to use domain-specific STT and/or SLU models for the particular usage domain of the application. Developers use the COMPRISE Cloud platform to manage collected domain-specific neutral data, process collected data (e.g. apply machine translation, launch annotation tasks) and train domain-specific neutral STT and/or SLU models. After successful training, models are downloaded and used in developed applications. The collected data for each application are grouped into separate corpora, speech data is appended to the application speech corpus, text data is appended to the application text corpus. As collected data needs to be annotated, the developer shall be able to give access to the collected corpora to the other users - annotators.

Data annotator uses the COMPRISE Cloud platform to label domain-specific neutral speech and text data. Data annotators are granted access to speech or text corpora by Developers. Data annotators can have access to multiple corpora simultaneously. For speech corpora, annotators will provide transcription for each audio recording, but each user prompt in text data - intent label or next dialog state label. Labeled data is then used for the training of domain-specific neutral models.

The administrator maintains the COMPRISE Cloud platform and manages global access to its resources by creating, approving and deleting user accounts.

3.2 Architecture

The COMPRISE platform is expected to work in a cloud environment as several web-services using Containerization (e.g. Docker[2], Kubernetes[3]) technique.

Therefore, hardware and system software management will be greatly simplified.

As seen in Figure 3 the COMPRISE platform consists of five main services:

• Authentication service authenticates users using a standard OpenID Connect protocol. As there are a lot of high-quality existing authentication solutions and providers, a new solution is not implemented in the scope of the project. Instead, existing authentication solutions or service providers (like Azure B2C) are utilized.

• API service provides COMPRISE platform functionality through an API. The service is implemented in the scope of the project.

• Storage service provides object storage through web service. Existing cloud storage solutions like Amazon S3 will be utilized as they provide scalability, high availability, low latency, durability and does not require hardware administration.

• Training service provides training of STT and SLU models. The service will be implemented in the scope of the project and use model training modules that are developed in the project's research activities. For machine translation of the training data, the service will use external machine translation service Tilde MT.

• Web UI provides a user interface for general COMPRISE platforms functions like registering applications, corpus annotation, triggering model training, etc.

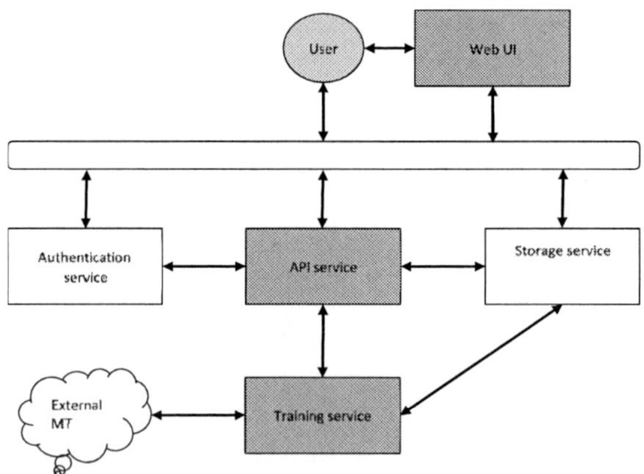

Figure 3. COMPRISE platform services

In order to efficiently balance the load between services and avoid unnecessary resource consumption COMPRISE platform API clients will request a special upload URL from API service, which allows uploading data to the Storage service directly without API service acting as an intermediary.

All services will be deployable as Docker containers which will allow to run them on almost any cloud provider infrastructure. For Docker container orchestration we use Kubernetes.

---

[2] https://www.docker.com/

[3] https://kubernetes.io/

Kubernetes scheduler and Horizontal Pod Autoscaler (HPA) are used to run containers only when they are requested and scale to multiple replicas when needed.

An optional gateway or proxy can be used for load-balancing, network administration, and protection.

3.3 Model Training

The training service is responsible for the training of in-domain neutral models for STT and SLU using model training modules provided by COMPRISE partners. These modules are packaged as Docker containers.

The training service is not exposed to the outside and is available only inside the cluster. It receives training requests from API service and initiates model training by starting training containers as a Kubernetes job. Started containers have direct access to the training data and models in the Storage service. Such an approach allows to run very different training workloads, improves portability and simplifies dependency maintenance (dependencies and environment are maintained inside containers). The limitation is that it does not allow to do traditional distributed training on multiple machines. We plan that in future this limitation can be lifted by using one or both of the following solutions:

• Model training containers can call Training service API to initiate sub-tasks.

• Training service can be extended to submit jobs to a classic High-Performance Cluster (HPC).

Also, in the future submission of training jobs to an external entity like the European Language Grid[4] will be considered. For machine translation of the training data, the service uses external machine translation service Tilde MT. In the future, support for other MT providers can be integrated.

3.4 User interface

The Web-based UI will provide the user interface for general COMPRISE Cloud platforms functions.

It is implemented using the Angular web framework and packaged as a Docker container as other services. It can be run directly in the cloud without an explicit virtual machine using services like Azure AppService or in the same Kubernetes cluster as other COMPRISE Cloud platform services.

The Web-based UI allows developers to sign-up, register applications, access API documentation and try-out forms. An important feature of the web-based UI is an interface for speech and text data annotation. This interface will be available without creating user accounts using a special URL with an embedded Annotator key, which will be created by the Developer and shared with annotators.

4. Development Status

The development of the platform started in November 2019 and is scheduled to be completed and made publicly available in August 2020. The platform architecture and API have already been specified and the first version of the API is already available in the test environment so that it can be integrated with the COMPRISE SDK.

5. Acknowledgements

COMPRISE has received funding from the European Union's Horizon 2020 Research and Innovation Programme under Grant Agreement No. 825081.

6. Bibliographical References

Byambakhishig, E., Tanaka, K., Aihara, R., Nakashika, T., Takiguchi, T., & Ariki, Y. (2014). Error correction of automatic speech recognition based on normalized web distance. In Fifteenth Annual Conference of the International Speech Communication Association (INTERSPEECH) (pp.2852–2856).

Chou, J. C., Yeh, C. C., & Lee, H. Y. (2019). One-shot Voice Conversion by Separating Speaker and Content Representations with Instance Normalization. In Proc. INTERSPEECH, (pp. 664–668)

H2020 COMPRISE project (2019). Deliverable D2.1: Baseline speech and text transformation and model learning library, Version 1.0, Retrieved from: https://www.compriseh2020.eu/files/2019/08/D2.1.pdf

Kang, S., Kim, J. H., & Seo, J. (2014). Post-error correction in automatic speech recognition using discourse information. Advances in Electrical and Computer Engineering, 14(2), 53-57.

Oualil, Y., Schulder, M., Helmke, H., Schmidt, A., & Klakow, D. (2015). Real-time integration of dynamic context information for improving automatic speech recognition. In Sixteenth Annual Conference of the International Speech Communication Association (INTERSPEECH), (pp 2107-21111).

Qian, J., Du, H., Hou, J., Chen, L., Jung, T., & Li, X. Y. (2018, November). Hidebehind: Enjoy Voice Input with Voiceprint Unclonability and Anonymity. In Proceedings of the 16th ACM Conference on Embedded Networked Sensor Systems (pp. 82-94).

Srivastava, B. M. L., Vauquier, N., Sahidullah, M., Bellet, A., Tommasi, M., & Vincent, E. (2020). "Evaluating voice conversion-based privacy protection against informed attackers", in Proc. ICASSP.

Sundermann, D., & Ney, H. (2003, December). VTLN-based voice conversion. In Proceedings of the 3rd IEEE International Symposium on Signal Processing and Information Technology (IEEE Cat. No. 03EX795) (pp. 556-559). IEEE.

Tam, Y. C., Lei, Y., Zheng, J., & Wang, W. (2014, May). ASR error detection using recurrent neural network language model and complementary ASR. In 2014 IEEE International Conference on Acoustics, Speech and Signal Processing (ICASSP) (pp. 2312-2316). IEEE.

Zhou, Z., Song, X., Botros, R., & Zhao, L. (2019, May). A Neural Network Based Ranking Framework to Improve ASR with NLU Related Knowledge Deployed. In ICASSP 2019-2019 IEEE International Conference on Acoustics, Speech and Signal Processing (ICASSP) (pp. 6450-6454). IEEE.

---

[4] https://www.european-language-grid.eu/

Proceedings of the 1st International Workshop on Language Technology Platforms (IWLTP 2020), pages 112–120
Language Resources and Evaluation Conference (LREC 2020), Marseille, 11–16 May 2020
© European Language Resources Association (ELRA), licensed under CC-BY-NC

From Linguistic Research Projects to Language Technology Platforms :
A Case Study in Learner Data

Annanda Sousa[1], Nicolas Ballier[2], Thomas Gaillat[3], Bernardo Stearns[1], Manel Zarrouk[4],
Andrew Simpkin[1], Manon Bouyé[2]
National University of Ireland Galway[1], Université de Paris[2], Universités de Rennes 1&2[3], Université Sorbonne Paris Nord[4]
Insight Centre for Data analytics[1] , CLILLAC-ARP F-75013[2], LIDILE[3] , LIPN [4]
{a.defreitassousa1, bernardo.stearns, andrew.simpkin}@nuigalway.ie,
nicolas.ballier@u-paris.fr, thomas.gaillat@univ-rennes2.fr, mbouye@eila.univ-paris-diderot.fr, zarrouk@lipn.univ-paris13.fr

Abstract

This paper describes the workflow and architecture adopted by a linguistic research project on learner data. We report our experience and present the research outputs turned into resources that we wish to share with the community. We discuss the current limitations and the next steps that could be taken for the scaling and development of our research project. Allying NLP and language-centric AI, we discuss similar projects and possible ways to start collaborating towards potential platform interoperability.

Keywords: NLP text processing, Machine Learning, Linguistic Data workflow, User Interface (UI)

1. Introduction

This paper illustrates the current shift from language sciences to linguistic data science. We intend to describe the prototype of an Automatic Essay Scoring system (AES) user interface predicting proficiency levels in English and discuss scalability, interoperability and some development issues when sharing our models and other research outputs of our project.

Automating language assessment is a task conducted with Automatic Essay Scoring systems (AES). Initially based on rule-based approaches (Page, 1968), more modern systems now rely on probabilistic models. Some of these models depend on the identification of features that are used as predictors of writing quality. Some of these features operationalise complexity and act as criterial features in L2 language (Hawkins and Filipović, 2012). They help build computer models for error detection and automated assessment and, by using model explanation procedures, their significance and effect can be measured. Recent work on identifying criterial features has been fruitful, as many studies have addressed many types of features. However, most of the studies (one notable exception is found in (Volodina et al., 2016), with a system designed for Swedish) are experimental and do not include any automated pipeline that can handle user data from input to output. In other words, pre-processing and data analysis are not necessarily connected to any machine learning module and a user interface. Most experiments include several experimental stages of data modeling, which impedes any real-life exploitation of the models such as a student typing a text to have it graded.

The work on criterial features has also raised the need to build systems dedicated to linguistic feature extraction. The purpose of such a task is to build datasets reflecting the multi-dimensionality of language. Several tools have been developed to suit the needs of specific projects in the extraction of linguistic complexity features (Lu, 2014; Crossley et al., 2014; Crossley et al., 2019; Kyle et al., 2018). These tools provide features of different dimensions of language.

However, it is not possible to apply them to a single data set in one operation. The researcher who wants to weigh the significance of all these features would benefit from a single tool applied uniformly to any data set.

Our proposal stems from a project dedicated to predicting proficiency levels in learner English. This system is made up of a user interface in which learners of English can type in a text and immediately be prompted with an assessment of their proficiency level after submission. The system was designed following a modular approach which provides room for other researchers' models. We show that it is possible to use what we have called 'the DemoIT infrastructure' to implement other models dedicated to processing texts with a view to classify them according to predetermined classes. In addition, we have derived a feature extraction pipeline from the demo and it enables researchers to build datasets by applying several state-of-the-art tools for further analysis.

In an effort to contributing to the FAIR paradigm, we have made available the code of the interface, the initial dataset and our statistical model (the .sav file). This how-to paper guides the computationally literate linguist from the data modelling to the actual web-interface for the deliverables of her linguistic project. Our case study is at the crossroads of

- research projects in applied linguistics,

- containerisation and virtualisation technologies for Language Technology Platforms,

- development of Language Technology platform interoperability: we present our web application and our workflow, as well as the exchange models, data and metadata...

The rest of the paper is organised as follows: section 2 presents some comparable tools for the analysis of complexity. Section 3. describes the context that triggered the need of the implementation of the infrastructure, which is a project aiming to automatically predict the CEFR level of a language learner. Section 4 details the tool we are proposing in this paper as well as some suggestions of improvements. The solution we adopted, "DemoIt", is a web-based infrastructure that allows users to demo their text processing systems easily in a scheduled asynchronous way. Section 5 presents the infrastructure we have adopted and the sub-components that can be re-used. Section 6 details the resulting resources we make available as deliverables of the project. Section 7 discusses our next steps in relation to other similar infrastructures, taking into account interoperability, multilingualism, scalability and legal restrictions (GDPR and copyright).

2. Existing tools for linguistic complexity feature extraction

A number of projects already exist in the domain of complexity feature extraction. Specific tools are dedicated to a specific dimension of complexity. A number of tools focus on lexical complexity, e.g. LCA (Lu, 2012) and TAALES (Kyle et al., 2018). Other tools focus on syntactic complexity, e.g. L2SCA (Lu, 2010) and TAASC (Kyle et al., 2018). Other tools focus on pragmatic dimensions, e.g. cohesion with TAACO (Crossley et al., 2019) and Coh-Metrix (McNamara et al., 2014). All these tools provide many metrics of one dimension to build datasets for further analysis.

More recently, work has been invested in developing common frameworks to support data interoperability with shared tools. CTAP (Chen and Meurers, 2016) is such a tool and allows a researcher to select various types of linguistic features to extract prior to building a customised data set. This approach provides the benefit of letting researchers choose and apply complexity analyses from a broad set of available features.

3. The Project: a Machine Learning Driven Language Proficiency Level Prediction

This section presents the experimental setup, the components of our project.

3.1. Aims of the Project

Our project aims to investigate criterial features in learner English and to build a proof-of-concept system for language proficiency level assessment in English. Our research focus is to identify linguistic features and to integrate them within a system with a machine learning component. The purpose is to create a system to analyse learner English essay writings and map them to specific language levels of the Common European Framework of Reference (CEFR) for Languages (European Council, 2001).

The proposal is a supervised learning approach in which we build several models designed to assign levels of the CEFR, which, to the best of our knowledge is novel. The system is trained on a database of more than 40,000 texts (approx. 3,298,343 tokens) that have already been labeled and grammatically annotated (Geertzen et al., 2013; Huang et al., 2018). The model relies on error-independent features of English to build a multi-dimensional feature representation of written essays. Figure 1 recaps the pipeline of the project.

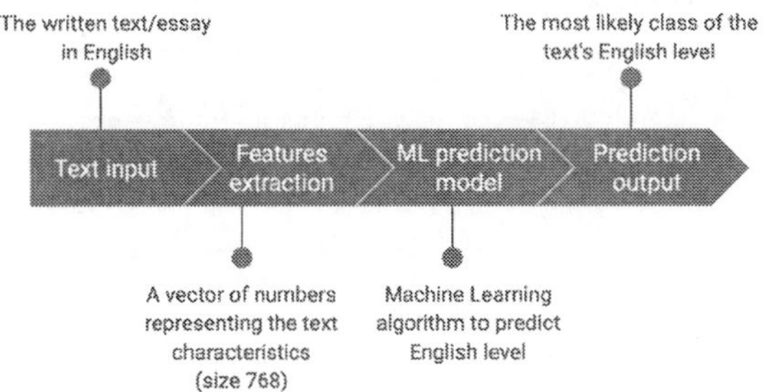

Figure 1: The pipeline for our project

3.2. Experimental Setup

3.2.1. Corpora and Dataset

The model was trained and tested on the Spanish and French L1 subsets of the Education First-Cambridge Open Language Database (EFCAMDAT) (Geertzen et al., 2013), an 83-million-word corpus collected and made available by Cambridge University and its partner, the organization Education First. Data [1] from 49,813 texts written by 8,851 learners were extracted. The model was also tested[2] on the CEFR ASAG corpus (Tack et al., 2017), another collection of learner texts made up of short answers to open-ended questions and written by French L1 learners of English. The texts were graded with CEFR levels by three experts.

By using the aforementioned corpus subsets, we implemented a program pipeline which is designed to convert the texts into series of values, subsequently used as features. Several state-of-the-art tools are exploited to extract features of several linguistic dimensions and create three datasets. Two internal sets are created from the 49,813 observations, i.e. the training set (75% randomly extracted from the EFCAMDAT corpus) and a test set (25% randomly extracted). One external data set was created from the ASAG-CEFR corpus including 299 observations. The internal dataset will be made available online for the research community on the EFCAMDAT website. Programming scripts will also be made available via an online software development platform. In order to ensure compliance with the General Data Protection Regulation (GDPR), data will be anonymised and no personal identification of learners will be used and published.

3.2.2. Feature Extraction

The model relies on a dataset of linguistic complexity metrics of different dimensions: syntactic, lexical, semantic, accuracy and pragmatic. These metrics form numeric feature vectors of values and characterise the learner texts. The vectors are matched with the CEFR levels assigned to the texts. We use several tools to compute the met-

---

[1]The University of Cambridge and English First took no part in the data manipulation. The dataset including the EFCAMDAT texts will be hosted by Cambridge, in accordance with the corpus regulations. Access is free for academic non-commercial uses, provided potential users request permission using an academic email address.

[2]Evaluation results are discussed in (Gaillat et al., submitted)

rics. Syntactic complexity measures are computed with the L2 Syntactic Complexity Analyzer (L2SCA). These tools rely on the Tregex module of Stanford CoreNLP (Manning et al., 2014) for phrase constituent retrieval. The Tool for the Automatic analysis of Syntactic Sophistication and Complexity (TAASC) is also used to compute ratios and scores of syntactic complexity such as prepositions per nominal, adjectival modifiers per object of the preposition, and also probability that two items occur together. For lexico-semantic features, the pipeline implements the Lexical Complexity Analyzer (LCA) relying on Treetagger (Schmid, 1994) to compute lexical diversity metrics. The Automatic Assessment of Lexical Proficiency (TAALES) tool computes includes 130 lexical indices with classic lexical complexity metrics and psycholinguistic properties of words. These properties are based on judgments of concreteness, familiarity, imageability, or supposed age of first exposure. The TAALES indices include frequencies, ratios of lexical words and n-grams as well as comparative metrics sourced from reference corpora. The textstat Python library[3] was used to compute readability metrics that indicate the level of difficulty of texts. Accuracy features are computed with the pyenchant Python library (Kelly, 2016) [4] for misspelt words. Regarding pragmatic features, the pipeline includes the Tool for the Automatic Analysis of Cohesion (TAACO) which computes metrics based on referential and discourse characteristics such as pronouns, lexical overlaps and connectives. In total, 768 different features were extracted and merged into one dataset to input into the classification models.

3.2.3. CEFR Level Classifier

The aim was to construct a classification model of learner CEFR levels (A1, A2, B1, B2, C1, C2, ie from beginners to advanced speakers). Among several model types tested, the optimal classification performance in the testing data set was found using multinomial logistic regression . The classifier using all features reached 82% accuracy (0.80 mean F1-score) on a six-point scale classification.

Given that the levels are ordinals, one of the reviewers suggested misclassifications B1 for B2 should incur different costs than, say, misclassifying B1 for C2. We did not resort to cost matrix, a system [5] used in the Cap2018 data challenge (Ballier et al., 2020) with the same classification task. The cost matrix used in this data challenge penalised a default assignment to A1 (because of a skewed dataset) and rewarded B1 versus B2 distinction (a sensitive boundary for some educational institutions like engineer schools). With hindsight, the robustness of such a cost matrix should be tested among several candidates to assess the consequences of penalisation weights.

3.3. The Infrastructure

To be able to demonstrate and test our model in order to have a proof-of-concept, we decided to create a web-based infrastructure that i) handles the Input/Output from and to

the user and ii) schedules the tasks to and from the classifier. The infrastructure's primary requirement was to process new texts for on-the-fly metric computation followed by classification. As a result, a web interface outputs the CEFR level predicted for the new texts. This infrastructure is composed of Docker modules (Merkel, 2014), which are interconnected to handle data ingestion, processing and model classification. The infrastructure is built to allow model switching. The system can be modified in three points. The feature extraction pipeline can be modified so as to compute different metrics. The classification model can be changed to match the extracted features. The User Interface (UI, cf. Figure 2) can be modified according to the task at hand.

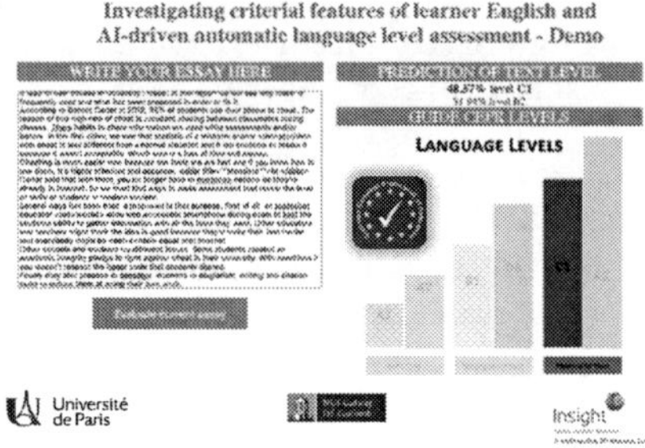

Figure 2: The user interface prototype

4. A Web-based Scheduling Infrastructure for Easy Text-Processing System Demonstration

4.1. Description of the Infrastructure Flow

Front-end. The UI demo has two main components (Figure 3), i) the web app component that interacts with the user on the web browser by receiving and responding text, and ii) the background component that manages the text processing system (in our case, extracting features and using them to classify the text's English level). These two components communicate with each other using a message broker - Redis, the third component of the UI demo. We created these different components in order to decouple the web app from the processing part, so the web app interface would not be blocked by a given request. This architecture provides the benefit of availability for new input, while processing feature extraction and classification to get a response for the current user.

Back-end. The environment of the web app and the processor are separated into two different docker containers, both of them having an instance of a Celery app. Celery works in an asynchronous way, from one side the Celery scheduler is responsible to create tasks, and from the other side the Celery worker is responsible to process the Celery scheduler created before. The web app is an instance of a Celery scheduler while the processor is an instance of a celery worker. When the web app receives a request with a text to process, it uses Celery to create a task and put it into the Celery queue by sending the text to be processed together

---

[3] see https://pypi.org/project/textstat/

[4] see https://pypi.org/project/pyenchant/

[5] http://cap2018.litislab.fr/competition_en.pdf

with the task ID through Redis. The processor docker, a Celery worker, communicates with Redis polling for tasks to process. When it receives a task from Redis, the worker processes it and uses Redis again to communicate the processed prediction level of the text. In the end, the web app can consult Redis, via the ID task, to get the result of the processing.

4.2. Plugging into the Model

Prior to plugging in a new model, it is necessary to conduct a supervised learning method on some data in order to fit a model. Once the model is tuned, a .sav file can be retrieved and placed into the architecture as shown in Figure 3. This .sav format stores models as a binary file. It is also essential to match the input features of the new model with the output features of the processing pipeline. The features created by the tools need to be filtered in order to pass only the data with the required features into the model.

4.3. Tests and Redeployment

We deployed our docker on an a web platform hosted by the French Linguistic Platform infrastructure HUMA-NUM [6]. The deployment of our UI was tested on HUMA-NUMm for a deployment on a Virtual machine using our docker virtualization. The system is fast and the HUMA-NUM team is very reactive. We needed to change the port 80 as the web interface required a different access port. [7] The feature extraction tool was also tested on this virtual machine. You need at least 32 CPUs 32 Gigabytes. We processed a 2019 version of the entire EFCAMDAT and it processes 100 files every five minutes. This confirms our desire to optimise the feature extraction. The feature extractor is optimised in the sense that each repertory is turned into an individual .csv files for the output data, so that the calculated features are regularly saved in case of crash (in the case of non-utf8 files, or unexpected sequences of commas, as experience seem to show).

4.4. Infrastructure Requirements

The system relies on the open-source Docker technology[8]. It is made up of three Docker containers, each designed for a specific purpose as detailed in 4.1. In order to run the system, docker must be installed. Docker-compose[9] is also required to run the three container Docker applications. Note that the infrastructure relies on a number of data handling technologies and a framework that do not require installation as they are located within Docker containers. This includes Redis[10], a database management system, as well as the Flask web application framework[11].

5. Available Resources

This section describes the current state of our platform-related project and research outputs.

5.1. Research Output

The project has yielded a number of resources and tools presented in Table 1 and all referenced in the project's web page [12]. The first tool is dedicated to end users, i.e. learners of English. A User Interface (UI) demo program provides a prototype for real-time proficiency assessment of new texts. Texts in English of more than 70 tokens are assigned probabilities of belonging to A1, A2, B1, B2, C1, C2 of CEFR levels. A documentation is available and it can be installed from NUIG Insight's Gitlab repository on request. Once installed, the demo acts as a web server, handles the text processing pipeline and interfaces with the results sent from the classification model as explained in Figure 3.

The second tool aims at the research community and focused on criterial features and AES systems. Researchers in this domain need to test different types of linguistic features to assess whether they are potentially criterial in determining CEFR levels (Hawkins and Filipović, 2012). We provide a tool that allows researchers to process batches of learner texts and output data sets ready for analysis. This tool includes the same processing pipeline as the UI demo and is only operated with the shell or command line. Users only have to place texts in a directory used as program input. It is available from NUIG Insight's Gitlab repository on request.

In the course of developing these tools, a number of data resources were created. First, the data set used for modeling in the UI demo system is available and can be exploited for other types of analyses grounded in linguistic complexity. The data set is composed of a list of metric values matched with CEFR levels. Secondly, the classification model implemented in the UI demo program is also available for download. Following the latest version of Nakala, the dataset warehouse hosted and managed by HUMA-NUM, we will upload our datasets with the corresponding permanent handles and DOIs to be attributed by HUMA-NUM [13].

5.2. Technical Aspects

For the web architecture, we have adopted Celery to avoid bottlenecks and nevertheless allow several users to query the system at the same time. As one of the reviewers pointed out, this decision has some consequences as opposed to an event-based approach. We intended to create the UI demo as a proof-of-concept for the project with time limitation. Celery seemed to be the best choice for us considering i) we were using a Python web application, ii) our team did not include specialists of event-based technologies, so the learning curve to implement using Celery was shorter than using an event-based approach, iii) our provisional goal for the project's scope was to make the UI demo available for more than one user, although we did not have the budget to support a massive number of users connecting to the system at the same time. We feel we can recommend this solution for a small-scale implementation but definitely, because of scalability limitation , future developments of our project could include an

---

[6]https://www.huma-num.fr/about-us

[7]http://linguisticdataprocessing.huma-num.fr/

[8]see https://www.docker.com/

[9]see https://docs.docker.com/compose/install/

[10]see https://redislabs.com/

[11]see https://www.palletsprojects.com/p/flask/

[12]see www.clillac-arp.univ-paris-diderot.fr/projets/ulysse2019

[13]https://humanum.hypotheses.org/5989

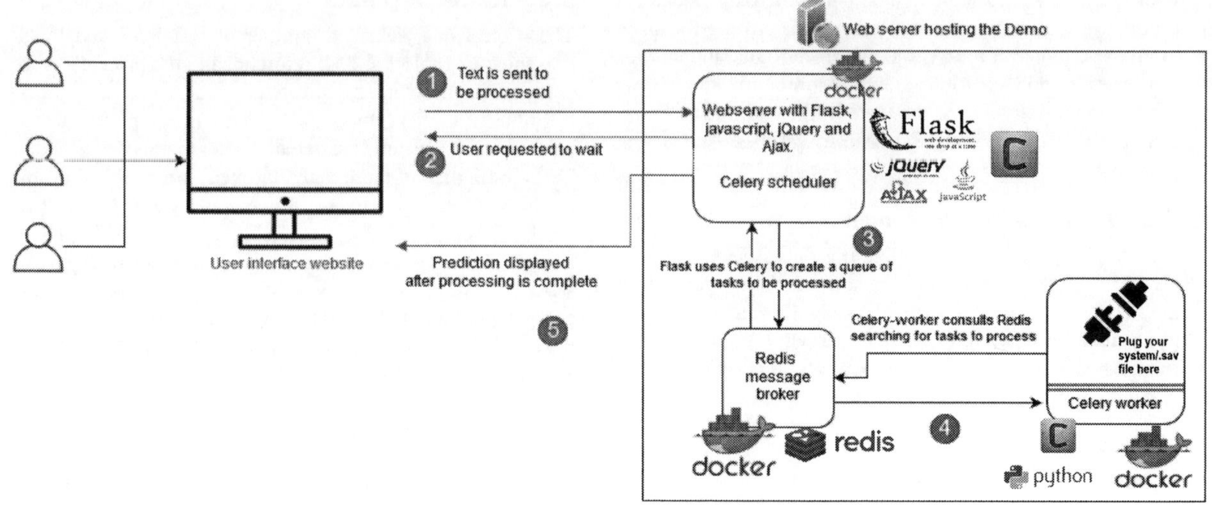

Figure 3: The customisable infrastructure

Resources	Availability
DemoUI (Web-based interface) http://ulysses.datascienceinstitute.ie:8080	Universal
Fully functional batch feature extraction tool (with pipeline modification access)	Restricted private Gitlab
Numerical Dataset metrics.csv file	Universal
Hybrid Dataset Texts_metrics.csv file	Universal (registration)
Statistical model	Universal model.sav file
"DemoIt" insfrastructure's source code https://gitlab.com/ulysses2019/ulysses	Universal

Table 1: The granularity of availability of the resources

event-based distributed approach for services communication/scheduler. This would make our system more robust and able to deal with more users at the same time.

For the feature extractor and individual distribution of the UI for researchers, we tested the Docker setup on MS Windows 10, iOS (Mojave) and Linux (Ubuntu 18.06). Because TAALES loads greedy frequency inventories and parsing the data is also memory-demanding, 16 Go of RAM are necessary for the execution (3 CPUs and 7 Gigas recommended for preferences in the docker). We wrote a user's guide in English for the installation of each tool. The whole annotation pipeline is in python, building from the former blocks from the tools. We have opted for a 3.6 version of python.

5.3. Governance and Uptake

The project was funded by the two partner countries and partners abode by the standard legal framework in use for this binational scheme [14]. Research papers were signed by the members of the projects of the two teams. Though we acknowledged respective percentages of ownership in relation to the input of the programming team, we agreed on Creative Commons Non Commercial Share Alike Licence for all our research outputs.

In terms of social aspects and community, we targeted two types of audiences. Our on-line prototype aims at learners of English and teachers in classroom environments. It is maintained until end of 2020 on the Irish partner infrastructure. To ensure sustainability afterwards, we have adopted the HUMA-NUM infrastructure [15] to host our project. As a prototype, it may experience scalability issues. The feature extraction tool was designed to be of interest to a potential consortium of researchers sharing a similar aim. Researchers working on linguistic complexity and conducting feature extraction tasks (for instance, for text classification purposes) may find the tool a useful assistant as it avoids coding. Specialists in Second Language Acquisition or Learner Corpus Research may benefit from the customisable micro-systems implemented in LS2CA_MS. For this tool parsing English data based on LS2CA (Lu, 2014), simple Tregex syntax (Levy and Andrew, 2006) can be used to create new features for the analysis of micro-systems (Gaillat et al., submitted).

6. Perspectives and Improvements

This section discusses developments in the making.

---

[14]A Guideline (in French) of recommended good practices for holders of this grant is available here: https://www.campusfrance.org/sites/default/files/medias/documents/2017-11/guide_bonnes_pratiques_ulysses.pdf

[15]https://www.huma-num.fr/about-us

6.1. Crowdsourcing Derived Applications and GDPR

To improve our model, we would like to store users' input to exploit it in further analyses. For the time being, the essays /texts submitted for assessment are not stored. We would like to make sure further crowdsourcing developments are compliant with GDPR and consider publishing general conditions of use warning the user that the texts used as queries will be stored to fine-tune the models. Anonymising the data for crowdsourcing will be carried out in accordance with (Klavan et al., 2012).

More generally, and more theoretically, the question is the compatibility of the models with the features when the system needs to evolve. If we collect more data (and possibly add other features), we will probably need to fine-tune the statistical models. We do not know whether this should lead to a standardization of (linguistic) features and interfaces as one of the reviewers suggested, but we suggest that an adaptation of the models can be reimplemented in the architecture by modifying the .sav file. We are not aware of any interface or standards to cater for this need.

6.2. Engineering and Interoperability

This section sums up current (and future) developments in the making of our project, with a view to offer more interoperability with existing platforms or similar projects.

6.2.1. Feature Engineering and Dimensionality Reduction

We spent much time integrating the various tools, and necessarily more time on feature collection and extraction than on dimensionality reduction. We are currently processing a complete dump of the EFCAMDAT dataset to address these issues and (Gaillat et al., submitted) reports preliminary findings on the French and Spanish datasets. The project was to build a proof-of-concept for the automation of proficiency level assessment. Further developments are required to improve the system. In its current version the model relies on a broad set of features (over 750) which makes it prone to overfitting. It is thus necessary to find a simpler model based on less features. This, in turn, will impact the data processing pipeline as only those tools related to selected features will be kept. We have obtained preliminary results with a new model based on the elastic net regression method (Zou and Hastie, 2005) trained on the EFCAMDAT training set and tested on another data set extracted from a totally different corpus, i.e. the CEFR-ASAG corpus (Tack et al., 2017). This method comes with the benefit of including feature dimensionality reduction. Using just 44 features classification showed 75.0% accuracy (CI [74.3, 75.8], p<0.001) and 59.2% (CI [53.4, 64.8], p <0.001) on the EFCAMDAT and CEFR-ASAG test sets respectively

For more generic linguistic feature processing and analysis, it would be relevant to design a tool and feature selection assistant for the batch feature extraction tool. This would enable researchers to select features and tools as needed very much like CTAP (Chen and Meurers, 2016). The latter tool supports a modular approach to feature extraction allowing for reusability. Users can compose their dataset variables prior to running an NLP pipeline that processes texts to produced the desired variable values. As the authors mention, additional functionality including machine learning modules is required to combine the collected evidence with specific outcome variables such as CEFR levels. An interface between CTAP and our Web demo UI could be developed in order to allow data exchange between the CTAP output and our CEFR classifier. Another advantage of a feature selection assistant would be to support multilingual processing. The current pipeline makes use of a number of tools that are language agnostic for the computation of some of the metrics. By allowing researchers to select language-agnostic metrics, it would be possible to build data sets used for modeling CEFR classification in other languages than English. Conversely, some metrics are language-dependent, as in the case of many lexical sophistication metrics which are based on lexical frequency inventories extracted from reference corpora of English. One line of research is to adapt some metrics to French as a Foreign Language, especially readability metrics (François, 2015) or to Dutch (Tack et al., 2018). Developing the interoperability of our feature extracting tool in the sense of multilingualism is also made possible by adapting our microsystem features to other languages, probably French as a Foreign Language for the next phase.

6.2.2. Pre-processing

One of the reviewers enquired about the implications of spoken data for our system. The short answer is that some written-based metrics may not be adequate for spoken data but speech data could be pre-processed to be fully tested by our system. The team discussed implementing a speech-to-text system, with the proviso that a single acoustic model should be chosen (eg preferably French speakers with available data). (Mariko and Kondo, 2019) reported successful use of IBM Watson Speech-to-text technology to transcribe learner speech for Japanese learners of English and give examples of the output. They reported Word Error Rates on 50 randomised speech samples and concluded that the automatic procedure was worth it. An important caveat for the calculation of the metrics is the absence of punctuation marks and the potentially useful insertion of "%HESITATION" for filled pauses (no threshold reported for the duration of filled pauses, though). The Watson system runs on Python 3.4. but is in the cloud and is not free. They do not seem to indicate whether the quality of the voice recognition improves over time for their longitudinal data. Following a uniformly python pipeline, we would try to use SpeechRecognition (Zhang, 2017) as a pre-processing stage of spoken data. We would have the added benefit of analysing spoken production, but this would probably imply a semi-automatic solution as the speech-to-text outputs would probably need to be manually edited. We also have initial reservations as to the applicability of written-designed metrics to spoken data (Ballier and Gaillat, 2016), in particular the transferability of the T-unit (a crucial concept for some complexity metrics) for spoken utterances, but we could experiment a speech-to-text module to pre-process learner recordings in order to test our model on spoken data, at least for fluency.

6.2.3. Post-processing

Collecting metrics to assess learner performance could be used for didactic purposes. It sounds plausible to select some features to guide learners in ICALL systems for self-assessment of their performance. A member of our team has begun applying some of the features to produce immediate feedback for learners, elaborating on a prototype (Ballier et al., 2019). This data visualisation application of our feature extractor takes the form of a dashboard where learner scores are compared to means of students of the same cohort and to native scores on similar essays.

6.3. Sustainability and the FAIR Paradigm

We have reached the final stage of our one-year project, and have tried to work in line with the FAIR paradigm (Mons, 2018) for our resources to be:

- **Findable** : the tools and resources are available from the project's web page, possibly from the LREC resource map and our datasets are to be linked with permanent handles and DOIs thanks to the Nakala HUMA-NUM services.

- **Accessible**: Some copyright restrictions apply to the corpus we used and to some of the tools. Access is either universal or restricted. There are copyright restrictions to the TAALES tool and to the initial EF-CAMDAT corpus data.

- **Interoperable**: our project is multi-platform and our UI infrastructure could be compared in terms of interoperability with similar existing language platforms. A project is in the making with the curators of the REALEC corpus (Vinogradova, 2016) and of the REALEC-inspector web interface [16] to analyse the relevance of the automatically extracted features for Russian learners of English.

- **Re-usable** : The UI interface can be customised for on-the-fly processing of texts. For example, to improve comparability with other language platforms, a three-point scale of learner levels could be re-implemented on our system with a different statistical model (.sav file). Maybe our datasets will be reused as well. Data Management Plans were not required for this level of funding, but we tried to produce comparable information for our datasets. Following the DMP Template of the EU Recommended practises (European Research Council, 2017) and few examples or guidelines for EU-funded research projects (Reymonet et al., 2018), we documented the Dataset reference and name, Data set description, Standards and metadata, Data Sharing, Archiving and preservation for our two datasets.

7. Conclusion

This paper has presented two tools and a set of of resources implemented in a Language Technology project. These tools rely on a modular implementation of a Docker architecture. As a result, this architecture is reusable in other

LT contexts such as L1 identification or Text Classification. We provide a web-based user demo tool and a linguistic complexity metric extraction tool. These tools can be modified to accommodate other projects relying on text features and classification. Our idea was to showcase the full workflow from the linguistic modelling to the web-based user interface to help linguists to disseminate their research projects. In this sense, this paper was intended as a 'how-to' for corpus linguistics to possibly publish web-based interfaces exploiting their data modelling.

Our project is a case study for linguistics as a cumulative data science. We showcase the data life cycle and some of its uses. We were able to reuse part of the EFCAMDAT data collection, we were able to concatenate several existing tools in a single workflow, we added our own micro-system features based on our analysis of learners' issues (the LS2CA_MS component of our pipeline) and our modelling (the .sav file), we shared the demoIT infrastructure we designed to exploit it. More data production can be expected with the UI and the feature extraction tool. Customisation is expected for our demoIT UI infrastructure and micro-system features. Our collaboration between corpus linguists, computational linguists, statisticians and computational scientists pertake of the current shift towards linguistic data science.

8. Acknowledgements

This work was undertaken with a PHC Hubert Currien Ulysse 2019 grant (project ref. 43121RJ) with the financial support of:

- Science Foundation Ireland (SFI) under Grant Number SFI/12/RC/2289_P2, co-funded by the European Regional Development Fund.

- The French Ministry of Higher Education, Research and Innovation (Ministère de l'Enseignement supérieur, de la Recherche et de l'Innovation, MESRI)

- The French Ministry for Europe and Foreign Affairs (Ministères de l'Europe et des affaires étrangères, MEAE)

We wish to thank the three anonymous reviewers for their comments. We are grateful to Kristopher Kyle and Scott Crossley for providing us with the source code of the TAALES tool and to Xiaofei Lu for showing us his L2SCA as visiting scholar and allowing us to implement the micro-system features. We thank Theodora Alexopoulou and Carlos Balhana for their willingness to help us in our project by hosting our resulting dataset on the EFCAMDAT website, in accordance with the corpus maintenance regulations. We thank Detmar Meurers for his enthusiasm and for letting us access an early stage version of the CTAP annotation platform. We also thank Felipe Arruda who provided us with substantial software development advice. We also thank the audience of the Paris workshop (30 Oct.2019) for their feedback on the presentation of the deliverables of the project.

---

[16]https://linghub.ru/inspector/

9. Bibliographical References

Ballier, N. and Gaillat, T. (2016). Classification d'apprenants francophones de l'anglais sur la base des métriques de complexité lexicale et syntaxique. In *JEP-TALN-RECITAL 2016*, volume 9, pages 1–14.

Ballier, N., Gaillat, T., and Pacquetet, E. (2019). Prototype de feedback visuel des productions écrites d'apprenants francophones de l'anglais sous moodle. In Julien Broisin, et al., editors, *Actes de la 9ème Conférence sur les Environnements Informatiques pour l'Apprentissage Humain (EIAH2019)*, pages 395–398.

Ballier, N., Canu, S., Petitjean, C., Gasso, G., Balhana, C., Alexopoulou, T., and Gaillat, T. (2020). Machine learning for learner English. *International Journal of Learner Corpus Research*, 6(1):72–103.

Chen, X. and Meurers, D. (2016). CTAP: A web-based tool supporting automatic complexity analysis. In *Proceedings of the Workshop on Computational Linguistics for Linguistic Complexity (CL4LC)*, pages 113–119.

Crossley, S. A., Kyle, K., Allen, L. K., Guo, L., and McNamara, D. S. (2014). Linguistic Microfeatures to Predict L2 Writing Proficiency: A Case Study in Automated Writing Evaluation. *The Journal of Writing Assessment*, 7(1):1–34.

Crossley, S. A., Kyle, K., and Dascalu, M. (2019). The Tool for the Automatic Analysis of Cohesion 2.0: Integrating semantic similarity and text overlap. *Behavior Research Methods*, 51(1):14–27.

European Council. (2001). *Common European Framework of Reference for Languages: Learning, teaching, assessment*. Cambridge University Press, Cambridge.

European Research Council. (2017). *Guidelines on the implementation of Open Access to scientific publications and research data in projects supported by the European Research Council under Horizon 2020*.

François, T. (2015). When readability meets computational linguistics: a new paradigm in readability. *Revue française de linguistique appliquée*, 20(2):79–97.

Gaillat, T., Simpkin, A., Ballier, N., Stearns, B., Sousa, A., Bouyé, M., and Zarrouk, M. (submitted). Predicting CEFR levels in learners of English: the use of microsystem criterial features in a machine learning approach. *Journal With Anonymous Submission*.

Geertzen, J., Alexopoulou, T., and Korhonen, A. (2013). Automatic Linguistic Annotation of Large Scale L2 Databases: The EF-Cambridge Open Language Database (EFCamDat). In R. T. Miller, et al., editors, *Proceeedings of the 31st Second Language Research Forum*, Carnegie Mellon. Cascadilla Press.

Hawkins, J. A. and Filipović, L. (2012). *Criterial Features in L2 English: Specifying the Reference Levels of the Common European Framework*. Cambridge University Press, United Kingdom.

Huang, Y., Murakami, A., Alexopoulou, T., and Korhonen, A.-L. (2018). Dependency parsing of learner English.

Kelly, R. (2016). Pyenchant a spellchecking library for python. *available: https://pythonhosted. org/pyenchant*.

Klavan, J., Tavast, A., and Kelli, A. (2012). The legal aspects of using data from linguistic experiments for creating language resources. In Arvi Tavast, et al., editors, *Human Language Technologies The Baltic Perspective: Proceedings of the Fifth International Conference Baltic HLT 2012*, pages 71–78. IOS Press.

Kyle, K., Crossley, S., and Berger, C. (2018). The tool for the automatic analysis of lexical sophistication (TAALES): version 2.0. *Behavior Research Methods*, 50(3):1030–1046.

Levy, R. and Andrew, G. (2006). Tregex and Tsurgeon: tools for querying and manipulating tree data structures. In *Proceedings of LREC2006*, pages 2231–2234.

Lu, X. (2010). Automatic analysis of syntactic complexity in second language writing. *International Journal of Corpus Linguistics*, 15(4):474–496.

Lu, X. (2012). The Relationship of Lexical Richness to the Quality of ESL Learners' Oral Narratives. *The Modern Language Journal*, 96(2):190–208.

Lu, X. (2014). *Computational Methods for Corpus Annotation and Analysis*. Springer, Dordrecht.

Manning, C. D., Surdeanu, M., Bauer, J., Finkel, J., Bethard, S. J., and McClosky, D. (2014). The Stanford CoreNLP Natural Language Processing Toolkit. In *Proceedings of the 52nd Annual Meeting of the Association for Computational Linguistics: System Demonstrations*, pages 55–60.

Mariko, A. and Kondo, Y. (2019). Constructing a longitudinal learner corpus to track l2 spoken English. *Journal of Modern Languages*, 29:23–44.

McNamara, D. S., Graesser, A. C., McCarthy, P. M., and Cai, Z. (2014). *Automated Evaluation of Text and Discourse with Coh-Metrix*. Cambridge University Press, USA.

Merkel, D. (2014). Docker: lightweight linux containers for consistent development and deployment. *Linux journal*, 2014(239):2.

Mons, B. (2018). *Data stewardship for open science: Implementing FAIR principles*. Chapman and Hall/CRC.

Page, E. B. (1968). The Use of the Computer in Analyzing Student Essays. *International Review of Education / Internationale Zeitschrift für Erziehungswissenschaft / Revue Internationale de l'Education*, 14(2):210–225.

Reymonet, N., Moysan, M., Cartier, A., and Délémontez, R. (2018). Réaliser un plan de gestion de données "fair" : modèle 2018.

Schmid, H. (1994). Probabilistic Part-of-Speech Tagging Using Decision Trees. In *Proceedings of the International Conference on New Methods in Language Processing*, pages 14–16, Manchester: UK.

Tack, A., François, T., Roekhaut, S., and Fairon, C. (2017). Human and Automated CEFR-based Grading of Short Answers. In *Proceedings of the 12th Workshop on Innovative Use of NLP for Building Educational Applications*, pages 169–179, Copenhagen, Denmark, September. Association for Computational Linguistics.

Tack, A., François, T., Desmet, P., and Fairon, C. (2018). NT2Lex: A CEFR-graded lexical resource for Dutch as a foreign language linked to open Dutch WordNet. In *Proceedings of the Thirteenth Workshop on Innovative Use of NLP for Building Educational Applications*, pages 137–146, New Orleans, Louisiana, June. Association for Computational Linguistics.

Vinogradova, O. (2016). The role and applications of expert error annotation in a corpus of English learner texts. *Computational Linguisitics and Intellectual Technologies. Proceedings of Dialog 2016*, 15:740–751.

Volodina, E., Pilán, I., and Alfter, D. (2016). Classification of Swedish learner essays by CEFR levels. In Salomi Papadima-Sophocleous, et al., editors, *CALL communities and culture ; short papers from EUROCALL 2016*, pages 456–461. Research-publishing.net.

Zhang, A. (2017). Speech recognition (version 3.8) python library. *Available from https://pypi.org/project/SpeechRecognition/.*

Zou, H. and Hastie, T. (2005). Regularization and variable selection via the Elastic Net. *Journal of the Royal Statistical Society, Series B*, 67(2):301–320.

Association for Computational Linguistics
209 N. Eighth Street
Stroudsburg, Pennsylvania 18360